The Independent Hostel Guide

England
Wales
Scotland
Northern Ireland

Edited by
Sam Dalley and Alice Lockett

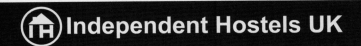

Independent Hostels UK

ISBN 978-0-9565058-7-3

Independent Hostel Guide 2018: England, Wales, Scotland & Northern Ireland. 27th Edition. Editors: Sam Dalley and Alice Lockett.

British Library Cataloguing in Publication Data. A catalogue record for this book is available at the British Library **ISBN 978-0-9565058-7-3**

Published by: Independent Hostels UK, Speedwell House, Upperwood, Matlock Bath, Derbyshire, DE4 3PE. Tel: +44 (0) 1629 580427.

© Independent Hostels UK, 2018
Proof read by Penny MacGregor. Printed by: Deltor, www.deltoruk.com

Front Cover Photo: Deepdale Backpackers Hostel (pg 152) © Robert Morris.
Back Cover Photos: Mawddach Estuary near Bunkorama (pg 299) © Robert Morris. Penrose Bunkhouse kitchen (pg 95) © National Trust Images/Mike Henton. Cards at Deepdale Backpackers (pg 152) © Robert Morris. Bunks at Brancaster Activity Centre (pg 155) © National Trust.

Internal Photographs: Photos on page 318 credited to Tony Jones. Photo on page 382 credited to Brain Sutherland. Photo on page 392 credited to Ike Gibson. Photo on page 298 credited to Martin Thirkettle. Photo on page 247 credited to Mike Emmett. Photo on page 224 credited to Mick Garratt. Photos on page 207 credited to Rob Nobal. Photos on page 218 credited to Elliott Simpson. Photos on page 401, 379 and 387 credited to VisitScotland/Paul Tomkins. Photos on page 351 credited to Allan Sutherland, Colin McLean and Tom Daly. Photos on pages: 95,97,105,109,111,112,115,118,126,127,129, 130,134,150,154,155,158,167,175,193,208,225,230,240,242,254,255,270,276, 278,286,304 © National Trust/Ross Hoddinott, Joe Cornish, Sarah Bailey, Robert Morris, Mike Henton, Roy Jones, Alex Green, John Millar, Peter Muhly, Roger Coulam, Paul Harris, Graham Bettis, James Dobson, Andrew Butler, Stuart Cox, Paul Delaney, David Noton, John Malley, Drew Buckley, Tracey Willis, Rob-Joules, Sarah Harris, Justin Seedhouse, Arnhel de Serra, David Sellman, Hywel Lewis, Chris Lacey, David Noton.

Other photos were donated by the accommodation and all copyright is retained.

ISBN 978-0-9565058-7-3

9 780956 505873

Distributed in the UK by:
Cordee Books and Maps,
3a De Montfort Street, Leicester,
LE1 7HD.
Tel: (0116) 2543579

CONTENTS

INDEPENDENT HOSTELS UK

Independent Hostels UK is a network of over 400 bunkhouses, hostels, camping barns and group accommodation centres. These provide a unique form of accommodation, ideal for groups, individuals and families who enjoy good company, travel and the outdoors.

IndependentHostels.co.uk

INDEPENDENT HOSTELS

Independent hostels have shared areas, self-catering kitchens and bedrooms with bunks. They are great for group get-togethers and for those who enjoy the outdoors and independent travel. Bunkhouses, camping barns, boutique hostels, backpackers' hostels and outdoor centres are all types of independent hostel. Independent hostels have :-

- Self-catering facilities

- Stays of just one night

- Private bedrooms, en suite rooms and dorms

- Wild locations for outdoor activities

- City centre locations for independent travel

- Welcome families, individuals and groups

- Can be booked 'sole use' for get-togethers or groups

- No membership requirements

- 95% are extra to the hostels in the YHA / SYHA.

BEST PRICE GUARANTEE

The hostels and bunkhouses displaying the Best Price symbol on our website promise that you will get their accommodation at the lowest price if you contact them direct. Contact them via our website, by phone, email, or the accommodation's website and you are guaranteed the best rates.

Why do we offer a Best Price Guarantee? Most websites take a large commission from your money before they pass it on to the accommodation, giving the hostels less money to spend on your stay. Independent Hostels UK gives you direct access to the accommodations' own booking systems so you can book direct.

Independent Hostel networks across the world have united to give their members the opportunity to offer a Best Price Guarantee. See **www.bestprice-hostels.com** for details of hostels worldwide who are offering the Best Price Guarantee.

KEY TO SYMBOLS

	Dormitories
	Private rooms (often ideal for families)
	Sleeping bags required
	Hostel fully heated
	Some areas heated
	Drying room available
	Cooking facilities available
	Meals provided or available locally
	WiFi available
	Simple accommodation, basic, clean and friendly
	Dogs by prior arrangement
	Bike shed
	Bronze, Silver, Gold, Green Tourism Award
	Affiliated to Hostelling International
	Operated by the National Trust
GROUPS ONLY	**Accommodation for groups only**
pp	**per person**
GR	**Ordnance Survey grid reference**

IndependentHostels.co.uk

Follow our social media @indiehostelsUK for special offers.

SELF CATERING

Hostels and bunkhouses have
kitchens for guests to use.

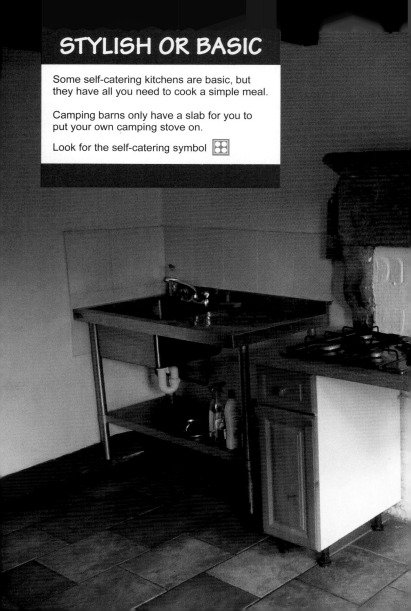

STYLISH OR BASIC

Some self-catering kitchens are basic, but
they have all you need to cook a simple meal.

Camping barns only have a slab for you to
put your own camping stove on.

Look for the self-catering symbol

CAMPING BARNS
AND BOTHIES

Camping barns and bothies offer simple accommodation in stunning rural locations. There is a platform to lay your sleeping roll, a table and benches and a safe area for you to use your camping stove. Some barns and bothies also have a wood-burning stove to gather around. Created to provided shelter for walkers but also ideal for family escapes, many camping barns were started by the Youth Hostel Association but they have always been owned and run by local farms and community. These barns continue to provide simple accommodation as part of the Independent Hostels network.

**Independenthostels.co.uk/
camping-barns-bothies**

Underbank Camping Barn, pg 179

SELF-CATERING

Many hostels and bunkhouses have large tables, ideal for group meals.

MEALS

Some hostels provide pre-ordered breakfasts and evening meals, or there are meals available locally.

Look out for this symbol

DINNER SERVED AT 7 PM PLEASE O...

SERVED WITH BROWN BREAD AND BU...

...MEMADE. FRENCH ONION SOUP (v)

...MEMADE. MUSHROOM AND ROASTED GARLIC SOUP (v)

...HT HOUR BEEF STEW WITH PROPER MASH AND PEPPERED CABBAGE

...RISA SPICED LAMB STEW WITH HERB COUSCOUS AND GREEN SALAD

...OKED SALMON TAGLIATELLE WITH GARLIC BREAD

...AL STEAK BURGER WITH CHEESE, CHIPS AND HOMEMADE COLESLAW

...MEMADE BEET 'N' BEAN BURGER WITH CHIPS AND HOMEMADE COLESLAW

...LUTEN FREE AND
...GAN OPTIONS
...LWAYS AVAILABLE.

SIDES HARICOT VERT, GARLIC BREAD, CHIPS, GREEN SAL...

...OMEMADE. WARM CHOCOLATE BROWNIE

...OMEMADE. WARM GINGER CAKE

...OMEMADE APPLE AND BERRY CRUMBLE

...ORTHEN BLOC

SERVED WITH CUSTARD
OR
YORKSHIRE DALES ICECREAM

ICE CREAM - BLACK TREACLE, CHOCOLATE AND SEASALT,
WHITE CHOCOLATE AND POPCORN
SORBET - RASPBERRY AND SORREL (VEGAN, GLUTEN FREE)

120 ML POTS

BUNKS

Most bunkhouses and hostels have bunks in the bedrooms

PRIVATE ROOMS

Many bunkhouses and hostels have private rooms. Sometimes with en suite facilities.

Look for this symbol

DORMS

Shared dorms are great value and a good way to get to know other guests.

Look out for this symbol

BE SOCIAL

Open-plan living areas are ideal for group hire and chatting with other guests.

Calico Barn Bunkbarn pg 244

LOUNGES

Many hostels and bunkhouses have lounges and log burners for relaxing evenings after outdoor days.

Gauber Bunk Barn pg 196

OPEN ALL YEAR

Most independent hostels and bunkhouses are open all year

Mid Wales Bunkhouse pg 291

DRYING ROOMS

Many have drying facilities, so you can go out in all weathers and be sure of a dry start the next day

Look out for the symbol

Hardraw Old School Bunkhouse pg 197

NATIONAL PARKS

All of the UK's National Parks are well provided for with independent hostels, bunkhouses & camping barns.

independenthostels.co.uk/national-parks/

Pindale Farm Outdoor Centre pg 173

VILLAGES & TOWNS

There are hostels and bunkhouses in rural villages and thriving market towns.

Puttenham Camping Barn pg 128

Tomlinsons Bunkhouse pg 241

FARMS & CITIES

There are bunkhouses on farms and hostels in cities.

Dacres Stable pg 210

CITY, BACKPACKERS
& BOUTIQUE HOSTELS

Independent city hostels, backpackers and boutique hostels cater for independent travellers exploring the UK. Close to public transport hubs, they are ideal for young travellers from overseas. They are also perfect venues for UK groups and individuals attending city events. These hostels are great places to meet people and make new friends, with many offering social evenings such as pub crawls and quizzes. Backpackers hostels are situated in cities and notable tourist locations around England, Wales and Scotland.

**Independenthostels.co.uk/
city-backpackers-boutique-hostels-
independent-travellers**

MOUNTAINS

There are hostels and bunkhouses in the popular mountain regions of the UK.

BEACHES & COAST

There are lots of hostels and bunkhouses along the coasts and islands of the UK.

**/independenthostels.co.uk/
bunkhouses-by-the-sea/**

FAMILIES

Hostels and bunkhouses provide ideal accommodation for families.

FRESH AIR

Many bunkhouses and hostels are in ideal locations for holidays in the fresh air.

FOUR LEGS

Some hostels welcome dogs by arrangement.

DOG FRIENDLY
ACCOMMODATION

There are over a hundred hostels and bunkhouses in the network which offer dog friendly accommodation. Situated in rolling countryside and National Parks, along stunning coastline and in picturesque villages. They provide ideal self-catering accommodation for holidays, dog friendly by arrangement and perfect for family groups. Many provide accommodation for periods as short as one night so are ideal for a stop-over on a long journey.

Look out for this symbol

Always contact the accommodation in advance to find out about arrangements for your dog.

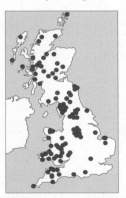

**Independenthostels.co.uk/
/dog-friendly-accommodation**

Corris Hostel pg 297

GROUPS

Bunkhouses and hostels are ideal for groups.
School groups, outdoor clubs and gatherings
of friends all use independent hostels.

SOLE USE

Hostels and bunkhouses can be booked 'sole use' for get-togethers and reunions.

Old Brooder Bunkhouse pg 137

Hardraw Old School Bunkhouse pg 197

CHRISTMAS
ACCOMMODATION

Christmas is a time for family, but hosting everyone can be tricky. Most hostels and bunkhouses welcome groups at Christmas and are an economical way to get the accommodation you need. Hire the whole place and share the fun of hosting the festive season, with everyone chipping in. Many places are in gorgeous locations, ideal for a Boxing Day walk. They range from large houses to farm barns, they have self-catering facilities and often large dining tables ideal to sit the whole family for the big dinner.

**Independenthostels.co.uk/
christmas-accommodation**

CONFERENCES

Some hostels and bunkhouses are ideal for team building events and conferences.

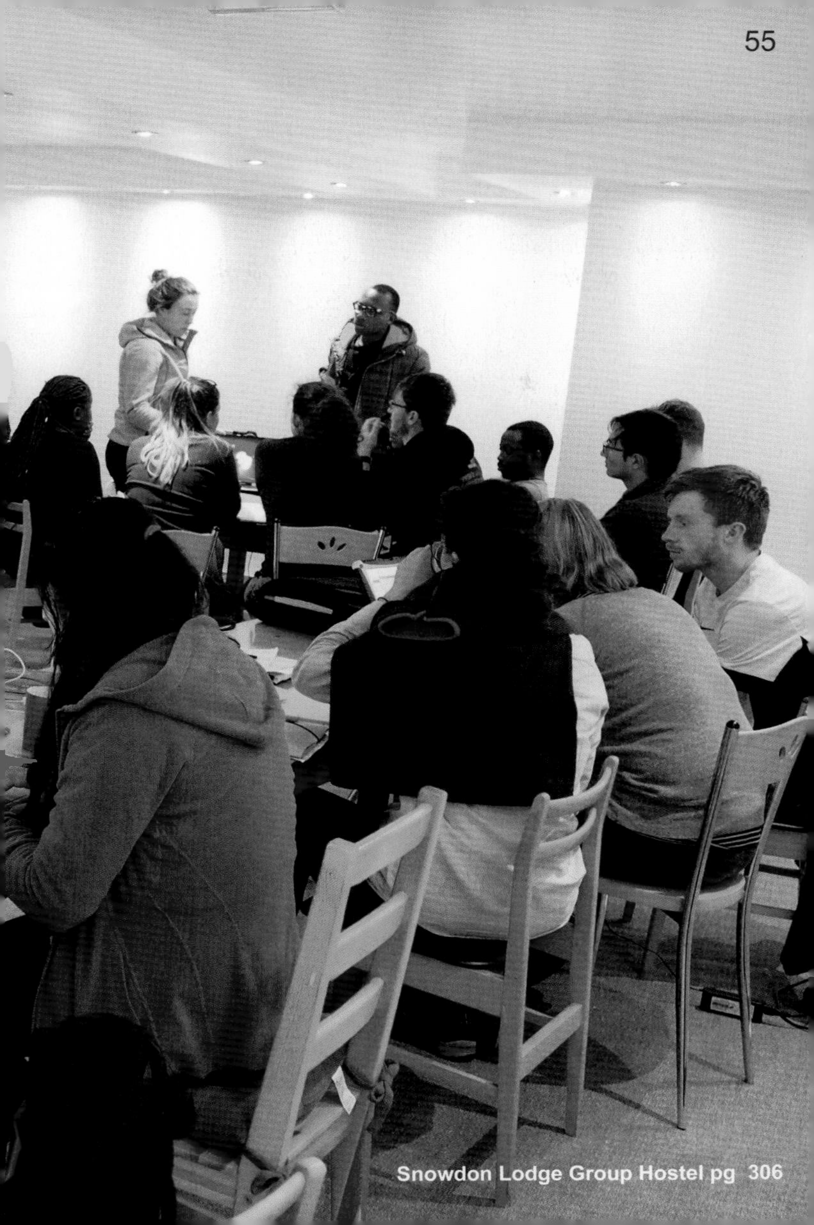

Snowdon Lodge Group Hostel pg 306

NO MEMBERSHIP

There are no membership requirements at
Independent Hostels.

YOUTH HOSTELS
PAST AND PRESENT

The YHA has sold many hostels over the last twenty years and some of these have been rescued from closure by private individuals or local interest groups. There are now over 70 former YHA properties in the Independent Hostels network including many hostels, bunkhouses and camping barns. These hostels continue to provide great value self-catering accommodation to help all, especially those of limited means, to a greater knowledge, love and care of the countryside.

**Independenthostels.co.uk/
/private-youth-hostels/**

NATIONAL TRUST
BUNKHOUSES AND BOTHIES

There are over 30 National Trust bunkhouses and bothies in the Independent Hostel Guide, all in spectacular locations. The bunkhouses are ideal for groups and provide self-catering accommodation in the grounds of National Trust Estates, within National Parks or along unspoiled coastlines. Most bunkhouses provide sleeping in bunk bed dormitories, a social area to gather and cook, showers, electricity and heating. National Trust bothies are often in isolated locations, and are the perfect getaway for those who really want to escape from modern life. Fitted with wooden sleeping platforms, there is usually no electricity and water often comes from a hand pump.

**Independenthostels.co.uk/
NationalTrust**

Dalehead Bunkhouse pg 175

WILDLIFE

Many hostels and bunkhouses are in remote locations, ideal for watching wildlife.

Knoydart Bunkhouse pg 375

ECO HOSTELS
AND BUNKHOUSES

Hostels and bunkhouses have a naturally low CO_2 footprint. Shared accommodation results in shared resources, making the accommodation sustainable as well as friendly. Self-catering facilities enable guests to eat local produce as part of their holiday. Cyclists and walkers use the ultimate in carbon free travel and some hostels and bunkhouses provide a discount for people who arrive without a vehicle. The hostels and bunkhouses on the map below make a special effort to run their accommodation in a sustainable way, on top of these natural green advantages. Some of them have achieved Green Tourism Awards and these have the symbols shown opposite on their pages.

**Independenthostels.co.uk
/eco-hostels**

Palace Farm Hostel pg 131

OUTDOOR ACTIVITIES

Hostel owners and staff will be able to tell you about the best outdoor activities in their area and some have activity providers on site.

67

© Hardraw Old School Bunkhouse pg 197

CRAFTS & YOGA

Some hostels run craft weekends, retreats and yoga holidays.

CYCLE TOURING

Hostels and bunkhouses are ideal for tours by bike.

Castle Creavie Haybarn Hostel pg 328

MORE THEN A BED

Many hostels and bunkhouses provide a particular welcome for those who arrive without a vehicle.

For a bike shed look for this symbol

73

Edens Yard Backpackers pg 98

BIKE HIRE

Some hostels have bike hire and repair facilities on site.

Comrie Croft pg 342

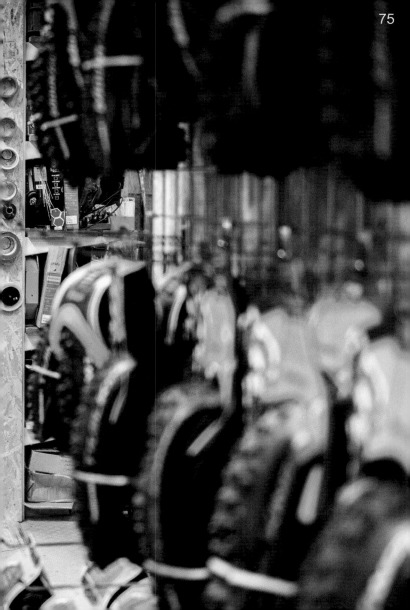

BIKE TRAILS

Many hostels and bunkhouses are on cycle routes and long distance cycle trails.

DUNARD HOSTEL

Dunard Hostel on the Hebridean Way pg 388

LONG DISTANCE WALKS

There are many hostels and bunkhouses along the Long Distance Paths of the UK. Over 20 classic walks are featured on the Independent Hostel Guide website with the locations of bunkhouses and hostels along the route. New walks are added regularly.

Footpath to Blencathra from White Horse Inn Bunkhouse, pg 219

CAMBRIAN WAY
ACCOMMODATION

The Cambrian Way is a mountain walking route from Cardiff on the south coast of Wales to Conwy on the north coast. The route is 291miles (485km) in length. It starts at Cardiff Castle and travels over some of the best mountain scenery in Wales including the Brecon Beacons, the Carmarthen Fans, the Cambrian Mountains, Cadair Idris, the Rhinogs, the Moelwyns, Snowden, the Glyders and the Carneddau. Bunkhouses and hostels along the route provide ideal accommodation for walkers with drying rooms, boot stores and a warm welcome.

**Independenthostels.co.uk/
cambrian-way-accommodation**

Cambrian Mountains, Dolgoch Hostel pg 288

HADRIAN'S WALL
ACCOMMODATION

Hadrian's Wall Path National Trail follows the line of Hadrian's Wall from the Solway Coast in the west to the Northumberland Coast in the east. The 84 mile path passes through a landscape of wild moorland with sky-filled vistas to woods and meadows and eventually to the city streets of Newcastle. Hostels and bunkhouses along the route provide good value self-catering accommodation tailored specifically to the needs of walkers on the trail.

**Independenthostels.co.uk/
hadrians-wall-path-accommodation**

Hadrians Wall © Slack House Farm pg 237

WEST HIGHLAND
WAY

The West Highland Way is Scotland's oldest long distance walk and is scattered with hostels and bunkhouses where you can experience true Highland hospitality. The 96 mile route follows drover's trails, scrambles along remote loch sides and passes over high moorland. The Way starts in Milngavie just north of Glasgow follows Loch Lomond and passes over Rannoch Moor by Glencoe to finish in Fort William in the Scottish Highlands.

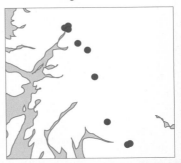

**Independenthostels.co.uk/
west-highland-way-accommodation**

Glencoe © Blackwater Hostel pg 361

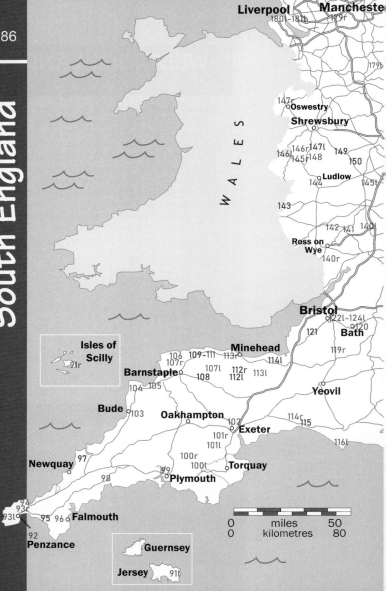

Liverpool 180l–181b
Manchester 179r

179l

147r Oswestry
Shrewsbury

146r 146l 147l 149
145l 148 150
144 Ludlow 145t

143

142 141 140

Ross on Wye
140r

Bristol 122l–124l
121 120
Bath

119r

Minehead
106 109–111 113r
107r 114l
Barnstaple 107l 112r 113l
108 112l

104 105

Bude 103

Oakhampton 102
101r 114r 115
101l Exeter

Newquay 97 100r 116r
100l Torquay
98 99 Plymouth

94
93t
93l
93r
92 95 96 Falmouth
Penzance

Yeovil

Isles of Scilly 91r

Guernsey
Jersey 91l

0 miles 50
0 kilometres 80

W A L E S

South England

KEY

45 – Page number

45l – Left side of page

45r – Right side of page

45 – Groups only

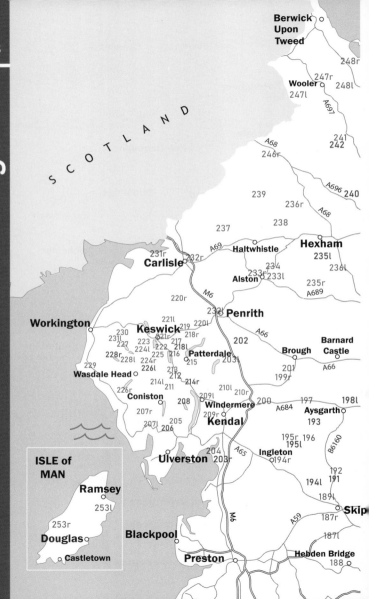

Berwick Upon Tweed

248r

Wooler 248l
247r
247l

A697

241
242

A68
246r

A696 240

239

236r

A68

237

238

Hexham

231r
232r
Carlisle

Haltwhistle

235l

A69

234
233r
Alston 233l

236l

235r
A689

220r

M6

232l Penrith

Workington

221l

230
231l 227 223 221r 219 220l
228r 224l 222 217 218l
228l 225 216
224r
226l
229
214l 213
Wasdale Head 212
226r 214r
Coniston 208

Keswick

218r

Patterdale

215

203l

202

A66

Brough

Barnard Castle

A66

201
199r

197

198l

200

209l
207r
207l 206

205

210l 210r

209r

A684

Windermere

Kendal

Aysgarth

193

B6160

Ingleton
194r

195r 196
195l

192
191

A65

194l

189l

A59

187r

Skip

187l

Ulverston 203r

ISLE of MAN

Ramsey

253l

253r

Douglas

Castletown

Blackpool

188

Hebden Bridge

Preston

M6

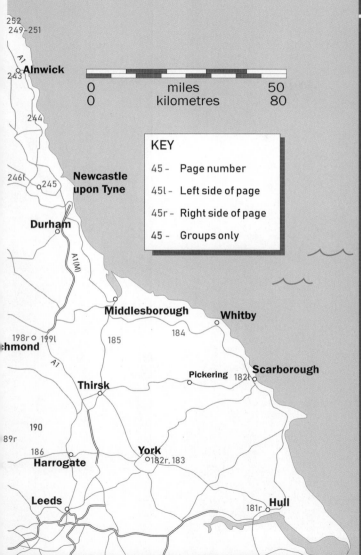

252
249-251

A1
Alnwick
243

244

246l 245

Newcastle upon Tyne

Durham

A1(M)

198r 199l
chmond

A1

KEY

45 – Page number

45l – Left side of page

45r – Right side of page

45 – Groups only

0   miles   50
0   kilometres   80

Middlesborough   **Whitby**

185   184

Pickering 182l
Scarborough

Thirsk

190

89r

186
Harrogate

York
182r, 183

Leeds

Hull
181r

North England

England

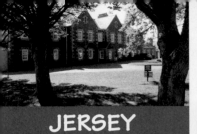

JERSEY
ACCOMMODATION
91l

Close to the pretty fishing port of Gorey in St Martin, with a range of B&B rooms including private en suites and dorms with shared showers plus camping. On & off-site activities include zip wire (U12s), archery, bush craft and SPLAT, low velocity paintball or "Escape from a Castle" by completing physical & problem solving tasks.

DETAILS
- **Open** - Feb-Dec. Reception 8:30-16.00 or 20:00 depending on the season
- **Beds** - 113: Bunks: 1x10, 6x8, 1x6, 4x4 En suite: 1x8, 1x4, 1x5, 2x3, 4x2, 2x1
- **Price/night** - B&B:Bunks £30.50-£32.50pp. En suites: bunks, sgle, family 3, 4, 5 & 8 £32.50-£34.50pp. Twin £65-£69/room. Youth groups £27.75pp.

CONTACT: Anna Stammers
Tel: 01534 498636
info@jerseyhostel.co.uk
www.jerseyhostel.co.uk
Faldouet, St Martins, Jersey, Channel Islands JE3 6DU

LONGSTONE
LODGE
91r

Opening on the 1st May 2018 the Isles of Scilly's first every hostel! Longstone Lodge will sleep 25 in single, twins and family rooms as well as dorm beds. The hostel has a large communal kitchen/lounge/diner and a laundry room, as well as large grounds with children's play. Situated in the heart of St Mary's, Scilly's largest island, it's the perfect base for visiting these stunning islands.

DETAILS
- **Open** - Check in 8.30-10am, 12.30-2pm & 5-6.30pm check out before 10am. Hostel closed for cleaning 11am-1pm
- **Beds** - 25: 2x1, 4x2, 1x4, 1x5, 1x6
- **Price/night** - Dorm: £24pp. Single Room: £26. Twin: £60. 4 bed room: £96. 5 bed room: £120.00. Sole Use: £625.

CONTACT: Colin, Amy & Suzy
Tel: 01720 422410
longstonelodge@yahoo.com
www.longstonelodge.co.uk
Longstone Lodge & Cafe, St. Marys Isles of Scilly TR21 0NW

PENZANCE
BACKPACKERS

Whether you're looking for sandy beaches and sheltered coves, the storm lashed cliffs of Land's End, sub-tropical gardens, international artists, the remains of ancient cultures, or just somewhere to relax and take time out, Penzance Backpackers is for you. Situated close to the sea front, and the town centre. Linen is provided. Lots of local information and a warm welcome all included.

DETAILS

■ **Open** - All year, 10.00-12.00, 17.00-22.00
■ **Beds** - 30: 2 double, 1x 4 (double + 2 bunks), 3x6, 1x7.
■ **Price/night** - From £17 per person. £38 for 2 people in private room.

CONTACT: Mathew
Tel: 01736 363836
info@pzbackpack.com
www.pzbackpack.com
The Blue Dolphin, Alexandra Road,
Penzance, TR18 4LZ

LANDS END
HOSTEL AND B&B

93l

Land's End Hostel and B&B provides accommodation in an idyllic location situated 1/4 mile from Land's End. Converted from a mill barn, the hostel is double glazed and centrally heated with a fully equipped kitchen, dining/ social area and modern bathrooms. The rooms have TVs, WiFi and USB ports, bedding and towels included. There is a double/twin ensuite B&B room in the farmhouse. Outside courtyard, bicycle storage and parking available.

DETAILS
- **Open** - All year.
- **Beds** - 14: 2×2, 1×4, 1×6 plus double B&B ensuite bedroom in the farmhouse.
- **Price/night** - £30pp, DIY Breakfast £5pp. B&B £85 per room

CONTACT: Lou
Tel: 07585 625774
lou@landsendholidays.co.uk
www.landsendholidays.co.uk
Mill Barn, Trevescan, Sennan, Nr Lands End, Penzance, TR19 7AQ

LOWER PENDERLEATH
FARM HOSTEL

93r

Just three miles from St Ives' beaches and 5 miles from Penzance, Lower Penderleath Farm Hostel provides self-catering accommodation in four twin rooms, one room with an alpine dormitory for 12 and family maisonette. The water on site is natural mineral water sold as bottled mineral water in 1989 and visitors can cook, drink and shower in it! Pub food in two local villages is within walking distance.

DETAILS
- **Open** - Easter-Oct. Arrive between 9.00am-8pm depart by 10 am.
- **Beds** - 24: 4x2 + dorm platform of 12, 1x4 self contained maisonette
- **Price/night** - £17pp, £38 twin room. £80 maisonette. BYO sleeping bag/pillow.

CONTACT: Russell Rogers
Tel: 07723 014567
rusrogers60@gmail.com
www.stivescampingandhostel.com
Lower Penderleath Farm, Towednack, St.Ives, Cornwall, TR26 3AF

COHORT
HOSTEL

94

Located in the centre of St Ives, Cohort is a stylish, friendly hostel. Great facilities include a hot shower in the courtyard for surfers, through to a laundry/drying room. The on-site bar is cheap; there's free WiFi, Netflix and comfortable pod beds - all with USB ports, lights, curtains and under-bed storage – and a big guest kitchen. Free tea and coffee before 10am. Walk outside to find cafes, bars, galleries, 5 spectacular beaches & the coastal path!

DETAILS

■ **Open** - February - December. 8am - 10pm

■ **Beds** - 61: 1x8, 7x6, 1x4, 2x twin, 1x twin/triple

■ **Price/night** - Beds from £15

CONTACT: Reception
Tel: 01736 791664
hello@stayatcohort.co.uk
www.stayatcohort.co.uk
The Stennack, St Ives, Cornwall,
TR26 1FF

PENROSE
BUNKHOUSE

95

On the edge of the Penrose Estate, the gateway to The Lizard Peninsula.

Penrose bunkhouse is right next to the SW Coast Path and has great access to many local walks, trails and cycling routes. Penrose, is home to many rare species of wildlife as well as Cornwall's largest freshwater lake, the Loe. The perfect location to base your group for wildlife adventures, walking and activity holidays or a break away from it all. The bunkhouse sleeps 16 in three rooms and is well equipped for self catering.

GROUPS ONLY

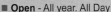
DETAILS

- **Open** - All year. All Day
- **Beds** - 16: 2x7, 1x2,
- **Price/night** - From £300 for two nights.

CONTACT: National Trust Holidays
Tel: 0344 335 1296
bunkhouses@nationaltrust.org.uk
www.nationaltrust.org.uk
Penrose Bunk House, Gunwalloe,
Helston, Cornwall TR12 7PY

FALMOUTH
LODGE

96

Judi has moved back from Grenada in the West Indies to be your host at Falmouth Lodge. Relaxed, friendly and clean, Falmouth Lodge Backpackers is just two minutes' walk from the Blue Flag Gyllyngvase beach and the South West Coast Path plus only eight minutes' walk into town with its exotic gardens, Art Galleries and Princess Pavilions and the harbour. Free parking. No curfew. Complimentary tea, coffee and breakfast. Well-equipped kitchen and cosy lounge with TV/DVD, and free WiFi.

DETAILS

- **Open** - All Year. Reception from 5pm
- **Beds** - 28: 2x2/3, 2 x4/5, 1x6/7, 1xdbl/ family en suite (some sea views).
- **Price/night** - From £19 per person

CONTACT: Judi
Tel: 01326 319996 or 07525 722808
judi@falmouthlodge.co.uk
www.falmouthbackpackers.co.uk
9 Gyllyngvase Terrace, Falmouth, Cornwall, TR11 4DL

BEACH HEAD
BUNKHOUSE

With fantastic views out to sea and along the north Cornish coast to Trevose Head, National Trust run Beach Head Bunkhouse provides great value basic self-catering holiday accommodation.

The great self-catering facilities and location just 1.5 miles from the beach at Porthcothan and close to the South West Coast path make it the perfect base for family holidays (but not those with very young children) and walking groups alike.

    GROUPS ONLY

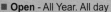

DETAILS

- **Open** - All Year. All day
- **Beds** - 14: 2x1 2x6
- **Price/night** - 2 nights from £340.

CONTACT: National Trust Holidays
Tel: 0344 335 1296
bunkhouses@nationaltrust.org.uk
www.nationaltrust.org.ukl
Park Head, St Eval, Wadebridge,
Cornwall, PL27 7UU

EDENS YARD
BACKPACKERS

98

Welcome to this quirky, Camino inspired eco hostel up-cycled from an old stable block to include mixed bunk rooms, a courtyard kitchen & a communal lounge. It's just a short leafy lane from the Eden Project situated on National Cycle routes 2 & 3, two miles from the North West Coast Path at Carlyon Bay and close to the historic Saints Way pilgrimage trail. Walkers and cyclists welcomed and offer pick-ups offered from the station or parking on request. Come and be welcome in Cornwall at Edens Yard.

DETAILS

- **Open** - Easter to mid October. Arrive between 4pm and 10pm please.
- **Beds** - 1x6, 1x8
- **Price/night** - £15

CONTACT: Neal or Julia
Tel: 01726 814907
info@edensyard.uk
www.edensyard.uk
17 Tregrehan Mills, St. Austell, Cornwall,
PL25 3TL

STAYKATION HOTEL
FOR BACKPACKERS

Perfect for backpackers and budget travellers. This friendly hostel offers a warm welcome to all its guests. In the centre of Plymouth just 10 mins from the train and bus stations and within easy walking distance of the ferry port. Located near some of the top bars, clubs, restaurants and theatres with friendly staff on site. Security is taken seriously with 24hr CCTV. Facilities include a small, well equipped, self-catering kitchen, common room, free linen, towels & WiFi. Dorm beds each have their own power light and lockers.

DETAILS
- **Open** - All year. Check in from 2pm, check out 10am.
- **Beds** - 10: 1x4, 1x6
- **Price/night** - £17pp

CONTACT: Carole Reynolds
Tel: 01752 269333 Mob:07455971473
carolereynolds99@hotmail.co.uk
Staykation.co.uk
94 Union Street, Plymouth, PL1 3EZ

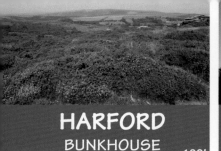

HARFORD
BUNKHOUSE

FOX TOR
BUNKHOUSE

Harford Bunkhouse & Camping offers comfortable budget accommodation on the edge of stunning South Dartmoor. An ideal choice if you are planning to start the Two Moors Way walk from south to north. Run alongside a working Dartmoor farm, the bunkhouse offers dormitory style accommodation with self catering facilities for up to 50 people. The campsite is on two of the farm's meadows. There are also two camping pods and a cabin which sleep up to 6 people each.

An ideal base for anyone wishing to spend time on Dartmoor whether it is to walk, climb, cycle, kayak or just relax and enjoy the spectacular scenery. This Bunkhouse is situated near the centre of Princetown. Guests can book packed lunches and breakfasts. The café has wood stoves and provides lovely home made food cooked to order. Guided walks & mountain biking are available as is mountain bike hire.

DETAILS

- **Open** - All year. All day.
- **Beds** - 40-50 beds
- **Price/night** - From £17pp. Camping pods/cabin £50 each. Camping £7.50pp

DETAILS

- **Open** - All year. All day. Arrive from 4.30pm, leave by 10.30am.
- **Beds** - 12: 3 x 4
- **Price/night** - From £11pp. Private room: £33/1person. £36.50/2people. £40/3people. £44/4people.

CONTACT: Julie Cole
Tel: 07968566218
julie.cole6@btinternet.com
www.harfordbunkhouse.com
West Combeshead, Harford, Ivybridge, Devon, PL21 0JG

CONTACT: Abbi or Dave
Tel: 01822 890238
enquiries@foxtorcafe.com
www.foxtorcafe.co.uk
Two Bridges Road, Princetown, Dartmoor, Devon, PL20 6QS

SPARROWHAWK
BACKPACKERS
101l

BLYTHESWOOD
HOSTEL
101r

A small, friendly eco-hostel in the centre of Moretonhampstead, Dartmoor National Park. Popular with cyclists, hikers, bikers, wild swimmers, artists and photographers, A beautifully converted stone stable, with solar-heated showers, kitchen, courtyard, BBQ and secure bike shed. High open moorland, rocky tors, ancient burial sites, stone circles, woods and clear rivers close by. Moretonhampstead has shops, cafés, art galleries and pubs. Cicerone LEJOG & Dartmoor Way cycle routes pass by.

In secluded, native woodland on the eastern edge of Dartmoor, the cabin has been a hostel since the 1930s. Friendly and peaceful, with a homely living room, wood burner, self-catering kitchen, picnic tables, BBQ and fire pit. Walk straight from the door to Heltor and Blackingstone Rock or along the river to Fingle Bridge and Castle Drogo. Cross stepping stones to Dunsford village. Moretonhampstead and Chagford are nearby. On the LEJOG cycling route.

DETAILS

- **Open** - All year
- **Beds** - 18: 1x14 + double/family room.
- **Price/night** - Adults dorm £19. U14 £10. Double room £42 (for 2 people).

DETAILS

- **Open** - All year.
- **Beds** - 16: 1x6, 1x4 (family), 1x2 (cabin) and 1x4 (cabin)
- **Price/night** - £16 per adult. U16 £10. Sole Use: £240pn 2+nights. £280 1night.

CONTACT: Alison
Tel: 01647 440318 - 07870 513570
ali@sparrowhawkbackpackers.co.uk
www.sparrowhawkbackpackers.co.uk
45 Ford Street, Moretonhampstead, Dartmoor, Devon, TQ13 8LN

CONTACT: Lewis and Sarah
Tel: 07758 654840
hello@blytheswood.co.uk
www.blytheswood.co.uk
Steps Bridge, Dunsford, Devon, EX6 7EQ

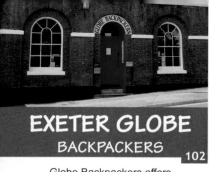

EXETER GLOBE
BACKPACKERS
102

Globe Backpackers offers clean, comfortable, self catering accommodation. It is just a few minutes' walk from Exeter's city centre with its cathedral, picturesque historic waterway, quay and wide range of shops, pubs, clubs, cafés and restaurants.

DETAILS

■ **Open** - All year (phone for Xmas). Check in/check out: Mon-Fri: 8.30-12 noon and 3.30pm to 11pm. Sat,Sun: 8.30am-11pm. Earlier check out by arrangement only.,

■ **Beds** - 46-52: 1x10, 3x8, 1x6, 3x2/4 (dbl/twin plus bunk bed)

■ **Price/night** - Dorms from £18.50pp or £80pp per week. Private rooms from £50 for two people, £80 for four people. 50p for card payments. £5 key deposit.

CONTACT: Duty Manager
Tel: 01392 215521
info@exeterbackpackers.co.uk
www.exeterbackpackers.co.uk
71 Holloway Street, Exeter, EX2 4JD

NORTHSHORE
BUDE
103

An ideal base to see the South West's attractions: The Eden Project, Tintagel Castle, The Tamar Lakes, Dartmoor and Bodmin Moor or as a stop off on the South West Coast Path. There are competition standard surfing beaches nearby. Families with children aged over 5 welcome. Meet old friends or make new ones, on the deck, in the lounge or around the dining room table after cooking up a storm in the fully fitted kitchen. No stag groups please.

DETAILS

■ **Open** - All year, except Christmas week. 8.30am-1pm & 4.30pm- 10.30pm.
■ **Beds** - 41: 2x6, 4x4, 1x3, 1x2, 4xdbl
■ **Price/night** - From £22pp dorm rooms (single night supplement)

CONTACT: Sean or Janine
Tel: 01288 354256
sean@northshorebude.com
www.northshorebude.com
57 Killerton Road, Bude, Cornwall,
EX23 8EW

ELMSCOTT
HOSTEL

Elmscott Hostel is surrounded by unspoiled coastline with sea views of Lundy Island. Great for walking, cycling, surfing and bird watching. The South West Coast Path is just a few mins' walk away. The hostel is well equipped for all your self-catering needs and has a games room and shop. In winter it is only available for sole use bookings.

DETAILS

■ **Open** - All year.
■ **Beds** - 32 (35 in winter): 1 unit of 20: 2x6, 2x4; 1 unit of 12: 1x6, 1x4, 1x2. Extra 3 bed room for sole use in winter.
■ **Price/night** - Adult £20-£22, under 16s £15.50-£17. Discounts for groups or longer stays.

CONTACT: John, Thirza and Kate
Tel: Hostel 01237 441367/ Owners
01237 441276/ Kate 01237 441637
john.goa@virgin.net
www.elmscott.org.uk
Elmscott, Hartland, Bideford, Devon,
EX39 6ES

PEPPERCOMBE
BOTHY
105

Located in a quiet, tranquil, wooded valley with views across Bideford Bay towards Lundy, Peppercombe Bothy is effectively a "stone tent".
A perfect stopover on the South West Coast Path which passes through the valley close by or for those who really do want to get away from it all. With access to it's own secluded beach you will not be disappointed. There is no light or heating so bring your own sleeping, cooking and eating equipment and a torch!

DETAILS
■ **Open** - All year. All day
■ **Beds** - 4-BYO mats and sleeping bags
■ **Price/night** - Low season September-May £20, High season June- August £25.

CONTACT: National Trust Holidays
Tel: 0344 335 1296
bunkhouses@nationaltrust.org.uk
www.nationaltrust.org.uk
Peppercombe, Bideford, Devon,
EX39 5QD

OCEAN
BACKPACKERS
106

Close to the picturesque Ilfracombe Harbour, this clean and friendly hostel offers fantastic facilities for walkers, cyclists, surfers, families, schools and activity groups. Providing self-catering accommodation with great facilities including, communal lounge (free WiFi), bike/surfboard storage, drying area and free parking. Ilfracombe is full of cafés, galleries, shops and restaurants and is home to Damien Hirst's statue, Verity.

DETAILS
- **Open** - Feb-Nov. Reception 9-12pm and 4pm-10pm. No curfew.
- **Beds** - 54:- 1x8, 5x6, 1 x single, 2 x double, 3 x double & bunk
- **Price/night** - Dorm beds £13.00-£19.00. Double rooms £42-£48 per room.

CONTACT: Chris and Abby
Tel: 01271 867835 Mob: 07866 667716
info@oceanbackpackers.co.uk
www.oceanbackpackers.co.uk
29 St James Place, Ilfracombe, Devon,
EX34 9BJ

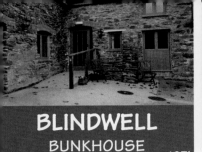

BLINDWELL
BUNKHOUSE
107l

On an Exmoor hill farm, with far reaching views of Devon and Dartmoor. Red deer, buzzards and Exmoor ponies on the doorstep. Perfect for Sustrans cycle route 3, with off-road mountain bike trails and many beautiful walking routes as well as Exmoor's beauty spots nearby.

High quality comfortable bunks and mattresses, shared toilets and showers with underfloor heating and disabled facilities. Traditional local pubs nearby.

DETAILS
- **Open** - All year.
- **Beds** - 16 1x6,1x6,1x4
- **Price/night** - £18pp excl bedding. Any week night whole bunkhouse £288. Weekend Fri/Sat £576. Christmas and New Year by arrangement. Bedding £5pp

CONTACT: Carol Delbridge
Tel: 01598 740246
delbridge.carol@googlemail.com
www.blindwellbunkhouse.co.uk
Blindwell Farm, Twitchen, Sandyway, South Molton, EX36 3LT

MULLACOTT
CAMPING BARN
107r

Set in 30 acres on the North Devon coast, the farm boasts sea views overlooking Woolacombe, Lundy Island, Lee Bay, Ilfracombe, and the Welsh coast. A former stable block with all accommodation on ground level with raised sleeping areas with mattresses. BYO sleeping bag/bedding and warm clothing. There is a dining area and well equipped kitchen. Toilets/coin operated showers are in a nearby block. No stag/hen parties. Dogs welcome with sole use bookings. B&B, camping and static caravan also on site.

DETAILS
- **Open** - March - November
- **Beds** - 20
- **Price/night** - £10 per person per night. Sole use: by arrangement.

CONTACT: Alison and Adrian Homa
Tel: 01271 866877
relax@mullacottfarm.co.uk
www.mullacottfarm.co.uk
Ilfracombe, Devon, EX34 8NA

ROCK AND RAPID
BUNKHOUSE

108

Perfect for an adventurous or relaxing break. The Rock and Rapid Adventure Centre offers activities such as climbing (climbing wall on site for lessons or use by experienced climbers) coasteering, canoeing and surfing.

The bunkhouse can be rented out for sole use, for an activity package or a full programme, including food, can be put together for your group. Just 15 mins from the North Devon coastline, so surfing lessons and other water sports are on offer. Hen and stags welcome as are family or school groups.

DETAILS

- **Open** - All year. 24 Hours.
- **Beds** - 40: 2 x 18, 2 x 2
- **Price/night** - £235 per night sole use.

CONTACT: Jade Evans
Tel: 0333 600 6001
bunkhouse@rockandrapidadventures.co.uk
www.rockandrapidadventures.co.uk
Hacche Mill, South Molton, EX36 3NA

BUTTER HILL
BARN

109

This cosy National Trust run bunkhouse can be found at Countisbury close to Lynton and Lynmouth on the North Devon Coast. Surrounded by the dramatic Watersmeet Valleys and Exmoor, it is perfect for accessing the South West Coastal Path and the Atlantic surf beaches. Also great for those wanting to experience Exmoor's dark skies. Perfect for families, groups and walkers, the barn is just along the road from Exmoor Bunkhouse (see page 110) so can be used as an overspill for larger groups.

     GROUPS ONLY

DETAILS

- **Open** - All Year. All day
- **Beds** - 6: 1x6
- **Price/night** - 2 nights from £120.

CONTACT: National Trust Holidays
Tel: 0344 335 1296
bunkhouses@nationaltrust.org.uk
www.nationaltrust.org.uk
Countisbury Hill, Lynmouth, Devon,
EX35 6NE

EXMOOR
BUNKHOUSE

110

Owned and managed by the National Trust and providing comfortable, high standard accommodation, Exmoor Bunkhouse is the perfect base for families or groups wanting to visit Exmoor National Park. Located at Countisbury, the bunkhouse is close to the Watersmeet Valleys and the North Devon coastal villages of Lynton and Lynmouth. Take part in the many activities Exmoor has to offer such as walking and horse riding or go surfing on nearby Atlantic coast beaches. Larger groups overspill at Butterhill Barn pg109.

       GROUPS ONLY

DETAILS

- **Open** - All year. 24 hours.
- **Beds** - 18: 2x8, 1x2
- **Price/night** - 2 nights minimum stay from £270 mid week and £390 weekend.

CONTACT: National Trust Holidays
Tel: 0344 335 1296
bunkhouses@nationaltrust.org.uk
www.nationaltrust.org.uk
Countisbury, Lynton, Devon, EX35 6NE

FORELAND
BOTHY

111

Foreland Bothy on the National Trust Foreland Point estate on the Exmoor coast offers very basic accommodation, but rewards you with a fantastic location right on the South West Coast Path. Treat it like camping but without the tent, so you need to bring camping mats, sleeping bags and cooking equipment. There is a composting loo but no hot water. The perfect location for a night or two for those who want to explore the area on foot or want to escape technology in this wilderness under some stunning dark skies.

DETAILS
- **Open** - All year. All day
- **Beds** - 4: 1x4 platforms
- **Price/night** - 2 nights from £40

CONTACT: National Trust Holidays
Tel: 0344 335 1296
bunkhouses@nationaltrust.org.uk
www.nationaltrust.org.uk
Lighthouse Road, Countisbury, Lynton, Devon, EX35 6NE

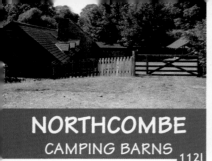

NORTHCOMBE
CAMPING BARNS
112l

EXMOOR
BUNKBARN
112r

Located a mile outside the town of Dulverton on Exmoor, Northcombe Camping Barns nestle in the Barle river valley with good canoeing, walking and bridleways. The perfect base for groups wanting to explore Exmoor. The barns sleep 16 and 28 in partitioned dormitories. Smaller groups can be catered for. Heated by wood-burning stoves with a well equipped kitchen, you just need to bring your own pillows, sleeping bags or duvets.

Converted from a former granary on a working farm, this eco-friendly bunkbarn is just 1km from Winsford Hill. Perfect for exploring Exmoor on foot, bike or canoe and close to the local attractions. Well equipped with open-plan kitchen, dining/seating and patio for BBQ. BYO sleeping bags, bedding & towels and also shoes/slippers to protect feet from rough barn floor. Sole use at weekends (2 nights min). Rooms can be booked and facilities shared in the week.

DETAILS

- **Open** - All year. Arrive after 4pm, depart before 10.30am
- **Beds** - 44: Barn16: 1x6, 1x10, Barn 28: 1x6, 1x10, 1x12
- **Price/night** - Sole use: Barn16 from £140, Barn28 from £240. Showers 20p

CONTACT: Sally Harvey
Tel: 01398 323602
sallyeharvey17@gmail.com
www.northcombecampingbarns.co.uk/
Hollam, Dulverton, Somerset, TA22 9JH

DETAILS

- **Open** - All year. All day.
- **Beds** - 25: 1x14, 1x8, 1x3
- **Price/night** - Weekend sole use: £350. Mon-Thur sole use: £300. Rooms: 14/bed £240, 8/bed £150, 3/bed £75.

CONTACT: Julia or Guy Everard
Tel: 01643 851410
bookings@exmoorbunkbarn.co.uk
www.exmoorbunkbarn.co.uk
Week Farm, Bridgetown, Dulverton
TA22 9JP

CHITCOMBE FARM
CAMPING BARNS
113l

A small family farm in West Somerset, on the edge of Exmoor, Chitcombe Farm provides inexpensive, basic, warm & dry accommodation. Perfect after a day hiking on Exmoor, or training for an event. The Hay Barn, is a dormitory style open plan barn whilst The Cart Shed is an open plan chalet. Both have well equipped kitchens, bathroom with showers, seating areas and central heating. Beds are in bunks. BYO pillows and sleeping bag.

DETAILS
- **Open** - All year.
- **Beds** - 16: The Hay Barn 14, The Cart Shed 4. More by arrangement.
- **Price/night** - £20pp. Sole use: The Hay barn £200. The Cart Shed £75.

CONTACT: Ali Kennen
Tel: 01398 371274
stkennen@hotmail.co.uk
chitcombebarns.co.uk/
Chitcombe Farm, Huish Champflower, Taunton, Somerset, TA4 2EL

BASE LODGE
113r

Base Lodge is your perfect base for exploring Exmoor, the Quantocks and North Devon. The South West Coast Path starts in Minehead and there is excellent mountain biking. Guided biking, navigational training, climbing, surfing, pony trekking and natural history walks can all be arranged. Base Lodge is clean, comfortable with self-catering and a cosy log burner.

DETAILS
- **Open** - All year. All day access once booked (reception open from 3pm).
- **Beds** - 22: 2x2, 1x7, 1x6, 1x5
- **Price/night** - Dorms £17.50, private single £7.50 supplement, twin/double £40. Sole use of Base Lodge from £200. Family room discount.

CONTACT: Wendy or Graham
Tel: 01643 703520 or 0773 1651536
togooutdoors@hotmail.com
www.togooutdoors.co.ukl
16 The Parks, Minehead, Somerset, TA24 8BS

CAMPBELL ROOM

114l

The Campbell Room offers self-catering group accommodation for youth organisations, schools, walkers, cyclists and others. Set in the Quantock Hills AONB within 10 minutes' walk of the forest, it offers a main hall which can also sleep 18, 2 bedrooms each sleeping 3, a multi-use cabin, kitchen, showers, drying room, campfire and space for 1 or 2 tents. Activities include walking, hiking, mountain biking, beaches and high-ropes.

DETAILS
- **Open** - All year. By arrangement.
- **Beds** - 24 recommended (but see website). 2x3, 1x18 max, 1x8 max
- **Price/night** - £4.50 pp (2 leaders free for groups over 12), min £54 per night.

CONTACT: Katie Newell
Tel: 01278 726 000
info@campbellroom.org.uk
www.campbellroom.org.uk
Campbell Room Group Accommodation, Aley, Over Stowey, Somerset.

MONKTON WYLD
COURT

114r

This Victorian Neo-Gothic mansion in Dorset's AONB, has easy access to the Jurassic Coast at Lyme Regis, and the Wessex and Monarch's Way long distance footpaths. Guests can use the vegetarian self-catering kitchen to prepare their own meals or purchase pre-booked vegetarian meals. There is camping in the grounds. Run by a charity that promotes sustainable living. Fruit and vegetables are grown in the organic garden and eggs come from free-range chickens.Jersey cows provide the milk.

DETAILS
- **Open** - All year. Office opening hours: 9am-5pm.
- **Beds** - 42 beds in a variety room sizes
- **Price/night** - £20 - £35pp.

CONTACT: Office Team
Tel: 01297 560 342
info@monktonwyldcourt.org
www.monktonwyldcourt.co.uk
Elsdon's Lane, Charmouth, Bridport, Dorset, DT6 6DQ

STONE BARROW

On the National Trust Golden Cap Estate, this bunkhouse has been converted from an old MoD radar station and provides fantastic group accommodation for families, walkers or special interest groups.

With great views over Golden Cap, Lyme Bay and Chesil Beach it is the perfect base for a walking or beach holiday with Charmouth beaches only half a hour walk away. Golden Cap Bunkhouse sleeps 8 in two 4 bed dorms and is well equipped for group self-catering.

DETAILS

- **Open** - All year. All day
- **Beds** - 8: 2x4
- **Price/night** - From £160 for two nights.

CONTACT: National Trust Holidays
Tel: 0344 335 1296
bunkhouses@nationaltrust.org.uk
www.nationaltrust.org.uk
Stonebarrow Lane, Charmouth, Dorset, DT6 6RA

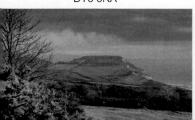

BUNKHOUSE
PLUS
116l

In the heart of Weymouth, the gateway to the Jurassic coast. With a mixture of bunk rooms with the 'Plus' of double en suite rooms. Close to the town centre, the safe swimming waters of the beach and the old harbour which hosts fantastic festivals of the sea. Go wind and kite surfing, fishing, sailing, diving or rock climbing. Sole use is available for 23. Facilities include large self-catering kitchen, lounge with Freeview TV and DVD. Not stag/hen or party groups.

DETAILS
- **Open** - All year. Arrivals 4 pm onwards.
- **Beds** - 23: 3×4, 1×3, 2×2, 2x double en suites
- **Price/night** - From £16.50. Sole use of building from £150 winter, £300 summer.

CONTACT: Bunkhouse Plus
Tel: 01305 775228
bunkhouseplus@gmail.com
www.bunkhouseplus.co.uk
Bunkhouse Plus, 47 Walpole Street,
Weymouth, DT4 7HQ

MYTIME
OUTDOOR CENTRE
116r

Located on the Isle of Purbeck, just outside the picturesque village of Worth Matravers, the rustic MyTIME Outdoor Centre provides ideal accommodation for groups wishing to explore the magnificent Jurassic coastline and experience the enviable range of outdoor activities nearby; from walking and cycling to coasteering and kayaking. Groups have sole use of the centre.

DETAILS
- **Open** - All year.
- **Beds** - 40: 24 inside: 1x2, 1x4 en suite, 1x8, 1x10. 16 camping.
- **Price/night** - Whole centre from £330 (24 people). 16 more can camp (BYO tents) at £7pp. Bedding £5pp. Dog £15. Winter fuel supplement £10 (Oct–Mar).

CONTACT: MyTIME Outdoor Centre
Tel: 01202 710701
enquiries@mytimecharity.co.uk
www.mytimecharity.co.uk/Outdoor_Centre.html
Off Renscombe Rd, Worth Matravers,
Isle of Purbeck, Dorset. BH19 3LL

SWANAGE
AUBERGE
117

Family run, Swanage Auberge, the bunkhouse that cares, is a refuge for climbers, walkers and divers, at the eastern end of the Jurassic Coast. In the centre of Swanage, a stone's throw from the South West Coast Path, there is excellent walking, diving and rock climbing on the doorstep. Swanage Auberge has a fully equipped self-catering kitchen, and a meals (inc packed lunch) service if required. Parking for 2 vehicles and on the street.

DETAILS

■ **Open** - All year (phone mobile if no reply). All day.
■ **Beds** - 15: 1x6, 1x4,1x5
■ **Price/night** - £20pp, £18 for 2+ nights. Inc bedding/towel, cereal breakfast, tea & coffee. Group rates. No credit cards.

CONTACT: Pete or Pam
Tel: 01929 424368. Mobile:07711 117668
bookings@swanageauberge.co.uk
www.swanageauberge.co.uk
45 High St, Swanage, Dorset, BH19 2LX

SOUTH SHORE
LODGE

118

South Shore Lodge on Brownsea Island in Poole Harbour provides accommodation for groups in a Victorian lodge. Located on the south coast of the island it has its own garden, beach access and views of the Purbeck Hills. Open all year for group hire including youth, community, special interest, corporate and school groups, it sleeps 24 in 5 rooms and is well equipped for self-catering. Access to Brownsea Island is by foot on a ferry from Poole.

        GROUPS ONLY

DETAILS

- **Open** - All year. All day
- **Beds** - 24: 3x6, 1x4, 1x2
- **Price/night** - 1 night £330.

CONTACT: National Trust Holidays
Tel: 01202 707744
brownseagroupbooking@nationaltrust.org.uk
www.nationaltrust.org.uk
Brownsea Island, Poole, Dorset, BH13 7EE

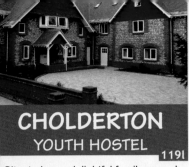

CHOLDERTON
YOUTH HOSTEL
119l

Situated on a delightful family owned farm, this 4* youth hostel provides family/child friendly accommodation for groups or individuals. The hostel is located 8 miles from historic Salisbury with its cathedral, and only 5 miles from Stonehenge. Cooked breakfasts are available from the Ewe Tree Café and packed lunches & evening meals can be pre-booked. Guests get free admission to Charlie's rare breeds farm and large indoor play barn, just next door. Or why not explore the tree top trail, zip wire and woodland walk in the grounds.

DETAILS

- **Open** - All year
- **Beds** - 70
- **Price/night** - Enquire for prices.

CONTACT: Reception
Tel: 01980 629438
info@choldertonyouthhostel.co.uk
www.choldertonyouthhostel.co.uk
Beacon House, Amesbury Road,
Cholderton, Salisbury, Wilts, SP4 0EW

MENDIP
BUNKHOUSE
119r

Larkshall (Mendip Bunkhouse) is the Cerberus Spelaeological Society's headquarters and offers well appointed, modern and comfortable accommodation on The Mendips. It is an ideal base for caving, walking, cycling, climbing and for exploring the Somerset countryside.

Popular tourist attractions, including Wells, Wookey Hole, Cheddar Gorge and the city of Bath, are all within reach. Camping available. Ample parking.

DETAILS

- **Open** - All year. All day.
- **Beds** - 30: (1x12, 1x18) plus camping
- **Price/night** - £8pp. Sole use of bunkrooms £87/£130 per night. Min charge £15 pp per stay (inc sole use).

CONTACT:
Tel: 0845 475 0954
hostelbookings@cerberusspeleo.org.uk
www.cerberusspeleo.org.uk
Cerberus Spelaeological, Larkshall,
Fosse Rd. Oakhill, Somerset, BA3 5HY

BATH YMCA

Bath YMCA offers great value accommodation. Centrally located, all the sights of this World Heritage city are easily reached on foot. With 210 beds, Bath YMCA specialises in making guests feel comfortable. There is a fully air conditioned lounge area with TV, laundry, lockers, pool & football table and WiFi. Couples, families, groups and backpackers are all welcome.

DETAILS

- **Open** - All year. All day.
- **Beds** - 210: Dorms: 1x10, 3x12, 1x15, 1x18. Rooms: 7 x quad, 6 x triple, 29 x twin, 5 x double, 9 x single
- **Price/night** - From: dorm £21pp, single £32pp, twin £28pp, double £30pp, triple £23pp, quad £22pp. Inc breakfast.

CONTACT: Reception
Tel: 01225 325900
stay@bathymca.co.uk
www.bathymca.co.uk
International House, Broad Street Place,
Bath, BA1 5LH

Are you ready for a great workout?

GOBLIN COMBE
LODGE
121

In the heart of Somerset, 10 miles outside Bristol, Goblin Combe Lodge is an Eco timber framed building set in 8 acres of private grounds with stunning views across the Severn Estuary. Run on a not-for-profit basis and surrounded by SSSI woodlands, it offers flexible accommodation for all groups with the possibility of additional tailored activities and learning programmes. Groups of up to 38 will sleep easy in 10 bedrooms of 2, 4 & 6 beds. Camping is also available.

       GROUPS ONLY

DETAILS

■ **Open** - All year. Ask about opening times.
■ **Beds** - 38
■ **Price/night** - Ask for prices. No min stay. Reductions for charities and schools.

CONTACT:
Tel: 01934 833723
goblin.combe@groundwork.org.uk
www.goblincombe.org.uk
Goblin Combe Lodge, Cleeve Hill, North Somerset, BS40 5PP

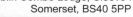

BRISTOL
BACKPACKERS
122l

Bristol's most central backpacker hostel. Clean & comfortable beds - mixed/single sex dorms - private rooms - individual bathrooms & free hot showers - free linen - large self-catering kitchen - free tea, coffee & hot chocolate. Late night basement bar - piano & guitar room - DVD lounge - free WiFi - luggage storage room - laundrette.
Run by backpackers for backpackers - No curfew after check in.

DETAILS
■ **Open** - All year. Reception hours 9am -11.30pm (no curfew).
■ **Beds** - 90: Bunk bed accommodation in private twin, private triple or 6, 8 and 10 bed dorms.
■ **Price/night** - From £13 for dorm beds. From £35 for private rooms.

CONTACT:
Tel: 0117 9257900
bristol.backpackers.hostel@gmail.com
www.bristolbackpackers.co.uk
17 St Stephen's Street, Bristol, BS1 1EQ

KYLE BLUE
HOSTEL BOAT
122r

Moored in the heart of Bristol's historic harbour, only a five minute stroll to the city centre. The Kyle Blue Hostel Boat is a converted Dutch Barge with private and shared cabins and a spacious upper deck providing fabulous views of the harbour from its tranquil lounge and well equipped self-catering kitchen. Great for independent travellers or small groups wanting to visit this vibrant city. Sleeping is in various sized cabins with private shower rooms. The Kyle Blue is moored in a residential area so no noise after 11pm.

DETAILS
■ **Open** - All year. All day
■ **Beds** - 30: 4x1 (2), 3x5 1x4 1x7
■ **Price/night** - from £25 per person

CONTACT:
Tel: 0117 929 0609
kylebluebristol@gmail.com
kylebluebristol.co.uk
Wapping Wharf, Museum Street, Bristol
BS1 6GW

ROCK AND BOWL

123

The Rock n Bowl Hostel is in the heart of Bristol. It occupies 2 floors of an historic 1930s building with The Lanes, a bowling alley, bar and club venue on the ground floor (hostel guests get great discounts).

With its huge range of rooms there will be a bed to suit your budget. And everyone gets a free breakfast! Facilities include a well equipped large kitchen, lounge with Sky TV including Sky Sports/ BT Sports, free WiFi & laundry.

DETAILS

■ **Open** - All year. All day.
■ **Beds** - 144: 1×20, 3×12, 1×10, 3×10 weekly bed dorm, 2×8, 2×6, 3×4, 1×4 female, 1xdouble/twin/3bed, 1xdouble
■ **Price/night** - Dorms from £10pp. Private rooms from £39. Weekly rooms from £90.

CONTACT: The Reception Team
Tel: 0117 325 1980
bookings@rocknbowlmotel.com
www.thelanesbristol.co.uk/hostel/
22 Nelson Street, Bristol, BS1 2LE

THE BRISTOL
WING
124l

This brand new hostel in the historic old police headquarters, is in the heart of the city centre. A mix of private, en suite and dorm rooms makes it ideal for single travellers, couples and families. The communal spaces on the ground floor include an award winning café offering tasty breakfast, great coffee and a super fresh lunch menu. Close to the bus station, just 20 minutes from Bristol Temple Meads and perfectly located for Bristol's best shopping from independent shops of Park Street & Clifton, big name brands in Cabot Circus or quirky market stalls in St Nicholas's Market.

DETAILS
■ **Open** - All year. All day.
■ **Beds** - 90
■ **Price/night** - From £18 per person

CONTACT: Reception
Tel: 0117 929 2975
enquiries@thebristolwing.co.uk
www.thebristolwing.co.uk/
5 - 7 Bridewell Street, Bristol, BS1 2QD

WETHERDOWN
124r
LODGE

An award winning eco-renovation in the heart of the South Downs National Park right on the South Downs Way National Trail. The perfect base for walkers, cyclists, business away-days and family get-togethers. The Lodge offers well appointed self-catering accommodation while the campsite has yurts and secluded woodland pitches. The centre has large grounds with woodland trails and a café. Pubs, shops within 2 miles.

DETAILS
■ **Open** - Hostel and campsite open all year. Yurts closed from Nov to April
■ **Beds** - 38: 10 x 3, 4 x 2
■ **Price/night** - See sustainability-centre website.

CONTACT: Dan
Tel: 01730 823549
accommodation@sustainability-centre.org
www.sustainability-centre.org
The Sustainability Centre, Droxford Road, East Meon, Hampshire, GU32 1HR

THE PRIVETT
CENTRE
125l

In glorious East Hampshire countryside (AONB), the Privett Centre offers low cost, comfortable, short-stay accommodation in a unique rural setting. It has been designed to accommodate small to medium-sized groups who like to have the place to themselves. Outside a large paddock and asphalt playground provide secure and spacious recreational and parking space. It is available for weekday, weekend and day use all year. The Privett Centre is an ideal residential setting for family & friends' get-togethers.

     **GROUPS ONLY**

DETAILS

■ **Open** - All year.
■ **Beds** - 29: 1x1, 1x2, 2x4, 1x6, 1x12
■ **Price/night** - From £15 pp. Minimum charges apply (Contact for exact prices).

CONTACT: Mehalah Piedot
Tel: 01256 351555
info@privettcentre.org.uk
www.privettcentre.org.uk
Church Lane, Privett, Hampshire,
GU34 3PE

SOUTH DOWNS
BUNKHOUSE
125r

Perfect for walkers, cyclists, horse riders & others wanting accommodation in the South Downs National Park. The Lock family provide a warm welcome to this beautifully converted barn on a working farm on the South Downs Way. Equipped with microwave, fridge, toaster, kettle & BBQ in the courtyard. Houghton and Amberley have pubs and cafés within walking distance. Secure bike storage/washing facilities. Horses welcome.

DETAILS

■ **Open** - All year. All day
■ **Beds** - 20: 3x4, 1x8. +6 B&B beds in the farmhouse 3x2 double/twin
■ **Price/night** - £22pp. BYO sleeping bag & towel, pillow supplied. Duvet, sheet & towel £4pn. Continental breakfast £4

CONTACT: Kate Lock
Tel: 01798 831100 Mob: 07710 630219
kate@southdownsbunkhouse.co.uk
www.southdownsbunkhouse.co.uk
Houghton Farm, Houghton, Arundel,
West Sussex, BN18 9LW

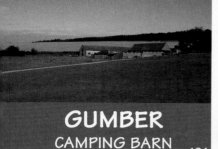

GUMBER
CAMPING BARN

A converted Sussex flint barn on a working sheep farm within the National Trust's Slindon Estate. It provides simple overnight accommodation or camping for walkers, horse riders and cyclists, just off the South Downs Way, or a tranquil and remote location for you to get away from it all. Just five minutes' walk from Stane Street, the Roman Road that crosses the South Downs Way at Bignor Hill. Sorry but NO CARS. Not suitable for under fives.

DETAILS

■ **Open** - Mar-Oct. Flexible opening hours
■ **Beds** - 25: 1x16, 1x5, 1x4 plus overflow area
■ **Price/night** - £12, £6 (under 16s).

CONTACT: Bothy Ranger
Tel: 01243 814484
gumberbothy@nationaltrust.org.uk
www.nationaltrust.org.uk/holidays/
gumber-camping-barn-and-campsite
Slindon Estate Yard, Slindon, Arundel,
West Sussex, BN18 0RG

SLINDON
BUNKHOUSE
127

This bunkhouse on the National Trust Slindon Estate has so much to offer all year round.

In the winter months enjoy the benefit of the wood burner in the lounge, and in the summer enjoy a barbeque in the walled garden.

Perfect for groups or groups of families wanting to get together and enjoy the fabulous South Downs National Park surroundings and the miles footpaths criss-crossing the estate.

GROUPS ONLY

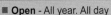
DETAILS

- **Open** - All year. All day
- **Beds** - 17, 1x6, 1x10, 1x1
- **Price/night** - 2 nights from £400.

CONTACT: National Trust Holidays
Tel: 0344 335 1296
bunkhouses@nationaltrust.org.uk
www.nationaltrust.org.uk
Slindon Estate Yard, Top Road, Slindon, Arundel, West Sussex, BN18 0RG

PUTTENHAM
CAMPING BARN

Eco project on North Downs Way offers simple overnight accommodation in a beautifully converted historic barn. Self-catering (or local pubs for food within walking distance); three shared sleeping areas; garden with picnic bench and cycle shed. NO CARS ON SITE, even for off-loading. Nearest railway stations: Wanborough 3.5 km, Guildford 7 km.

DETAILS

■ **Open** - Easter to Oct. arrive after 5pm leave before 10am. No access 10am-5pm.

■ **Beds** - Sleeping platforms for 11.

■ **Price/night** - £15 adults; £12 aged 5-17 (accompanied by adult). Sole use by arrangement. £3 `green` voucher if arriving on foot, cycle or public transport.

CONTACT: Bookings
Tel: 01483 811001
bookings@puttenhamcampingbarn.co.uk
www.puttenhamcampingbarn.co.uk
The Street, Puttenham, Nr Guildford,
Surrey, GU3 1AR

HENMAN
BUNKHOUSE

129

Perfect for groups wanting to walk or cycle around Leith Hill or beyond. This National Trust owned bunkhouse in the Surrey Hills AONB sleeps up to 16 in 6 and 4 bunk dorms. Well equipped with a self-catering kitchen, large dining table and comfy seating around an open fire. Walkers can directly access the Greensand Way and other local routes and there are many bridleways and tracks suitable for cycling. This is a great place for a holiday only 30 miles from London but in stunning countryside.

DETAILS

- **Open** - All year. All day except for Christmas and New Year
- **Beds** - 16: 2x6, 1x4
- **Price/night** - £200 Friday to Sunday, £150 Monday to Thursday

CONTACT: National Trust Holidays
Tel: 0344 335 1296
leithhill@nationaltrust.org.uk
www.nationaltrust.org.uk
Broadmoor, Dorking, Surrey, RH5 6JZ

OCTAVIA HILL
BUNKHOUSE
130

Converted from former farm buildings, Octavia Hill Bunkhouse is located on Outridge Farm on the National Trust Toys Hill Estate. Sleeping 14 in two rooms it is the perfect base for families or groups of walkers wanting to explore this lovely area of the Kent Downs Area of Outstanding Natural Beauty.

This bunkhouse has plenty of communal space and a well equipped kitchen for those who want to self-cater. Easily accessible by car, train and bus (the bus stop is just 15 minutes' walk away)

      GROUPS ONLY

DETAILS
- **Open** - All year. All day
- **Beds** - 14: 1x8,1x6
- **Price/night** - 1 night £250.

CONTACT: National Trust Holidays
Tel: 0344 335 1296
bunkhouses@nationaltrust.org.uk
www.nationaltrust.org.uk
Pipers Green Road, Brasted Chart, Westerham, Kent, TN16 1ND

PALACE FARM
HOSTEL
131

Palace Farm Hostel is a relaxing and flexible 4* hostel on a family run farm. Situated in the village of Doddington, (which has a pub!), in the North Kent Downs AONB, the area is great for walking, cycling (cycle hire available £10 a day) and wildlife. The accommodation consists of ten fully heated en suite rooms sleeping up to 39. Duvets, linen and continental breakfast included.

DETAILS

- **Open** - All year. 8am to 10pm flexible, please ask.
- **Beds** - 39: 1x8, 1x6, 2x5, 1x4, 1x3 and 4x2
- **Price/night** - From £18-£35 (all private en suite rooms). Reduction for groups.

CONTACT: Graham and Liz Cuthbert
Tel: 01795 886200
info@palacefarm.com
www.palacefarm.com
Down Court Road, Doddington,
Sittingbourne / Faversham, Kent,
ME9 0AU

KIPPS
CANTERBURY

Perfect for backpackers, visitors or small groups looking for self-catering budget accommodation in Canterbury. A short walk from the town centre and Canterbury Cathedral. A great base for day trips to Dover, Leeds Castle and local beaches. There is a dining room, TV lounge, garden, a fully equipped kitchen, a small shop & cycle hire.

DETAILS

■ **Open** - All year. No curfew. Reception 7.30am to 11pm.
■ **Beds** - 51:- 2x1, 2x2, 1x3, 1x5, 1x6, 1x7, 2x8, 1x9. Most rooms en suite
■ **Price/night** - From: dorms £14pp, singles £22pp, doubles £37, quads £50. Weekly and winter rates available. Credit cards accepted. Free on-street parking.

CONTACT: Reception
Tel: 01227 786121
kippshostel@googlemail.com
www.kipps-hostel.com
40 Nunnery Fields, Canterbury, Kent, CT1 3JT

ALPHA
HOSTEL
133l

Just 50m from Margate's Blue Flag, safe swimming beach and next to the Viking Coastal Trail for walkers and cyclists. The beach is perfect for sand castles and water sport. Visit the area or stop-over on the way to Europe. Facilities nclude; two lounges, a dining room, and large self-catering kitchen. Families and individuals welcomed as well as school and other groups with sole hostel use.

Classroom and catering available for 20+. Group self-catering also an option.

DETAILS
- **Open** - All year, 8am-10am, 5pm-10pm.
- **Beds** - 60: 2x6, 2x5, 4x5, 2x3, 6x2
- **Price/night** - £16.00pp. Groups: contact the hostel with requirements for meals etc. to obtain the best price.

CONTACT: Suzy Shears
Tel: 01843 221616
info@margatehostel.com
www.margatehostel.com
3 Royal Esplanade, Westbrook Bay, Margate, Kent CT9 5DL

HARLOW
INTERNATIONAL
133r

Harlow International Hostel is in the centre of a landscaped park and is one of the oldest buildings in Harlow. The town of Harlow is your ideal base for exploring London, Cambridge and the best of South East England. The journey time to central London is only 35 minutes from the hostel door and it is the closest hostel to Stansted Airport. National Cycle Route 1 passes the front door. Meals can be provided for groups. There's a children's zoo, orienteering course and outdoor pursuits centre in the park.

DETAILS
- **Open** - All year. 8am - 10.30pm (check in 3-10.30pm).
- **Beds** - 30: 2x1, 5x2, 1x4, 1x6, 1x8
- **Price/night** - Please see the website.

CONTACT: Richard Adams
Tel: 01279 421702
mail@h-i-h.co.uk
www.h-i-h.co.uk
13 School Lane, Harlow, Essex, CM20 2QD

CHILTERNS
BUNKHOUSE
134

Located on the National Trust's Ashridge Estate in the heart of the Chilterns Area of Outstanding Natural Beauty, This bunkhouse provides rustic, basic accommodation which comprises of two restored barns located amongst the woodlands and grassland of the estate. A well equipped, self-catering kitchen, lounge and outdoor eating area make it perfect for self-catering groups whilst the nearby village of Aldbury has pubs and cafés. The mobile reception here is limited making it the perfect place to get away from it all!

GROUPS ONLY

DETAILS
- **Open** - All year. All Day
- **Beds** - 16: 2x8
- **Price/night** - From £150

CONTACT: National Trust Holidays
Tel: 0344 335 1296
bunkhouses@nationaltrust.org.uk
www.nationaltrust.org.uk
Outwood Kiln, Aldbury, Tring,
Hertfordshire, HP23 5SE

CLINK78

In the centre of London in a 200 year old courthouse, Clink78 combines original features with modern interior design to create a friendly unique hostel. In the heart of King's Cross, with easy tube access the whole city. The friendly team will happily help with your itinerary and provide discounted attraction tickets. Kitchen, games area, TV/film lounge. Meet new people in The ClashBAR.

DETAILS

- **Open** - All year. 24 hours. No curfew or lockouts.
- **Beds** - 500: 4-16 bedded, triple, twin, single, en suite, cell rooms(for 2)
- **Price/night** - From £15pp, book b/fast online/on arrival. Bedlinen, WiFi & London walking tour inc. Group discounts.

CONTACT: Reservations
Tel: 020 7183 9400
reservations78@clinkhostels.com
www.clinkhostels.com
78 Kings Cross Road, King's Cross,
London, WC1X 9QG

CLINK261

One of London's best established backpacker hostels, Clink261 offers simple, comfortable, self-catering accommodation in the centre of London. King's Cross is a creative, upcoming area close to the British Museum, Covent Garden and Camden Market or a short tube ride to Piccadilly Circus & Leicester Square. Guests are invited round the corner to Clink78 for entertainment and good value drinks at the ClashBAR.

DETAILS

■ **Open** - All year. All day (except for Xmas) - no curfew or lockouts.
■ **Beds** - 170: 4-6 8-10 & 18 bed dorms, 4 private rooms (up to 3 beds)
■ **Price/night** - From £15pp, Breakfast bookable online/ arrival. Group discounts.

CONTACT:
Tel: 020 7833 9400
reservations261@clinkhostels.com
www.clinkhostels.com
261-265 Gray's Inn Road, King's Cross,
London, WC1X 8QT

OLD BROODER
BUNKHOUSE

137

Comfy, farm self-catering for 20 singles in four bedrooms. Mix of oak bunks/ conventional beds. Relax in cosy sitting room; BBQ, ping-pong, croquet & badminton in the garden; explore the farm, picnic in a meadow. 20 bikes included to explore quiet country lanes, or kayak down the River Stour, Go Ape, visit castles, print workshop courses.

 GROUPS ONLY

DETAILS

■ **Open** - Check booking arrangements
■ **Beds** - 20: 2x2, 2x8
■ **Price/night** - W/ends: 2nts from £1200, 1nt (occasionally) from £900. 3nts Bk Hols £1750. Xmas-New Yr (3nts+) £1750+. Extra nts from £300 m/wk: 2nts £600. Small groups/1 nt stays negotiable at short notice. Ask for a quote

CONTACT: Juliet Hawkins
Tel: 01787 247235
hawkins@thehall-milden.co.uk
www.thehall-milden.co.uk
The Hall, Milden, Lavenham, Sudbury,
Suffolk CO10 9NY

COURT HILL
CENTRE
138

Just 2 miles south of Wantage, and only a few steps from the historic Ridgeway National Trail, Court Hill Centre enjoys breathtaking views over the Vale of the White Horse. Reclaimed barns surround a pretty courtyard garden. Offering accommodation to families, groups and individuals, the centre offers evening meals, breakfasts and picnic lunches. There is a beautiful high-roofed dining room which retains the atmosphere of the old barn. A meeting/class-room camping and self-catering available.

DETAILS
■ **Open** - All year. To check availability please call 01235 760253.
■ **Beds** - 59: 1x15,1x9,1x6,1x5,6x4,1x2
■ **Price/night** - From £20.50. U18 £15.50

CONTACT: Reception
Tel: 01235 760253
info@Courthill.org.uk
www.Courthill.org.uk
Letcombe Regis, Wantage, OX12 9NE

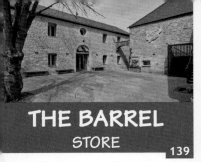

THE BARREL
STORE
139

Located in the heart of Cirencester, the newly converted Barrel Store provides stylish self-catering accommodation for up to 43 guests in 14 rooms. The rooms are designed to be simple but stylish and almost all are en-suite. Within easy reach of many well-known Cotswold attractions and accessible to transport links, the Barrel Store is perfect as a base from which to explore this fantastic area. Exclusive hire available, get in touch for details.

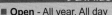

DETAILS

■ **Open** - All year. All day
■ **Beds** - 43:1x1, 2x2 bunks, 1x2 double, 3x3 single over double, 7x4 bunks.
■ **Price/night** - Bunks in shared room from £28, single room from £45.

CONTACT: The Barrel Store manager
Tel: 01285 657181
stay@newbreweryarts.org.uk
www.newbreweryarts.org.uk
New Brewery Arts, Brewery Court,
Cirencester, Gloucestershire, GL7 1JH

CROFT FARM
WATERPARK
140l

YE OLD FERRIE INN
BUNKHOUSE
140r

Just outside Tewkesbury in the scenic River Avon Valley, with it's own lake. Accommodation is in cabins, a pod village, chalets and camping. Great for touring the Cotswolds, Malverns, Bredon Hill and the Forest of Dean. There are also a wide range of watersports activities and tuition on offer providing added interest for those wanting a more active holiday. A footpath meanders through the meadow to the River Avon, and free river fishing is available to all guests.

This beautiful riverside pub has been standing on the banks of the River Wye since the 15th century. With charming traditional features, warming open fires and stunning views across the valley, Ye Old Ferrie Inn is the ideal base for your exploration of the Wye Valley. Ye Old Ferrie Inn Bunkhouse, adjoining the inn, is the perfect place for you to hang up your rucksack, kick off your walking boots and relax. Popular with canoeists, walkers and climbers. If you don't fancy self-catering there is B&B in the Inn.

DETAILS
- **Open** - All year. 9am-9pm.
- **Beds** - 250: 58x4 9x2
- **Price/night** - Bed £12, B&B £18, half board £24, full board £30

CONTACT: Martin Newell
Tel: 07736036967
alan@croftfarmleisure.co.uk
www.croftfarmleisure.co.uk
Bredons Hardwick, Near Tewkesbury,
Gloucestershire GL20 7EE

DETAILS
- **Open** - All year. All day.
- **Beds** - 20:1x14, 1x6 + dbl B&B rooms.
- **Price/night** - From £15 per person. For sole use please ring to enquire.

CONTACT: Jamie
Tel: 01600 890 232
hello@yeoldferrieinn.com
www.yeoldferrieinn.com
Ferrie Lane, Symonds Yat West,
Herefordshire HR9 6BL

BERROW HOUSE
BUNKHOUSE
141

Visit Berrow House Bunkhouse in the idyllic Malvern Hills with direct access to the hill and Eastnor Castle just down the road. Berrow House is near to the old spa town of Malvern and within half an hour of the Welsh Border and the Forest of Dean. It's an ideal base for walkers with the start of the Worcestershire Way walk near by. In the garden around Berrow House there is a selection of simple accommodation and camping with a wildlife picnic area, woodland, star gazing and grass sledging.

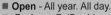
DETAILS

- **Open** - All year. All day.
- **Beds** - 7 (Bunkhouse), 4 (Fold), 3 (Nook), 3 (Bandsaw Barn) & 8 tents.
- **Price/night** - £14 per person

CONTACT: Bill or Mary Cole
Tel: 01531 635845
berrowhouse@tiscali.co.uk
www.berrowhouse.co.uk
Hollybush, Ledbury, Herefordshire,
HR8 1ET

WOODSIDE LODGES
BUNKHOUSE
142

Woodside Lodges Bunkhouse sits in a landscaped park with pools & wild flower meadows, along with Scandinavian self-catering lodges, a campsite and camping pods. The bunkhouse offers 5 self-catering units. Guests enjoy private rooms but share the campsite shower block. Close to the Herefordshire Trail, Malvern Hills & the Forest of Dean it's ideal for walkers, cyclists & nature lovers.

DETAILS

- **Open** - All year. All day.
- **Beds** - 15: 1x2, 3x3, 1x4 (max 20 using camp beds)
- **Price/night** - From £12.50 based on 4 sharing a room. Phone/check website for full prices. Sole use available. £5 per pet.

CONTACT: Woodside Lodges Country Park
Tel: 01531 670269
info@woodsidelodges.co.uk
www.woodsidelodges.co.uk
Woodside Lodges, Falcon Lane, Ledbury, Herefordshire, HR8 2JN

DUNFIELD
HOUSE

In rural Herefordshire, close to the Welsh border, Dunfield House provides accommodation for groups of up to 95 with sole use of the house, stables, parkland and swimming pool. From November to March the house and stables can also be hired individually by smaller groups. The house provides fully catered accommodation and the stables have a self-catering kitchen. A great choice for school, youth, music or church groups, training courses and family get-togethers.

       GROUPS ONLY

DETAILS

- **Open** - All year. All day.
- **Beds** - 95: main house 73, stables 22.
- **Price/night** - Sole hire of site from £25pp fully catered. Stables (sleeping 22) self-catering from £350 per night.

CONTACT: The Reception Team
Tel: 01544 230563
info@dunfieldhouse.org.uk
www.dunfieldhouse.org.uk
Kington. Herefordshire. HR5 3NN

LUDLOW MASCALL
CENTRE

144

Located in the heart of Ludlow and within walking distance of restaurants, shops, pubs and attractions. The nearby Shropshire Hills and Mortimer Forest offer miles of stunning landscapes to explore. This beautiful Victorian building has been extended to provide en suite accommodation with twin rooms, a family room, and a room designed for those with limited mobility. Fresh towels, bedlinen, complimentary toiletries, tea- and coffee-making facilities, parking and WiFi included. Breakfasts available for an extra charge.

DETAILS
- **Open** - All year except Christmas.
- **Beds** - 19: 7 x 2, 1 x 1, 1 x 4
- **Price/night** - From £44.30 per person

CONTACT:
Tel: 01584 873882
info@ludlowmascallcentre.co.uk
www.ludlowmascallcentre.co.uk
Lower Galdeford, Ludlow, Shropshire
SY8 1RZ

HAYE FARM
SLEEPING BARN
145l

FOXHOLES
CASTLE
145r

This bunkhouse on a working farm has a fully equipped self-catering kitchen, dining room and lounge. Enjoy the quiet rural location on the covered decking, patio (with BBQ) and lawn. The Wyre Forerst is one of the largest remaining ancient forests in England. On the Worcestershire Way and close to the Severn Way and Mercian Way (NCN route 45) at Bewdley (1 mile). The West Midland Safari Park and Severn Valley Railway are also very close.

Foxholes Castle Bunkhouse, is situated within a relaxed, family-run campsite, with glorious views of South West Shropshire's beautiful hills. Just a few minutes' walk from the Shropshire Way, Offa's Dyke Path and the Sustrans cycle network, it is the perfect base for walkers, cyclists, photographers, families or couples. The lively town of Bishops Castle with its pubs, cafés, restaurants and take-aways is just a 10 minute walk away. In addition to the bunkhouse there are 2 cabins nearby. The Datcha sleeps 6 and the Eco cabin sleeps 8.

DETAILS

- **Open** - All year. 24 hour access.
- **Beds** - 15: 1x2, 1x3, 1x4, 1x6
- **Price/night** - From £20pp. Book bed in dorm, private room or exclusive use of whole barn. Visit website for full prices.

CONTACT: Stuart Norgrove
Tel: 07732489195
enquiries@haye-farm.co.uk
www.haye-farm.co.uk
Haye Farm, Ribbesford, Bewdley,
Worcestershire, DY12 2TP

DETAILS

- **Open** - All year.
- **Beds** - 7
- **Price/night** - £15 pp. Sole use: £90.

CONTACT: Adam Smith/Wendy Jones
Tel: 01588 638924
foxholes.castle@googlemail.com
www.foxholes-castle.co.ukl
Foxholes Camping, Montgomery Rd,
Bishops Castle, Shropshire, SY9 5HA

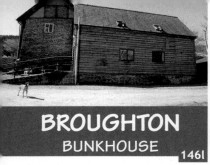

BROUGHTON
BUNKHOUSE
146l

BRIDGES
YOUTH HOSTEL
146r

Clean and cosy accommodation in a 17th century barn with a wealth of exposed beams and full of character. There is a fully equipped kitchen, central heating, hot water and showers. Clothes washing and drying facilities are also provided. Located just outside Bishops Castle in South Shropshire, perfect for walking on the nearby Stiperstones and Long Mynd. Ideal for cycling around Clun or just enjoying the real ale brewed in two of Bishop Castle's own pubs.

Tucked away in the tranquil Shropshire hills, close to Long Mynd & Stiperstones, Bridges Hostel is an ideal spot for walkers with the Shropshire Way passing close by. It is also handy for the End to End cycle route and good mountain biking routes. The hostel has a good kitchen, lounge with wood fire, a drying room, a shop and a large garden. Meals are available, camping is allowed and there is a pub nearby.

DETAILS
- **Open** - All year. 24 hours.
- **Beds** - 12: 2 x 6
- **Price/night** - From £10pp. Sole use hire by groups, weekend or mid week is welcomed. Please phone for prices.

CONTACT: Kate
Tel: 01588 638393
lbrfarm@fastmail.co.uk
www.broughtonfarm-shropshire.co.uk
Lower Broughton Farm, Nr Bishops Castle, Montgomery, Powys SY15 6SZ

DETAILS
- **Open** - All year. Reception open 8-10 am & 5-10 pm. Hostel closes at 11pm.
- **Beds** - 38: 2x4 en suite, 1x6 or 8, 1x10, 1x12 plus camping
- **Price/night** - Adults £19 one night, £16 two+ nights. Under 18's £13 one night, £11.50 two+ nights. Camping £8.

CONTACT: Bridges Youth Hostel
Tel: 01588 650656
bridges@yha.org.uk
Ratlinghope, Shrewsbury, Shropshire, SY5 0SP

WOMERTON FARM
BUNKHOUSE
147l

Womerton Farm Bunkhouse sits right next to the Long Mynd in the heart of the Shropshire Hills. It offers small select accommodation for 8 with a well appointed kitchen and living area. it is just 3 miles from Church Stretton, 12 miles from Shrewsbury and 15 miles from Ludlow. Local attractions include Acton Scott Working Farm Museum, Stokesay Castle and Museum of Lost Content. Well behaved dogs allowed.

       GROUPS ONLY

DETAILS
- **Open** - All year. All day. Closed from 11 am to 4pm on change over days.
- **Beds** - 8: 1x6 bunks + dble sofa bed.
- **Price/night** - £80 Christmas/New Year & Easter to Sept, £60 off peak. Discounts for 4+ nights and mid-week.

CONTACT: Ruth or Tony
Tel: 01694 751260
ruth@womerton-farm.co.uk
www.womerton-farm.co.uk
Womerton Farm, All Stretton, Church Stretton, Shropshire, SY6 6LJ

SPRINGHILL
FARM BUNKHOUSE
147r

Part of a Welsh hill farm on the Wales/ Shropshire border at 1475ft above sea level, with beautiful views over the Ceiriog Valley and Berwyn Mountains. Great for walking, riding, cycling, team building, meetings, or just to relax. There is a heated games and lecture room. The bunkhouse has under-floor heating, entrance hall with w/c and large kitchen plus lounge and dining room. The patio and lawn have a BBQ and hot tub. Horse riding and archery are available on site. Horses and pets welcome on request.

DETAILS
- **Open** - By arrangement.
- **Beds** - Bunkhouse: 25, Cottages: 2x6
- **Price/night** - £20pp (including bedding but not towels)

CONTACT: Sue Benbow
Tel: 01691 718406
sue@springhillfarm.co.uk
www.springhillfarm.co.uk
Springhill Farm, Selattyn, Oswestry, Shropshire, SY10 7NZ

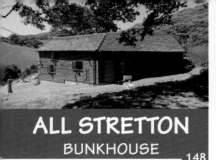

ALL STRETTON
BUNKHOUSE
148

All Stretton Bunkhouse offers comfortable, cosy, self-catering accommodation for individuals and groups of up to 10. It has easy access to the Long Mynd with walks and bike rides for all levels. It is within easy reach of the busy town of Church Stretton and just 10 minutes' walk from the local pub. There's a well equipped kitchen, a shower, two toilets and a tumble dryer. Sole use bookings may bring dogs.

DETAILS

- **Open** - All year. Winter 4pm-10:30am. Summer 5:00pm-10:30am.
- **Beds** - 10: 2x4, 1x2
- **Price/night** - £19; children half price; under 5's free. £1 pppn discount for those arriving without a vehicle.

CONTACT: Frankie Goode
Tel: 01694 722593   Mob: 0781 5517482
info@allstrettonbunkhouse.co.uk
www.allstrettonbunkhouse.co.uk
Meadow Green, Batch Valley, All
Stretton, Shrops, SY6 6JW

STOKES BARN
BUNKHOUSES

149

On top of Wenlock Edge, AONB, in the heart of Shropshire. Stokes Barn has two bunkhouses with comfortable, centrally heated, dormitory accommodation. Perfect for corporate groups, walkers, field study, schools, stag and hen parties, or a reunion with friends/family. Ironbridge World Heritage Site is 6 miles away. Much Wenlock is walking distance with shops, pubs and sports facilities.

DETAILS

■ **Open** - All year. All day.
■ **Beds** - Threshing Barn 28: 1x12,1x10,1x6 Granary 16: 1x10,1x4,1x2
■ **Price/night** - Prices per min 2 nights: Barn: £560 midweek, £910 weekend. Granary: £398 midweek, £615 weekend. Both units weekend 2 nights: £1365.

CONTACT: Helen
Tel: 01952 727491
info@stokesbarn.co.uk
www.stokesbarn.co.uk
Stokes Barn, Newtown Farm, Much Wenlock, Shropshire, TF13 6DB

BIG MOSE
BUNKHOUSE

150

Situated on the National Trust Dudmaston Estate, 4 miles south east of Bridgnorth, Big Mose Bunkhouse accommodates groups of up to 18 in 4 bunkrooms of varying sizes. As well as its spacious communal areas, a large multi-purpose room can be hired. The bunkhouse is perfect for groups of family/friends, walkers and clubs. Dudmaston has lots to offer with managed woodlands, beautiful walks, tranquil pools with plenty of wild life.

DETAILS

- **Open** - All year.
- **Beds** - 18: 1x2, 1x4, 1x6, 1x6
- **Price/night** - 2 nights: £306 (Jan-April), £342 (May-Sept & Xmas). £324 (Oct-Dec). Discounts for longer stays.

CONTACT: National Trust Holidays
Tel: 0344 335 1296
bunkhouses@nationaltrust.org.uk
www.nationaltrust.org.uk
Quatford, Bridgnorth, Shropshire, WV15 6QR

HATTERS
BIRMINGHAM

151l

Your perfect base for exploring central Birmingham, Hatters has combined hotel quality en suite accommodation with the social buzz of an international hostel.
Groups of all sizes and independent travellers will enjoy free WiFi & breakfast, large communal areas and helpful staff. Full/half board possible for larger groups. Ask about discounts for Cadbury World, Warwick Castle, The Sealife Centre and other attractions.

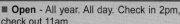
DETAILS
■ **Open** - All year. All day. Check in 2pm, check out 11am.
■ **Beds** - 100: single, double, twin, triple, 4, 6, 8 and 12 bed rooms.
■ **Price/night** - From £12 dorms, from £32 private rooms, inc b/fast & linen. Enquire for group bookings.

CONTACT: Reception
Tel: 0121 236 4031
birmingham@hattersgroup.com
www.hattersgroup.com/#bham
92-95 Livery Street, Birmingham, B3 1RJ

ACKERS
ADVENTURE

151r

Ackers Residential Centre (ARC) is a purpose built accommodation set in 70 acres of semi rural land just 2 miles from the centre of Birmingham. Perfect for The Sea Life Centre, Cadbury World, Thinktank, The Bull Ring shopping centre, National Motorcycle Museum, the NEC. With 9 sleeping rooms, a fully equipped self-catering kitchen, dining area and a rec room with TV, DVD, games and comfy seating. Akers Adventure provide instructor led outdoor activities on site which can be incorporated into your stay.

DETAILS
■ **Open** - All year.
■ **Beds** - 26: 4x4, 5x2
■ **Price/night** - Enquire for price.

CONTACT: Emma Simon
Tel: 0121 772 5111
emma.simon@ackers-adventure.co.uk
www.ackers-adventure.co.uk
Ackers (ARC), Waverley Canal Basin, Small Heath, Birmingham, B10 0DQ

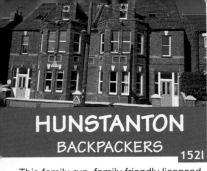

HUNSTANTON
BACKPACKERS
152l

This family run, family friendly licensed hostel is ideal for schools (classroom available) & groups as sole use or for families & individuals in private rooms. Close to the beach, town centre, Sealife sanctuary, cliff walks and buses serving the Norfolk Coast. Perfect for walking, cycling, birding and fun on the beach. Food served or self-cater in the kitchen. Enjoy sea views from the garden patio.

DETAILS
■ **Open** - All year. 8-10am, 5-9:30pm.
■ **Beds** - 48: 1x dbl, 2x3, 4x4, 1x5/6, 2x6/8, 1 grd floor 2 bed. Some en suite.
■ **Price/night** - Prices from: Dorms £24, 2 bed £55, 4 bed £80. Ask re multi night discounts, family rooms, sole use & schools/groups full board packages.

CONTACT: Neal or Alison Sanderson
Tel: 01485 532061 Mob: 07771 804831
enquiries@hunstantonhostel.co.uk
www.norfolkbeachholidays.co.uk
15-17 Avenue Road, Hunstanton,
Norfolk, PE36 5BW

DEEPDALE
BACKPACKERS
152r

Deepdale Backpackers offers a range of comfortable self-catering rooms with private en suite shower and toilet facilities, plus single sex dorms. All bedding is provided, just BYO towels. With underfloor heating throughout, laundry & drying facilities, all rooms have shared access to a large well equipped kitchen, communal dining area and living room with TV and woodburner.

DETAILS
■ **Open** - All year. All day. Collect key from Deepdale Visitor Information Centre
■ **Beds** - 50: 5xdbl, 1 twin, 1 quad, 1 family quad, 2 female dorms, 2 male dorms
■ **Price/night** - From £12 in a shared dorm room. From £30 twin/double room.

CONTACT: Deepdale Backpackers
Tel: 01485 210256
stay@deepdalebackpackers.co.uk
www.deepdalebackpackers.co.uk
Deepdale Farm, Burnham Deepdale,
Norfolk, PE31 8DD

DEEPDALE
GROUPS HOSTEL
153

Deepdale Groups Hostel is at the heart of Burnham Deepdale in an Area of Outstanding Natural Beauty on the beautiful North Norfolk Coast. The Groups Hostel offers comfortable, self-catering accommodation for groups. Sleeping up to 18 people in 4 bedrooms, it is perfect for friends, larger family gathering, clubs or reunions. A great base for a walking break, cycling tour or for bird/wildlife watching groups. The knowledgeable staff give advice and share their passion for the area.

 GROUPS ONLY

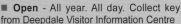
DETAILS

■ **Open** - All year. All day. Collect key from Deepdale Visitor Information Centre
■ **Beds** - 19: 2x6, 1x4, 1x3
■ **Price/night** - From £216 (19 people)

CONTACT: Deepdale Group Hostel
Tel: 01485 210256
stay@deepdalebackpackers.co.uk
www.deepdalebackpackers.co.uk
Deepdale Farm, Burnham Deepdale,
Norfolk, PE31 8DD

TOWER
WINDMILL
154

Built in 1816 and last used as a working corn mill in 1914, this National Trust bunkhouse has panoramic views of the surrounding countryside and the Norfolk coastline.

A perfect venue and location for groups of family and friends to get together and explore the local beaches and miles of public footpaths. Featuring a well equipped ground floor kitchen, sitting/dining area, a third floor library and large enclosed garden. BYO bedding and linen.

 GROUPS ONLY

DETAILS

- **Open** - All year.
- **Beds** - 19: 2 x8, 1x twin, 1x single
- **Price/night** - 3 night weekend break from £487 - £919

CONTACT: National Trust Holidays
Tel: 0344 335 1296
bunkhouses@nationaltrust.org.uk
www.nationaltrust.org.uk
Tower Windmill, Tower Road, Burnham Overy Staithe, Norfolk, PE31 8JB

BRANCASTER
ACTIVITY CENTRE
155

This National Trust Grade 2 listed flint cottage is located within the picturesque harbour of Brancaster Staithe on the North Norfolk Coast. With stunning sea views across the beautiful marshes. Groups of up to 22 or up to 48 can be accommodated. Self-cater in the well equipped kitchen, or eat out in nearby pubs and cafés. The upstairs 'snug' has a TV and woodburner and there is a garden with seating and gas BBQ. Perfect for sailing, walking, kite surfing, bird watching & the Norfolk Coast Path.

DETAILS

■ **Open** - All year. By arrangement.
■ **Beds** - 48:1x8, 1x7, 2x6, 3x5, 1x4, 1x2
■ **Price/night** - From £691 for 2 nights low. £920 for 2 nights high.

CONTACT: National Trust Holidays
Tel: 0344 335 1296
bunkhouses@nationaltrust.org.uk
www.nationaltrust.org.uk
Dial House, Harbour Way, Brancaster Staithe, Kings Lynn, Norfolk PE31 8BW

OLD RED LION

The medieval walled town of Castle Acre is on the Peddars Way, ancient track/long distance path. This former pub, continues to serve travellers who seek refreshment and repose. Stay in private rooms or dorms (bedding/linen supplied). There are quiet communal areas and 2 large areas suitable for group activities.

DETAILS

■ **Open** - All year. All day. Arrival times by arrangement.
■ **Beds** - 22: 1x8, 1x6, 1x double, 2 x double en suite, 2 x twin
■ **Price/night** - Twin £50, double en suite £70, double £65. Dorm beds £22.50. Includes self service, wholefood breakfast, bedding, towel, all day access and parking.

CONTACT: Alison Loughlin
Tel: 01760 755557
oldredlion@yahoo.co.uk
www.oldredlion.org.uk
Old Red Lion, Bailey Street, Castle Acre,
Norfolk, PE32 2AG

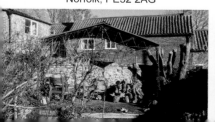

BROOK HOUSE
BARN
157l

Quality self-catering accommodation for families, groups or individuals, with panoramic views over the Lincolnshire Wolds. Scamblesby, is on the Viking Way and has footpaths, bridleways and country lanes. Louth and Horncastle: 10 mins' drive, Lincoln, Boston and coastal beaches: 30 mins. Close to Cadwell Park, Market Rasen Racecourse & Aviation Heritage. Cottage also available.

DETAILS

- **Open** - All year. Flexible access.
- **Beds** - Barn 22: 5x4/5. Cottage 4: 2x2
- **Price/night** - Whole barn hire (2 night min) weekend £450/night and midweek £325/night. Extra nights from £250. Room hire: Single £40, 2 sharing £50, 3 sharing £60, 4 sharing £80 and 5 sharing £90.

CONTACT: The Strawsons
Tel: 01507 343266
enquiries@brookhousefarm.com
www.barnbreaks.co.uk
Watery Lane, Scamblesby, Nr Louth,
Lincolnshire, LN11 9XL

IGLOO
HYBRID
157r

On Market Square, right in the centre of Nottingham, Igloo offers great value and comfort. Rooms are decorated using locally sourced, up-cycled furniture and feature street art murals. With a fully equipped self-catering kitchen, free WiFi, power showers, lockers, lounge, outdoor courtyard and laundry facilities. Igloo Annexe & Pods, offers further accommodation with the same standard.

DETAILS

- **Open** - All year. All day. Reception open 7am-1am weekday, 24hrs Fri / Sat.
- **Beds** - 49: singles, twins, doubles, triples, quads and family rooms.
- **Price/night** - Dorms: from £19pp. Residential rate of £95 per week after 10 nights' stay. Singles from £29.

CONTACT: Igloo Hybrid
Tel: 01159 483822
hybrid@igloohostel.co.uk
www.igloohostel.co.uk
Igloo Hybrid, 4-6 Eldon Chambers,
Wheeler Gate, Nottingham, NG1 2NS

CLUMBER PARK
BUNKHOUSE

A converted gardener's cottage situated on the National Trust's Clumber Park Estate. Once part of Sherwood Forest, this 538 hectare estate of undulating woodland, grassland, heathland, farmland and an ornamental lake, is one of the most valuable havens for wildlife in Nottinghamshire.

There are opportunities for walking and cycling on the estate making this a fabulous location for families. The bunkhouse is well equipped for self-catering with kitchen, dining area and lounge.

GROUPS ONLY

DETAILS

- **Open** - All year. All Day
- **Beds** - 12: 4x3
- **Price/night** - 2 nights from £240.

CONTACT: National Trust Holidays
Tel: 0344 335 1296
bunkhouses@nationaltrust.org.uk
www.nationaltrust.org.uk
Clumber Park, Worksop,
Nottinghamshire, S80 3AZ

SHINING CLIFF
HOSTEL
159l

With its own crags, streams, lakes and over 100-acres of mature woodland, the hidden Shining Cliff Hostel has nature on its doorstep. The hostel offers a full range of activities; on-site there's bushcraft, abseiling, ecology and environmental art, or travel a little further afield for climbing, caving & canoeing. Access is a ten minute walk, down a very rough track, from the nearest parking area. Paths lead through the woods to the A6 at Ambergate (20 mins' walk) which has a food shop, pubs, buses and trains to Derby. Sole use only.

 GROUPS ONLY

DETAILS
- **Open** - All year.
- **Beds** - 20: 1 x 4, 2 x 6, 2 x 2
- **Price/night** - Please enquire. Sole use only.

CONTACT:
Tel: 01433 620377
enquiries@shiningcliff.org
www.lindleyeducationaltrust.org/
Jackass Lane, Alderwasley, DE56 2RE

SHEEN
BUNKHOUSE
159r

Sheen Bunkhouse is in a quiet corner of the Peak District, close to the beautiful Dove and Manifold valleys. It offers a large TV lounge, well equipped self-catering facilities and two bunkrooms with wash basins.
The Manifold Track, Tissington Trail and High Peak Trail give easy access to beautiful countryside, ideal for families and cyclists. Dovedale, the Upper Dove Valley and the remote moors around Flash and Longnor offer stunning walking. Buxton (8miles), Leek (10 miles) and Bakewell (12 miles) & Alton Towers (20 mins by car) are all easily accessed

DETAILS
- **Open** - All year. 24 hours access, reception 8am - 9pm.
- **Beds** - 14: 1x8, 1x6
- **Price/night** - From: £16, U16s £11.

CONTACT: Jean or Graham Belfield
Tel: 01298 84501
grahambelfield11@gmail.com
Peakstones, Sheen, Derbys, SK17 0ES

GLENORCHY
CENTRE
160

The Glenorchy Centre is found on the edge of the Peak District National Park in the historic market town of Wirksworth. The High Peak Trail for walking, pony trekking and cycling and Black Rocks for bouldering and climbing are within a couple of miles. Nearby Cromford has Arkwright's mills, a World Heritage Site, and Cromford Canal. Suitable for self-catering groups, the accommodation is well appointed and boasts a spacious multi-purpose room with a large stage.

         GROUPS ONLY

DETAILS

- **Open** - Mid Feb to early Dec. 24 hours.
- **Beds** - 26: 1x12, 1x8, 1x4, 1x2
- **Price/night** - Mon-Thurs £975; Fri-Sun £605; Sat-Sat £1375. Small groups £18pp. 1 night: min charge £400.

CONTACT: The Secretary
Tel: 01629 824323
secretary@glenorchycentre.org.uk
www.glenorchycentre.org.uk
Chapel Lane, Wirksworth, Derbyshire,
DE4 4FF

THE RECKONING
HOUSE
161

Renovated to a high standard including double glazing and insulation, the Reckoning House is situated 3 miles from Bakewell. It is on the edge of the Lathkill Dale National Nature Reserve, full of interesting flora and fauna as well as outstanding geological features. Horse riding, fishing, golf and cycle hire are available locally. Local walks include the Limestone Way. Facilities include: cooking area, 4 calor gas rings (gas supplied), hot water for washing up & showers, storage heaters in all rooms.

DETAILS

- **Open** - All year. By arrangement.
- **Beds** - 12: 2x6 bunk rooms.
- **Price/night** - £15 per person. Sole use £95 per night.

CONTACT: Rachel Rhodes
Tel: 01629 812416 / 07540839233
mandalecampsite@yahoo.co.uk
www.mandalecampsite.co.uk
Mandale Farm, Haddon Grove,
Bakewell, Derbyshire, DE45 1JF

ROYAL OAK
BUNKBARN

A refurbished stone barn next to an award winning Peak District country pub, The Royal Oak Bunkbarn, is perfectly situated with direct access onto the High Peak and Tissington Trails (disused railways for easy off-road cycling). The area is also very popular with climbers and walkers with limestone gorges and stone circles to explore. The bunkbarn offers comfortable, clean bunk bed style rooms. The five separate bunk rooms are all heated and lockable. Campsite and holiday cottages also available.

DETAILS

- **Open** - All year. All day.
- **Beds** - 34: 3x8, 1x6, 1x4
- **Price/night** - April to Sept £17pppn, Oct to March £15pppn.

CONTACT: The Royal Oak
Tel: 01298 83288
hello@peakpub.co.uk
www.peakpub.co.uk
The Royal Oak, Hurdlow, Nr Buxton,
SK17 9QJ

THORNBRIDGE
OUTDOORS

163

Thornbridge Outdoors offers excellent flexible group accommodation. With its superb location in the heart of the Peak District you have access to wonderful countryside, interesting places and the traffic free Monsal Trail, so popular with walkers and cyclists. The 3 buildings can be booked separately or together.

DETAILS

■ **Open** - All year. All day.
■ **Beds** - 86 + camping: Lodge 38: 4×5, 4×3, 1×6. Farm House 38: 2×8, 2×6, 1×5, 1×3, 1×2. Woodlands 10: 1×5, 1×4 1x1. Tipis & camping 45: 9 x 4/5.
■ **Price/night** - Weekend breaks from £360 (Woodlands), £1,056 (Farm House), £1,320 (Lodge). Ask for activity and additional meeting space costs.

CONTACT: Reception
Tel: 01629 640491
info@thornbridgeoutdoors.co.uk
www.thornbridgeoutdoors.co.uk
Great Longstone, Bakewell, Derbyshire,
DE45 1NY

MOORSIDE FARM
BUNKHOUSE

164l

A 300-year-old farmhouse set 1300 feet up in the beautiful Derbyshire/Staffordshire Peak District National Park. Five miles from historic Buxton and a perfect base for all the Peak District has to offer. The 2 sleeping areas sleep 14 and 6 - perfect for a small group or family. A 3 course breakfast, packed lunch and a substantial evening meal are provided, vegetarians catered for. Hot drinks can be made in the small kitchen. Ample parking space is provided.

DETAILS
- **Open** - All year. 24 hours.
- **Beds** - 20: 1 x 14, 1 x 6
- **Price/night** - Full board (b/fast, packed lunch, eve meal) £39pp. B&B only £29pp. Min booking 4 people. Groups only.

CONTACT: Charlie
Tel: 01298 83406
charliefutcher@aol.com
www.moorsidefarm.com
Hollinsclough, Longnor, Buxton, Derbyshire, SK17 0RF

ROACHES
BUNKHOUSE

164r

The Roaches Bunkhouse is at the foot of The Roaches gritstone edge in the Peak District. The area has some of the best climbing in the country plus walks and cycling in stunning scenery. An ideal base for climbers, walkers and cyclists. It has a drying room, secure bike storage and rooms sleeping 2 or 4 in bunks. The communal area has tables and chairs, log fire, TV and board games. Self-catering facilities are available in a small kitchen. Parking available on site. Close to Ye Old Rock Inn and 3 miles from shopping in the market town of Leek.

DETAILS
- **Open** - All year.
- **Beds** - 42: 9x4, 3x2
- **Price/night** - £10 per person per night.

CONTACT: Ken Baines
Tel: 01538 300308 Mob: 07836628868
info@roachesbunkhouse.com
www.roachesbunkhouse.com
Upper Hulme Mill, Roach Road, Upper Hulme, Nr Leek, Staffordshire, ST13 8TY

ALSTONEFIELD
CAMPING BARN
165

Close to Dovedale, the Manifold Valley Cycle Trail, Carsington Water, Alton Towers and the Roaches Rocks (great for climbers). Ideal for quiet group get togethers, families, cyclists, walkers, D of E, Scouts, school groups and team building. This is camping in the comfort of a remote cosy barn, with log burning stove. Having no electric and no distractions it is the perfect place to switch off from the hassles of a hectic life. BYO all camping equipment.

       GROUPS ONLY

DETAILS

■ **Open** - All year. All day apart from Christmas and New Year.
■ **Beds** - 12: BYO sleeping mats & bags
■ **Price/night** - 9pp or £108 for sole use.

CONTACT: Robert or Teresa Flower
Tel: 01335 310349
gateham.grange@btinternet.com
www.gatehamgrange.co.uk/
newwcampingbarn.htm
Gateham Grange, Alstonefield,
Ashbourne, Derbys. DE6 2FT

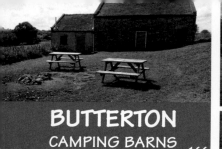

BUTTERTON
CAMPING BARNS
166

Waterslacks Camping Barn is perched on the edge of the Manifold Valley with breath-taking views of the surrounding hills. BYO all camping gear including stove and sleep mats.

Wills Barn is a fully equipped bunkhouse with stunning views of this unspoiled area of the Peak District National Park. A rustic log-burning stove provides heating and cooking facilities.

Fenns Barn 4* self-catering holiday let and camping are also available

       GROUPS ONLY

DETAILS

- **Open** - All year. All day
- **Beds** - Waterslacks: 15. Wills: 6. Fenns: 7 + Camping.
- **Price/night** - Waterslacks from £127, Wills from £130 + Electricity meter £1

CONTACT: Jason and Michelle
Tel: 07708 200282
fennsfarmaccommodation@gmail.com
www.peakdistrictbarns.co.uk/
Fenns Farm, Wetton Road, Butterton, Leek, Staffordshire, ST13 7ST

ILAM
BUNKHOUSE

167

The former 18th century stable block of Ilam Hall in the Peak District National Park close to Dove Dale.

Now managed by the National Trust and providing high quality group accommodation. Each bunk has a locker, night light and plug socket. The sociable main living area has a large dining table with benches, an open plan kitchen and large comfortable sofas. Explore the limestone hills, dales, rivers and woodland of the picturesque White Peak.

 GROUPS ONLY

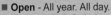

DETAILS

- **Open** - All year. All day.
- **Beds** - 16: 2x6, 1x4
- **Price/night** - Week: £170. Weekend £250. Minimum bookings apply weekends and bank holidays. Dogs: £15/dog/stay.

CONTACT: National Trust Holidays
Tel: 0344 335 1296
bunkhouses@nationaltrust.org.uk
www.nationaltrust.org.uk
Ilam Bunkhouse, Ilam Park, Ilam, nr Ashbourne, DE6 2AZ

EDALE BARN
COTEFIELD FARM
168l

Overlooking Mam Tor and at the start
of the Pennine Way - great for walking
holidays, Edale Barn is a traditional
camping barn or "stone tent" with a basic
sleeping platform and a small communal
living area. Within easy reach of the high
moorland of Kinder and the wooded
Derwent Valley. Adjoining the barn, but
with external access, is a cooking area
and separate toilet. There is no hot water
or electricity. BYO sleeping & cooking
equipment and torches. The Old Nags
Head pub at Edale serves hot food within
walking distance. 4 self-catering holiday
cottages also available.

DETAILS
■ **Open** - All year. All day
■ **Beds** - 8 on a sleeping platform
■ **Price/night** - Please enquire.

CONTACT: Sally Gee
Tel: 01433 670273
sallygee52@hotmail.com
www.fb.com/cotefieldfarmcottages/
Ollerbrook, Edale, Hope Valley, S33 7ZG

UPPER BOOTH
168r
CAMPING BARN

Next to a small campsite alongside
Crowden Clough. Hire the barn and
additional pitches on the campsite if
required. There is space for cooking
(BYO equipment) and tables for eating.
Toilets, sinks & showers are shared with
the campsite. On a working hill-farm,
the Pennine Way passes through the
farmyard and there is great mountain
biking locally.

DETAILS
■ **Open** - March-November. Arrival
between 3pm and 9pm. Departure before
10am. Not suitable for late night parties.
■ **Beds** - Sleeping space for 12
■ **Price/night** - Sole use (up to 12
persons) from £90 per night plus vehicles.
Individuals from £10 per person per night.

CONTACT: Robert, Sarah or Alice
Tel: (01433) 670250
mail@helliwell.info
www.upperboothcamping.co.uk
Upper Booth Farm, Edale, Hope Valley,
Derbyshire, S33 7ZJ

PEAK DISTRICT
HOLIDAY BARN
169

This beautifully converted, impressive holiday barn is situated in the heart of the Peak District, perfectly for large groups for celebrations, holidays or residential courses. Close to Chatsworth, Hathersage, Bakewell and Tideswell. With new games room plus lawned garden with BBQ, fire pit, hot tub & pizza oven. A 2 bed cottage is also available.

 GROUPS ONLY

DETAILS
- **Open** - All year. All day. Check in is available from 4pm.
- **Beds -** 24: 2x2 king, 2x2 double, 1x8, 1x6 (dbl + bunks), 1x2
- **Price/night -** Fri/Sat £2250/2 ngts, Fri/Sat/Sun £2800/3ngts. Mon-Thur £850pn. 12 or less: £600pn. Deals for midweek breaks. Wedding from £3250 inc 2 ngts.

CONTACT: Amanda or Mark
Tel: 07525 051226 or 07791 667027
bookings@peakdistrictholidaybarn.co.uk
www.peakdistrictholidaybarn.co.uk
Wardlow Mires, near Tideswell, Buxton, Derbyshire, SK17 8RW

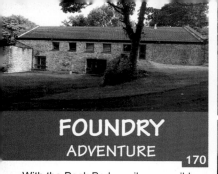

FOUNDRY
ADVENTURE

With the Peak Park easily accessible, the centre is an ideal location for outdoor activities and it welcomes a wide range of groups. The 2 units, Kinder & Howden can be booked together or separately. The spacious centre includes; comfy lounges with library, TV and wood burning stove, well equipped kitchens & dining areas, An extensive network of paths give access to the countryside. Adventure activities available-great for team building & courses.

🚻 🅿 ▦ 🏠 😶 🔜 📶 **GROUPS ONLY**

DETAILS

■ **Open** - All year. All day.
■ **Beds** - Kinder 31: 1x10, 1x2, 1x3, 2x8, Howden 21: 2x8, 1x3, 1x2
■ **Price/night** - From £20pppn Whole centre £680 pn

CONTACT: Tim Gould
Tel: 07786 332702
tim@foundrymountain.co.uk
foundryadventurecentre.co.uk
The Old Playhouse, Great Hucklow,
Derbyshire, SK17 8RF

ST MICHAELS
CENTRE
171

At the heart of Hathersage in the Hope Valley, close to Stanage and the other gritstone edges, the Derwent Valley Reservoirs, Chatsworth, Castleton and Hathersage outdoor pool. With limitless walking from the door. High quality accommodation for groups, with a well equipped self-catering kitchen, dining room, lounge & classroom. Outdoor activities available on request.

      GROUPS ONLY

DETAILS

■ **Open** - All year. Office open Monday – Friday 8.30 am – 4pm
■ **Beds** - 38: 2x2, 1x4, 2x6, 1x8, 1x10. Plus 4 in adjacent cottage.
■ **Price/night** - £22.50pp min, £450 a night, min stay: 2 nights. Activities: £280 per day (max 12 people) + transport cost.

CONTACT: Gary Richards
Tel: 01433 650309
stmichaels@nottscc.gov.uk
www.nottinghamshire.gov.uk
Main Road, Hathersage, Derbyshire, S32 1BB

THORPE FARM
BUNKHOUSES
172

Close to Hathersage and 2 miles west of Stanage Edge, the bunkhouses are on a family-run dairy farm. Popular areas for climbing, walking from meadows to moorland with fantastic views & mountain biking. Each bunkhouse is heated and has a living room, kitchen, bathrooms with two toilets, showers and washbasins. Sleep in dorms with bunks or the Hayloft has mattresses on the gallery floor. Camping is available. Secure bike storage and free parking.

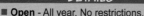

DETAILS

- **Open** - All year. No restrictions.
- **Beds** - Old Shippon 32: 2x12, 2x4. Old Stables 14 1x8, 1x6. Pondside 14: 1x8, 1x6. Byre 14: 1x6, 1x4 Living Room 4.
- **Price/night** - See own website.

CONTACT: Jane Marsden
Tel: 01433 650659
jane@hope-valley.co.uk
www.thorpe-bunk.co.uk
Thorpe Farm, Hathersage, Peak District,
Via Sheffield, S32 1BQ

PINDALE FARM
OUTDOOR CENTRE
173

A mile from Castleton in the heart of the Peak District, Pindale Farm offers a range of accommodation. There's B&B in the farmhouse. The Barn has 6 self-catering units. The Engine House is a self-catering unit and The Powder House is a small camping barn. There is also a campsite. The ideal base for many outdoor activities. Instruction is available.

DETAILS

■ **Open** - All year (camping March-October). 24 hours.
■ **Beds** - 64: Farmhouse: 4. Engine House: 8. Powder House: 4. The Barn 6x8-10 plus camping.
■ **Price/night** - Camping £8pp (hook up £4). Barns £16pp + £1 electric tokens. Enquire for B&B.

CONTACT: Alan Medhurst
Tel: 01433 620111
info@pindalefarm.co.uk
www.pindalefarm.co.uk
Pindale Road, Hope, Hope Valley,
Derbyshire, S33 6RN

HOMESTEAD
& CHEESEHOUSE
174

In the heat of Bamford these two bunkhouses are on a small farm just 3 miles from Stanage Edge. The Derwent Dams are close by. Perfectly located for visiting Castleton, Chatsworth House and Hathersage. Both bunkhouses are centrally heated have hot showers and have their own well equipped kitchens. Sheets and pillows are provided (BYO sleeping bags) Book separately or together. Sorry, no dogs.

DETAILS
- **Open** - All year. Arrive after 2pm on day of arrival and leave by 11am on departure.
- **Beds** - Homestead 22: 1x10, 2x6. Cheesehouse 4: 1x4.
- **Price/night** - From £15pp. Homestead £195, Cheesehouse £45. Minimum of 2 night booking for Homestead at weekends or phone for a quote for a single night fee.

CONTACT: Helena Platts
Tel: 01433 651298
The Farm, Bamford, Hope Valley,
S33 0BL

DALEHEAD
BUNKHOUSE
175

Dalehead Bunkhouse is on a working hill farm at the remote head of Edale Valley. Providing basic but comfortable accommodation heated by log burner & infrared radiant heat. There is a kitchen with fridge/freezer, a lounge, dining room and plenty of parking. Please bring sleeping bags, pillows and towels. Edale is a very popular destination for walkers, climbers, mountain bikers, hang-gliders or for enjoying the magnificent scenery.

GROUPS ONLY

DETAILS
- **Open** - All year. All day.
- **Beds** - 20: 1x6, 1x8, 1x6
- **Price/night** - Mon-Thurs £190 per night. Fri-Sun £275. Min 2 nights bookings Fri-Sun, 3 nights bank holidays. Dogs £15 per dog per stay.

CONTACT: National Trust Holidays
Tel: 0344 335 1296
bunkhouses@nationaltrust.org.uk
www.nationaltrust.org.uk
Dalehead Bunkhouse, Upper Booth, Edale, Hope Valley, S33 7ZJ

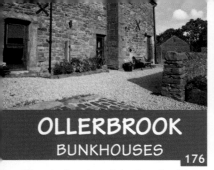

OLLERBROOK
BUNKHOUSES
176

Close to the start of the Pennine Way with easy access to Kinder Scout and the village of Edale via a network of footpaths from the doorstep. Castleton, Buxton, Bakewell and Chatsworth House are all within 40 minutes' drive. There are 2 bunkhouses each with a fully equipped kitchen and available for sole use by groups. Bring your own sleeping bags.

DETAILS

■ **Open** - All year. All day. Arrive after 4pm depart before 10.30am.
■ **Beds** - 34: Nab View 18: 3x6, Stables Bunkhouse 16: 4x4
■ **Price/night** - Nab View: £300 (min 2 nights), The Stables: midweek £200, weekends £210 (min 2 nights). Enquire for longer stays and prices/room or bed.

CONTACT: Sheila
Tel: 01433 670235
ollerbrookfarm@gmail.com
www.ollerbrookfarm.co.uk
Ollerbrook Booth, Edale, Hope Valley,
Derbyshire, S33 7ZG

JOHN HUNT
BASE

The John Hunt Base is situated in the High Peak on the site of Hagg Farm OEC (pg 178). The base offers comfortable, family friendly accommodation ideal for sightseeing, hillwalking, trail running and biking as well as quieter pursuits such as photography. There is a picnic area, wildlife garden with fire pit and a playing field with climbing boulder. Activities can be arranged including climbing, stream scrambling, caving & on-site high ropes.

 GROUPS ONLY

DETAILS

■ **Open** - All year. Office, Mon-Thur 8.30am- 4.30pm, Fri 8.30-3.30pm
■ **Beds** - 18: 1 x 8, 1 x 6, 2 x 2
■ **Price/night** - £289 min 2 nights. Instruction (12 people) from £280 per day.

CONTACT:
Tel: 01433 651594
haggfarm@nottscc.gov.uk
www.nottinghamshire.gov.uk/haggfarm
Hagg Farm OEC, Snake Rd, Bamford,
Hope Valley, S33 0BJ

HAGG FARM

Situated in the Peak District's Woodlands Valley Hagg Farm offers comfortable accommodation for up to 44 people with an additional 18 beds in the John Hunt Base (pg 177). Part of Nottinghamshire County Council's Environmental and Outdoor Education Service, Hagg Farm is available for private hire by groups of friends, families, clubs and charitable organisations and can be booked on a self-catering or catered basis.

DETAILS

- **Open** - All year. Office: Mon–Thurs 8:30am - 4.30pm Fri 8:30am – 4pm
- **Beds** - 44: 4 x 8, 2 x 4, 2 x 2
- **Price/night** - £23pp: min charge for 25 people, min 2 night stay. Outdoor activity instruction for 12 from £280 per day.

CONTACT: Kirsty Weatherall
Tel: 01433 651594
haggfarm@nottscc.gov.uk
www.nottinghamshire.gov.uk/haggfarm
Hagg Farm OEC, Snake Rd, Bamford,
Hope Valley, S33 0BJ

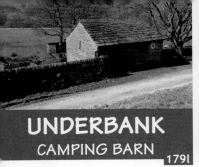

UNDERBANK
CAMPING BARN
179l

Blaze Farm dairy and sheep farm is in Wildbourclough valley on the western edge of the Peak District National Park with stunning views of Shuttlingsloe. A "stone tent", the barn provides a simple base for family escapes and for walking, climbing, fell-running and mountain biking. Bring equipment as if camping. There is a fridge, and a fire pit in the enclosed patio. Blaze Farm ice-cream parlour and café serves snacks & light meals and there are good pubs nearby.

DETAILS

■ **Open** - All year. Arrive: 4pm leave 10am (earlier arrivals by arrangement).
■ **Beds** - 10: BYO sleeping mats/bags
■ **Price/night** - £95 sole use. Bring £1 coins for electricity. £20 deposit for keys.

CONTACT: Caroline & Marshall Waller
Tel: 01260 227 266
underbankcampingbarn@gmail.com
underbankcampingbarn.co.uk
Blaze Farm, Wildboarclough,
Macclesfied, Cheshire, SK11 0BL

HATTERS
MANCHESTER
179r

Hatters on Hilton Street combines hotel quality en suite accommodation with the social buzz of an international hostel. Located in the heart of the bohemian Northern Quarter of Manchester, it's your perfect base for all city centre attractions & transport links. Full/half board options for larger groups. Ask about discounts to Alton Towers, about Man Utd & City football stadium tours and about all that is FREE to do in Manchester!

DETAILS

■ **Open** - All year. All day. Check in 2pm, check out 11am.
■ **Beds** - 155; single, twin, double, triple, 4, 6, 8, and 12 bed rooms. All en suite.
■ **Price/night** - From £12 dorms, from £32 private rooms inc linen & b/fast. Enquire for group bookings.

CONTACT: Reception
Tel: 0161 236 4414
hilton@hattersgroup.com
www.hattersgroup.com/#mcr
15 Hilton Street, Manchester, M1 1JJ

EMBASSIE
BACKPACKERS

180l

EURO HOSTEL

180r
LIVERPOOL

The Embassie is a majestic terraced house in an unspoiled Georgian square. Until 1986 it was the Consulate of Venezuela! Only 15 minutes' walk from the centre of Liverpool, known for its nightlife, it's in the perfect position. Recently refurbished, there are new kitchen facilities, a brand new shower suite and an all new games room & relax area with Sky Sports and HD television. The hostel is clean, safe and staffed 24 hours. Bedding is provided (including sheets) and free coffee, tea, toast and jam are available 24 hours.

DETAILS

- **Open** - All year. All day.
- **Beds** - 50
- **Price/night** - £18 (Sunday to Thursday), £24 Friday, £28 Saturday

CONTACT: Kevin
Tel: 0151 7071089
embassie@gmail.com
www.embassie.com
1 Falkner Square, Liverpool, L8 7NU

Right in the heart of the city and a perfect base from which to experience Liverpool's legendary night life, shopping and waterfront walks. Backpackers, couples, families and groups are all welcomed. Rooms vary from 8 bed dorms (mixed or female only), en suite private rooms for up to 8 people or VIP suites accommodating groups of 6 or 8 in bunks with private TV lounge and en suite facilities. The Hatch bar serves meals including breakfast and is a great live music venue as well as providing good quality food and drink. Car park discounts provided on check out.

DETAILS

- **Open** - All year All day.
- **Beds** - 220 approximately
- **Price/night** - From £14 pp

CONTACT: Reception
Tel: +44 (0) 845 490 0971
liverpool@eurohostels.co.uk
www.eurohostels.co.uk/liverpool/
54 Stanley Street, Liverpool L1 6AU

HATTERS
LIVERPOOL
181l

HULL TRINITY
BACKPACKERS
181r

Hatters Liverpool combines hotel quality en suite rooms with the social buzz of an international hostel. Conveniently located for all city centre attractions and transport links it's your perfect base for experiencing the heart and soul of Liverpool. Full/half board options for larger groups. Ask at the reception about discounts to Alton Towers, Beatles tours, football stadium tours, Albert Docks and many other FREE adventures.

In the heart of Hull, (European City of Culture 2017) this newly renovated backpackers hostel is aimed at the individual traveller, small groups, cyclists and families. With flexible room layouts including an en suite family room it is perfect for visiting Hull's art exhibitions and family friendly attractions such as The Deep. Self-catering kitchenette. The coffee lounge in reception welcomes you as well as passers by.

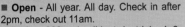

DETAILS

- **Open** - All year. All day. Check in after 2pm, check out 11am.
- **Beds** - 300; sgle, dble, twin, triple, 4, 6, 8 and 12 bed rooms. All en suite
- **Price/night** - From £12 for dorms and from £32 for privates inc linen and b/fast. Enquire for group bookings.

CONTACT: Reception
Tel: 0151 709 5570
liverpool@hattersgroup.com
www.hattersgroup.com/#lpool
56-60 Mt Pleasant, Liverpool, L3 5SH

DETAILS

- **Open** - All year. All day. Except 25 & 26th Dec
- **Beds** - 12: 1x6, 2x4, 1x4 en suite, 2xsingle/twin
- **Price/night** - From £19ppp (dorm) to £30pp single

CONTACT: Glenn Gavin
Tel: 01482 223229 mobile:0785 3000474
hulltrinitybackpackers@gmail.com
hulltrinitybackpackers.com
51/52 Market Place Kingston Upon Hull HU1 1RU

SCARBOROUGH
YOUTH HOSTEL
182l

For a fun filled, seaside break Scarborough is unbeatable: two safe, sandy beaches, penny arcades, pirate ship, three surf schools and the new Alpamare Waterpark. Once a 17th century water mill on a quiet riverside just outside the town, Scarborough Youth Hostel is also a perfect base for exploring the coast and country of the North York Moors and Wolds with miles of paths, tracks and quiet lanes for walkers and cyclists.

DETAILS
■ **Open** - All year. 7.30 - 10.00 am and 5.00 - 10.00 pm.
■ **Beds** - 46: 5x6, 4x4.
■ **Price/night** - Beds from £15, rooms from £55, discounts for YHA members

CONTACT: Robert Fletcher
Tel: 01723 361176
scarboroughhostel@gmail.com
www.scarboroughhostel.com
The White House, Burniston Road,
Scarborough, YO13 0DA

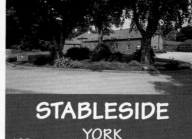

STABLESIDE
YORK
182r

Stableside, a quiet & welcoming 4* hostel situated right on the historic Knavesmire, is the perfect location for enjoying a break in the beautiful, historic city of York. Guests can take advantage of the varied room options catering for the single traveller and larger groups. Free parking, free WiFi and a fabulous Yorkshire welcome. Meals can be provided for groups. On the NCN Route 65 for easy access to the city centre.

DETAILS
■ **Open** - All year (except during race meetings). All day.
■ **Beds** - 133: 2x6, 21x4, 8x triple, 1x twin, 11 x single.
■ **Price/night** - B&B twin room £70 inc towels. Enquire for school group rates.

CONTACT: Fay
Tel: 01904 709174
fay.waudby@yorkracecourse.co.uk
www.stablesideyork.co.uk
Stableside, York Racing Stables, York,
YO24 1QG

HALIFAX COLLEGE
HOSTEL
183

Within walking distance of Heslington village and the University of York campus.

Halifax College is the perfect base for exploring York. The city is famous for the iconic York Minster, exquisite architecture, The Shambles, boutique shopping, a vibrant café and restaurant culture and world class museums such as the National Railway Museum and the unique Jorvik Centre. All rooms are self-catering and single occupancy with a wash basin and the use of shared bathroom and kitchen within each house.

DETAILS

- **Open** - July - September
- **Beds** - 51
- **Price/night** - £26.00

CONTACT: Reception
Tel: 01904 328431
conferences@york.ac.uk
yorkconferences.com/hostel/
Halifax College Reception, Garrowby Way, York, YO10 5GH

BANK HOUSE
FARM HOSTEL

A luxury bunkbarn, a camping barn and B&B on an organic farm in beautiful Glaisdale Dale, with stunning views of the North York Moors and just 1 mile from the Coast to Coast route. The newly converted bunkbarn is warm & well appointed with one large dorm. The camping barn provides simple, single-night shelter for walkers or cyclists.

DETAILS

■ **Open** - All year. Phone calls 9am-9pm
■ **Beds** - Bunkbarn: 1x11 (9 singles 1 bunk) Camping barn: 8: 2x4
■ **Price/night** - Bunkbarn: W/ends £500 (Fri-Sun), Bank Hols £600 (3 nights). Saturday £400. Midweek from £25pppn. Deals for longer stays. Camping Barn: £12pp. Farmhouse B&B: £40.

CONTACT: Chris or Emma Padmore
Tel: 01947 897297
info@bankhousefarmhostel.co.uk
www.bankhousefarmhostel.co.uk
Bank House Farm, Glaisdale, Whitby
YO21 2QA

COTE GHYLL
MILL

185

In a beautiful and secluded valley in the North Yorkshire Moors National Park, this converted linen mill is a perfect base for exploring the moors, dales & coast. Osmotherley has pubs, a tea room & shops. Explore the stream and woodlands or take part in organised activities for children and groups. Next to Cod Beck reservoir, Cleveland Way, Coast to Coast and at start of Lyke Wake Walk. All refurbished, en-suite bedrooms.

DETAILS

■ **Open** - All year. 7am -10am, 5pm-9pm.
■ **Beds** - 71: Mill 61: 4x2,6x4, 4x6 + 5 rollout beds. Annex: 10
■ **Price/night** - Adults from £24. U18's from £17. Family rooms from £42. Enquire for groups & sole use.

CONTACT: Reception
Tel: 01609 883425
mill@coteghyll.com
www.coteghyll.com
Osmotherley, Northallerton, North
Yorkshire, DL6 3AH

WEST END
OUTDOOR CENTRE

186

Amidst stunning landscape overlooking Thruscross Reservoir on the edge of the Yorkshire Dales National Park, this self-catering centre offers excellent facilities in bunkrooms plus an en suite leader's room with well equipped kitchen, dining, lounge & shower/toilet areas. Ideal for team building, youth groups & family parties. 12 miles from Harrogate & Skipton. Groups must include a 25+ adult. No stag or hens.

DETAILS

■ **Open** - All year. Flexible.
■ **Beds** - 30: 4x2, 3x4, 1x6, 1x4 en suite
■ **Price/night** - Sole use: Fri +Sat £375, Fri+Sat+BH £1100. Midweek £240 per night (min 2 nights). 4 nights midweek: £780, 7 nights £1250. £5 per dog pn.

CONTACT: Hedley or Margaret Verity
Tel: 01943 880207
info@westendoutdoorcentre.co.uk
www.westendoutdoorcentre.co.uk
West End, Summerbridge, Harrogate, HG3 4BA

TRAWDEN
CAMPING BARN

EARBY
FRIENDS OF NATURE

Trawden Camping Barn is a listed stone barn on Middle Beardshaw Farm. Surrounded by stunning landscape the nearby village of Wycoller has been much used by film crews. The barn is large and open with an ancient timbered roof. There is accommodation for 15; 7 beds/bunks and 8 mattresses (BYO sleeping bags) with plenty of communal space, a table tennis and pool table and a well equipped kitchen (in a separate building just 15m away). Pub & café just a short walk away.

Earby's newly refurbished Independent Hostel (Friends of Nature House), welcomes individuals, families and small groups to this historic, cosy cottage with picturesque garden. A perfect stop for Pennine Way walkers and great base for local day hikes, cyclists or discovering the countryside and local heritage. Featuring comfortable lounges, wood burning stove, a well equipped kitchen and dining areas that seat 18. Real ale pub and meals nearby. Adults must accompany U16s.

DETAILS

- **Open** - All year. Warm clothes and sleeping bags required in winter
- **Beds** - 15: 1x15
- **Price/night** - £15 pp plus £10 per night per group for electricity.

CONTACT: Ursula
Tel: 01282 865257
ursulamann@hotmail.co.uk
Middle Beardshaw Head Farm, Burnley
Road, Trawden Lancashire, BB8 8PP

DETAILS

- **Open** - March-Nov. All year for sole use
- **Beds** - 22: 1x2, 2x6 and 1x8.
- **Price/night** - From £16, U18's from £12. Discount for FoN & IFN members.

CONTACT: Warden
Tel: 01282 842349
earby@naturefriends.org.uk
www.thefriendsofnature.org.uk
9-11 Birch Hall Lane, Earby, Lancashire,
BB18 6JX

HEBDEN BRIDGE
HOSTEL

188

Expect a warm welcome at Hebden Bridge Hostel. Comfy and welcoming, with private rooms and dorm beds from £15. Nestled into woodland only a short walk from the town centre, and less than 500m from the Hebden Bridge Loop on the Pennine Way, the hostel makes the perfect base for hiking, sight-seeing, relaxing or experiencing Hebden Bridge's vibrant café, music, arts & culture.

DETAILS

■ **Open** - Easter to Nov. Sole use all year. Arrive 5-8pm, leave by 10am.
■ **Beds** - 33 : 6x4 (or 2), 1x3 (or 2), 1x6
■ **Price/night** - Bunkroom £15pp. Dorm £20pp. Twin £55. Double £60. Double+1 £75. Private 4-bed room £75. Midweek single £35. Sole use available.

CONTACT: Em or Dave
Tel: 01422 843183
mama@hebdenbridgehostel.co.uk
www.hebdenbridgehostel.co.uk
The Birchcliffe Centre, Hebden Bridge,
W Yorks, HX7 8DG

AIRTON BARN

189l

A friendly welcome awaits you in a unique setting at Airton Barn. Adjacent to the 17th century Friends Meeting House,

Airton Barn is a simple bunkhouse sleeping up to 18 people over two floors, with storage space for up to 5 bicycles. Located on popular walking and cycling routes, and surrounded by some of Yorkshire's finest tourist destinations, the Barn is ideally placed for walkers and cyclists as well as small group getaways.

DETAILS

■ **Open** - All year. Volunteer warden resident on site
■ **Beds** - 6 bunk beds + 6 mattresses + 6 air beds. Overflow camping for 2 tents.
■ **Price/night** - £17pp, reducing for larger groups. Call to discuss.

CONTACT: The Friend in Residence
Tel: 01729 830263
airtonbarn@gmail.com
www.airtonbarn.org.uk
The Nook, Airton, Skipton, North
Yorkshire, BD23 4AE

GRASSINGTON
BUNKBARN

189r

With spectacular views of Wharfedale, Grassington Bunkbarn offers comfortable group accommodation. Featuring a well equipped kitchen and a lounge/games area with Freeview TV plus WiFi, good mobile coverage and a BBQ area outside. With walking, cycling, climbing, fishing, horse riding, archaeology, bird watching, geology, botany and even golf, there's something for everyone.

DETAILS

■ **Open** - Reception 9am - 5pm Mon - Fri, Sat 10am - 2pm.
■ **Beds** - 34: 2x12, 1x6, 1x4
■ **Price/night** - Sole use: W/E: £980 (2 ngts). BH: £1250 (3 ngts). Midweek: £390pn. 4 ngts: £1180. 7 ngts: from £2040. Bed £25 (call for availability).

CONTACT: Paul, Mark or Janet Kent
Tel: 01756 753882
enquiries@grassingtonbunkbarn.co.uk
www.grassingtonbunkbarn.co.uk
Spring Croft, Moor Lane, Grassington,
BD23 5BD

NIDDERDALE
BUNKHOUSE
190

Exclusive hire in the stunning Nidderdale Valley overlooking Gouthwaite reservoir. The bunkhouse has a well equipped, open plan kitchen, beautiful dining & seating areas with great views. The Nidderdale Way goes right past the house. The Yorke Arms, Michelin star restaurant, is nearby. The award winning village of Pateley Bridge has pubs, cafés and festivities throughout the year. The Nidderdale Museum is a short drive away. Perfect for walkers, wildlife lovers or to explore Yorkshire. No dogs.

 GROUPS ONLY

DETAILS
- **Open** - All year. All day.
- **Beds** - 20: 1x8, 3x4
- **Price/night** - From just £18 per person. Exclusive group hire

CONTACT: Matt or Bev
Tel: 07597 645254
nidderdalebunkhouse@gmail.com
www.nidderdalebunkhouse.com
Ramsgill, Harrogate, North Yorkshire
HG3 5RH

SKIRFARE
BARN

Skirfare Barn, with its stunning backdrop of Upper Wharfedale & Littondale, nestles in the Yorkshire Dales with the climbers' challenge, Kilnsey Crag, on the doorstep. The area is famous for walking & cycling with many footpaths, including the Dales Way, close by. At nearby Kilnsey you can book day fishing & food at The Kilnsey Park, or bar snacks at The Tennant Arms Hotel. Pony & Llama trekking & many other activities are also nearby. The barn provides warm, comfortable accommodation for walking, cycling, friends or family groups.

DETAILS

- **Open** - All year.
- **Beds** - 20: 2x2 (twin), 2x4, 1x8.
- **Price/night** - From £16 per person.

CONTACT: Matt & Bev
Tel: 07597 645254
skirfarebarn@gmail.com
www.skirfarebarn.com
Kettlewell Rd, Kilnsey, North Yorkshire,
BD23 5PT

KETTLEWELL
HOSTEL

192

The Kettlewell Hostel is a stylish independent youth hostel in the heart of the Yorkshire Dales. Sleeping up to 42 in 11 bedrooms, it has a large dining room, a secondhand bookshop, a self-catering kitchen, a lovely lounge with wood-burning stove, a private garden & a big bike shed! There are great walks from the front door and world class cycling on the Tour de France Route of '14.

DETAILS

■ **Open** - All year. Reception 8-10.30am, 4-10pm.
■ **Beds** - 42: 1x2 twin, 1x2 double, 4x3, 2x4, 2x6
■ **Price/night** - Beds from £19, private rooms for 2 from £49. Sole use from £399/night.

CONTACT: Saul & Floss Ward
Tel: 01756 760232
saulward@hotmail.com
www.yha.org.uk/hostel/kettlewell
Whernside House, Kettlewell, Skipton,
North Yorkshire, BD23 5QU

TOWN HEAD
BARN
193

Town Head Barn is a converted barn, located in Upper Wharfedale and in the small village of Buckden. The accommodation sleeps 13 in 4 rooms including a single leader's room with en suite facilities. Close (just 3.5 miles) to the village of Kettlewell with pubs and shops and with easy access to Buckden Pike which at 702m high is just waiting to be climbed. This is the perfect location for groups or families wanting to get away from it all in the Yorkshire Dales National Park.

DETAILS

- **Open** - All Year. All day
- **Beds** - 13: 3x4,1x1
- **Price/night** - From £312 for two nights sole use. (min booking 2 nights)

CONTACT:National Trust Holidays
Tel: 0344 335 1296
bunkhouses@nationaltrust.org.uk
www.nationaltrust.org.uk
Buckden, Skipton, North Yorkshire,
BD23 5JA

HORNBY LAITHE
BUNKBARN
194l

Simple, comfortable accommodation in the Yorkshire Dales National Park, Hornby Laith Bunkhouse Barn occupies a secluded position within easy walking distance of the pretty village of Stainforth and the market town of Settle. It is within easy access of a wide variety of routes for walkers and climbers. Sleeping up to 50, there is a separate barn containing a recreational area, extra camping and space for a marquee for events/ weddings & ample parking. There's a self-catering kitchen but a full catering can be organised by arrangement.

     **GROUPS ONLY**

DETAILS
■ **Open** - All year.
■ **Beds** - 50.
■ **Price/night** - 36 people: £800 w/end. 50 people: £1,050 w/end. Enquire for prices for other party numbers.

CONTACT: Neil and Enid Caton,
Tel: 01729 822240
Hornby Laithe, Stainforth, Nr Settle,
North Yorkshire BD24 9PB

194r

INGLETON YHA
GRETA TOWER

On the edge of the Yorkshire Dales, surrounded by magnificent countryside with caves, waterfalls and mountains, Ingleton is dominated by Ingleborough, the best known of Yorkshire's Three Peaks (this is a great base for The Challenge). Known for its walking routes and waterfall trail, there is plenty here for walkers, climbers, mountain bikers and cavers. Licensed and serving tasty meals there is also a self-catering kitchen. Perfect for families and school trips.

DETAILS
■ **Open** - All year (sole use only Nov-Feb). Reception open 8am-12, 5-10pm
■ **Beds** - 64: 4x6, 7x4, 1x2, 2x5
■ **Price/night** - Beds from £16, rooms from £30. Sole use bookings welcome.

CONTACT: Manager
Tel: 015242 41444
ingleton@yha.org.uk
www.ingletonhostel.co.uk
Greta Tower, Sammy Lane, Ingleton,
North Yorkshire, LA6 3EG

THE OLD SCHOOL
BUNKHOUSE

BROADRAKE
BUNKBARN

195l 195r

Situated near Ingleton in the Yorkshire Dales, on the Yorkshire Three Peaks route. Old School Bunkhouse sleeps up to 30. It has a comfortable lounge, with TV, DVD and WiFi, a large kitchen diner, 4 bathrooms and a drying room with washing machine. Outside is parking for 12 cars and a large picnic bench to take in the views of Ingleborough and Whernside. The pub over the road is ideal for that celebratory drink.

Broadrake Bunkbarn offers direct access to the Three Peaks Challenge Walk, Wainwright's Pennine Journey & The Dales Highway. This popular accommodation for 20 has an upstairs open-plan living space with excellent self-catering & communal facilities. It is perfect for special birthday celebrations, extended family reunions, cyclists, cavers and dark sky enthusiasts. Small groups welcome, especially mid-week.

   GROUPS ONLY

DETAILS

- **Open** - All year. 24 hours.
- **Beds** - 30: 5x6
- **Price/night** - £320 per night (sole use) for up to 20 people with an extra £16 per person for groups over 20 people. Minimum of 2 nights at weekends.

DETAILS

- **Open** - All year. All day.
- **Beds** - 20: 1x8, 2x4, 2x twin.
- **Price/night** - Weekends (2 nights) £900, Bank Holiday WE (3 nights) £1350, or £25pppn. Mid-week £360 or £20pppn Week £2000. £5 bedding/towel hire.

CONTACT: Debbie Bryant
Tel: 01931 714874 Mob: 0788 4260 815
oldschoolbunkhouse@gmail.com
www.oldschoolbunkhouse.co.uk
Chapel-le-Dale, Ingleton, Carnforth,
Lancs, LA6 3AR

CONTACT: Mike & Rachel Benson
Tel: 01524 241357
info@broadrake.co.uk
www.broadrake.co.uk
Broadrake, Chapel-le-Dale, Ingleton,
LA6 3AX

GAUBER
BUNK BARN

In Yorkshire's Three Peaks country on the route down from Pen Y Ghent and in close proximity to the Dales Way and Dales High Way routes.Close to Ingleton with it's lido and waterfalls, Ribblehead Viaduct, White Scar Caves, Wensleydale Creamery, and the Settle to Carlisle railway. This warm comfortable bunkbarn sleeps up to 13 in three rooms. Walkers, cavers, cyclists & families all enjoy the Yorkshire Dales. Within easy driving distance of the coast and Lake District. Dogs welcome for sole use only

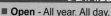

DETAILS

- **Open** - All year. All day.
- **Beds** - 13: 2x4, 1x5 (dbl + 3) ensuite.
- **Price/night** - £18 inc fitted sheet & pillow. Duvet & towel hire one off charge of £5. Simple breakfast by arrangement.

CONTACT: Jon Radda & Katie Hawkins
Tel: 01524 241150
gauberbunkbarn@gmail.com
www.gauberbunkbarn.co.uk
Ribblehead, Ingleton, Carnforth, LA6 3JF

HARDRAW
OLD SCHOOL

Next to the Pennine Way, in the village of Hardraw, The Old School Bunkhouse offers well appointed, practical accommodation for up to 26. The large hall (with games, table tennis, piano, log burner & sofas) and grounds are perfect for group activities. Hardraw has a café, inn and the famous Hardraw Force waterfall. The market town of Hawes is a 1.5 mile walk across fields. Instruction available in many outdoor activities.

DETAILS

- **Open** - All year. All day.
- **Beds** - 26:1x8,1x9,1x6,1x3 + 3 mattresses & 2 tent spaces
- **Price/night** - £15pp. Sole use £175–£300. Winter (Mid Nov to End Feb): min. 5 persons or min. charge of £65.

CONTACT: Andy or Helen
Tel: 01969 666034 Mob: 07546894317
enquiries@hardrawoldschoolbunkhouse.co.uk
www.hardrawoldschoolbunkhouse.co.uk
Schoolhouse, Hardraw, near Hawes,
Wensleydale, North Yorkshire, DL8 3LZ

THE JONAS
CENTRE
198l

DALES
BIKE CENTRE
198r

Twelve Scandinavian styled self-catering log cabins located at the heart of Wensleydale in the tranquil beauty of the Yorkshire Dales,. Nine lodges are located in Elm Wood away from the main complex & the other three are located near to Granary Barn, which has a shop, two lounges a meeting room and a kitchen for group use. The varied use of the centre means that facilities are comfortable rather than luxurious.

Dales Bike Centre, in Swaledale, Yorkshire Dales, is the centre of cycling in Yorkshire! Home of the Ard Rock Enduro, on Woodcocks Coast to Coast mountain bike route and close by the routes of the 2014 Tour de France and Yorkshire Dales Cycle Way. Facilities include an on-site café, well stocked bike shop, bike hire, bike wash, fully equipped workshop, drying room and lots of friendly advice. Close to 4 pubs.

DETAILS

■ **Open** - All year. Office open from 9am - 5pm Monday to Saturday.
■ **Beds** - 60: 12 lodges each sleeping between 5 and 7 people.
■ **Price/night** - See website for special offers. Discounts for full site use.

DETAILS

■ **Open** - All year. All day.
■ **Beds** - 14: Old barn 1x4, 1x2. New barn 1x4, 2x2,
■ **Price/night** - Single room £39, 2 bed bunkroom £58, 4 bed bunkroom £116, 3 people in 4 bed bunkroom £97. Inc b/fast.

CONTACT: Simon Eastwood
Tel: 01969 624 900
stay@jonascentre.org
www.jonascentre.org
Redmire, Leyburn. North Yorkshire, DL8 4EW

CONTACT: Stu Price
Tel: 01748 884908
enquiries@dalesbikecentre.co.uk
www.dalesbikecentre.co.uk
Parks Barn, Fremington, Richmond, Yorkshire Dales DL11 6AW

BROMPTON ON SWALE
BUNKBARN
199l

BENTS
CAMPING BARN
199r

Located on a small working farm, just 3 miles east of Richmond, Yorkshire. Brompton on Swale Bunkbarn offers a welcome break from walking or cycling the Coast to Coast.

A pot of tea for weary walkers upon arrival and safe storage for bikes makes this bunkhouse especially welcoming. Close to the Yorkshire Dales, Swaledale, Wensleydale, Easby Abbey, Richmond Castle & Ellerton Lakes. Dogs are welcome to stay but must be kept on a lead around the yard as there are ducks, hens and geese.

Bents Camping Barn, formerly a 17 century shepherd's cottage, is in the Yorkshire Dales National Park. There are 2 bunkrooms sleeping 14 in total (BYO sleeping bags), a well equipped kitchen and a dining area. Please bring £1 coins for the electric metre. The Coast to Coast path is nearby and the Howgill Fells, Wild Boar Fell and Crosby Garrett Common offer great fell walking. Smardale Gill Nature Reserve and Sunbiggin Tarn are also easily accessible.

DETAILS
- **Open** - All year. All day.
- **Beds** - 14: 1x8, 1x6
- **Price/night** - £11 per person. Full barn £140 per night.

CONTACT: Dorothy Ousby
Tel: Booking: 017687 74301, Dorothy: 01768 371760
info@bentscampingbarn.co.uk
www.bentscampingbarn.co.uk
Newbiggin-on-Lune, Kirkby Stephen, Cumbria, CA17 4NX

DETAILS
- **Open** - All year. All day
- **Beds** - 12: 3x4
- **Price/night** - £10pp. £120 sole use. Sleeping bag hire £1

CONTACT: Chris Wilkin
Tel: 01748 818326
chris01748@gmail.com
24 Richmond Road, Richmond, North Yorkshire, DL10 7HE

HOWGILLS
BARN

200

Howgills Barn offers a beautifully renovated self-catering barn in Sedbergh Yorkshire. Breathtaking views, plenty to see and do on the doorstep & set in a private location where the children can enjoy some freedom. A five minute walk into Sedbergh to nearby pubs, cafés and restaurants. Dogs welcome too. Hot tub available. Five stars on trip advisor from over 100 reviews, gives a flavour of the quality of the accommodation.

DETAILS
- **Open** - All year. All day.
- **Beds** - 35: 6x4 1x5 1x6 (all en suite) plus camping
- **Price/night** - From £30pp inc. breakfast. Duvet £6 sgle, £9 dbl. Please enquire for hot tub rates. Camping £12pp.

CONTACT:
Tel: 0800 832 1632 Mob: 07973 947753
info@howgillsaccommodation.co.uk
www.howgillsaccommodation.co.uk
Castlehaw Farm, Castlehaw Lane,
Sedbergh, Cumbria LA10 5BA

KIRKBY STEPHEN
HOSTEL
201

Former Methodist Church with a range of accommodation for individuals, families and groups amongst beautiful authentic features; stained glass, arches and panels. There's a large dining room & kitchen and a quiet lounge in the gallery. Kirkby Stephen is a market town in the upper Eden valley, On Wainwright's Coast to Coast path with easy access to the Pennine Journey, the Walney to Wear Cycle Route, the Howgill Hills, the Yorkshire Dales and the Lakes.

DETAILS

■ **Open** - All year. Please arrive after 5pm (or ring to arrange arrival).
■ **Beds** - 38: 1x8, 3x6, 2x4, 1x2, 1x2 en suite.
■ **Price/night** - £20pp. Group rates.

CONTACT: Denise
Tel: 07812 558525
kirkbystephenhostel@btconnect.com
www.kirkbystephenhostel.co.uk
Market Street, Kirkby Stephen, Cumbria, CA17 4QQ

GREENGILL
BARN

202

A converted traditional barn on the edge of Morland in Cumbria's rolling Eden Valley. Close to the Lake District and handy for the M6. Great for gatherings of family or friends wanting to visit the Lake District, the Pennines, the Yorkshire Dales and the Borders. There is a large, fully equipped kitchen/dining room and comfortable games room. On NCR 71 and Wiggo's Loop on C2C. Good local walking and easy access to lakes & fells. Local café and pub for meals & real ale.

GROUPS ONLY

DETAILS

■ **Open** - All year.
■ **Beds** - 16: 2x8
■ **Price/night** - Min 2 nights: £590 then £160 per night. Own sleeping bags free, or duvet, pillow, towel £5. Dogs £20.

CONTACT: Freddy Markham
Tel: 01931 714244 Mob: 07831 428541
freddy@greengillholidays.co.uk
www.greengillholidays.co.uk
Greengill Barn, Strickland Road,
Morland, Penrith, Cumbria CA10 3AX

NEW ING
LODGE

2031

This 10-bedroom, 10-bathroom B&B and hostel offers comfortable, friendly, accommodation with delicious food. Shap is in the Eden Valley, just off the M6, on the edge of the Lake District National Park. The Howgills and the Pennine Fells are a short drive away. On Wainwright's Coast to Coast, the Westmorland Way and the Miller's Way and perfect for large, sole use groups.

YEALAND
OLD SCHOOL

203r

Stroll from the doorstep to Warton Crag for views across the sands of Morecambe Bay. In early summer hunt out a host of wild flowers on the limestone scenery at nearby Gaitbarrows NNR and Hutton Roofs crags. Kids will enjoy Lakeland Wildlife Oasis, a small zoo close by. The New Inn is only 300m away. Relax in the grounds of the adjacent Quaker Meeting House. Car park. Groups only at weekends, except when there's a last minute vacancy

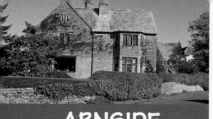

ARNSIDE
INDEPENDENT HOSTEL 204

This large, family run Edwardian house hostel overlooks Morecambe Bay with great views of the Lake District mountains. The Lakes, Yorkshire Dales, Arneside Knott and Leighton Moss are all easily accessed. Enjoy spectacular summer evening sunsets in the garden with fire pits and BBQ or winter evenings relaxing by the fire in the lounge, playing board games with a local ale from the bar. Self-cater in the large kitchen or book a delicious home cooked supper in the restaurant.

DETAILS

- **Open** - All year, except Christmas Day. Reception: 7.30-10am, 5.30-10.30pm.
- **Beds** - 67
- **Price/night** - from £18.50.

CONTACT: Martin or Leigha
Tel: 01524 761781
enquiries@arnsidehostel.co.uk
arnsideindependenthostel.co.uk/
Oakfield Lodge, Redhills Rd, Arnside,
Cumbria, LA5 0AT

ROOKHOW
CENTRE
205

In the Rusland Valley, surrounded by glorious woods where bonfires/BBQs are permitted, near Coniston, Windermere & Grisedale Forest, Rookhow is the perfect base for walking, orienteering, mountaineering, biking and other outdoor activities or quiet retreat. A small, cosy hostel converted from stables of the nearby Quaker Meeting House (available for group activities). The sleeping areas can be rented as private/family rooms.

DETAILS

■ **Open** - All year. All day.
■ **Beds** - 20: 1x9, 1x8, plus extra on bed settees. Also camping available
■ **Price/night** - From: £18 (U16 £9). Sole use from £225. Camping 1/2 the above. Duvet hire £5pp.

CONTACT: Warden
Tel: 01229 860231 Mob: 0794 350 8100
straughton@btinternet.com
www.rookhowcentre.co.uk
Rusland Valley, nr Grizedale, Ulverston,
Cumbria, South Lakeland, LA12 8LA

LOWICK SCHOOL
BUNKHOUSE
206

Within the old primary school at Lowick Green, which is nestled between Coniston (4 miles) and Ulverston, the bunkhouse has a lounge with wood-burning stove, large kitchen/dining room, great views of the mountains and an outdoor area with campfire. River Deep Mountain High Activity Centre provides a wide variety of outdoor activities. Group and family packages include activities in the price.

GROUPS ONLY

DETAILS

- **Open** - All year.
- **Beds** - 20: 2x8, 1x4 (one 8 bed can be expanded to 10)
- **Price/night** - Sole use from £550 at weekends (Club scheme), from £200 per night Mon-Thurs. £250 damage deposit. Family holiday packages.

CONTACT: Emma Hoving
Tel: 01539528666
info@riverdeepmountainhigh.co.uk
www.riverdeepmountainhigh.co.uk/
Lowick Green, Ulverston LA12 8EB

FELL END
CAMPING BARN
207l

Fell End is a traditional 18th century Lakeland stone barn, located within its own grass courtyard approximately ½ mile from the farm. It is within easy distance of Coniston (6 miles) and the Duddon Valley (5 miles). Come and stay and witness the star filled skies, a truly breathtaking sight. Experience the 'Sound of Silence' in the tranquil and calming Fell End Barn. BYO your own cooking equipment, torches, bedding and mat.

DETAILS
- **Open** - All year, all day.
- **Beds** - 12: 1x12
- **Price/night** - £11 per person.

CONTACT: Office or Jean Jackson
Tel: Office 017687 74301,
Farm 01229 716 340
info@lakelandcampingbarns.co.uk
www.lakedistrictcottages.co.uk
Thornthwaite Farm, Woodland,
Broughton in Furness, Cumbria,
LA20 6DF

HIGH WALLABARROW
CAMPING BARN
207r

High Wallabarrow is a traditional hill farm in the Duddon Valley; the Lake District's quiet corner. The well equipped camping barn, an old farmhouse, sleeps 10 upstairs. Downstairs there's a large living area with woodburning stove and fully equipped kitchen. Mattresses provided BYO sleeping bags/pillows. Toilet just outside and shower nearby. 15 mins walk to pub, 10 mins to climbing cragg. Not suitable for rowdy groups.

DETAILS
- **Open** - All year. Arrive after 4pm, (earlier by arrangement) vacate by 11am.
- **Beds** - 10: 1x10 with extra possible.
- **Price/night** - £12.50pp weeknights in school term. Two-night weekends sole-use £125/night. £1.50 per dog per night..

CONTACT: Chris Chinn (9am to 9pm)
Tel: 01229 715011
camden.chinn@gmail.com
www.wallabarrow.co.uk
High Wallabarrow, Ulpha, Broughton-in-Furness, Cumbria, LA20 6EA

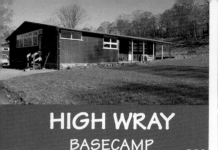

HIGH WRAY
BASECAMP

208

Situated in the heart of South Lakeland, in secluded woodland, 4 miles from the village of Ambleside, High Wray Basecamp provides an ideal base for groups wishing to explore the Lake District. Local attractions include rambling, fell walking, climbing and water sports. The Basecamp ranger will happily assist on local walks and activities. The Longland block has two 8 bed dorms, while the Acland block has two 10 bed dorms and a twin leaders room.

      GROUPS ONLY

DETAILS

- **Open** - All year. All day.
- **Beds** - 16 + 22
- **Price/night** - Prices from £11 per person per night (minimum 8 persons booking).

CONTACT: Philippa Barber
Tel: 01539 434 633
philippa.barber@nationaltrust.org.uk
nationaltrust.org.uk
High Wray, Ambleside, Cumbria, Lake District. LA22 0JE

LAKE DISTRICT
BACKPACKERS

209l

KENDAL
HOSTEL

209r

In the heart of Windermere, close to shops, cafés and pubs, 2 minutes from the train & bus station and opposite the TIC and tour offices. Easy access to the National Park by the 555 bus, 25 minute walk to the lake with steamer trips and boat hire and access to the fells from the door. Maps and guides available in this friendly, cosy hostel.

Kendal Hostel is a family run hostel set in a Georgian townhouse in the historic market town of Kendal, right in front of the well known Brewery Arts Centre and only a stone's throw from the town centre. 13 bedrooms sleep up to 68 guests which are welcome to use the kitchen, lounge, dining room, bike shed and FREE WiFi.

DETAILS

- **Open** - All year. 24 hours with key code for front door.
- **Beds** - 20:- 1x6, 2x4, 2 x double with single above.
- **Price/night** - From £16.95pp dorms, £19.95pp private rooms. £2pn discount for stays of 3+ nights (Nov-Mar) inc self serve continental b-fast & free tea/coffee.

DETAILS

- **Open** - All year. 7.30am to 11.30am, 4.30pm to 8.30pm and by arrangement.
- **Beds** - 68: 1x14, 1x8, 2x7 (family), 2x6, 1x5(family), 1x4, 1x3, 4x2, 1x double. Family rooms have private shower room and double bed.
- **Price/night** - £20 Sun -Thurs, £22 Fri & Sat. Sole use from £750pn

CONTACT: Paul
Tel: 015394 46374
info@lakedistrictbackpackers.co.uk
www.lakedistrictbackpackers.co.uk
High Street, Windermere, Cumbria,
LA23 1AF

CONTACT: Jan or Kristina
Tel: 01539 724066
kristina@kendalhostel.co.uk
www.kendalhostel.com
118-120 Highgate, Kendal, Cumbria,
LA9 4HE

MAGGS HOWE
CAMPING BARN
210l

In the quiet, unspoilt valley of Kentmere, a ramblers' paradise of woods, fields, lanes, a scattering of traditional farms & the fells covered with Wainwright walks. There is plenty to do including biking, riding & fishing, as well as quiet enjoyment. Maggs Howe provides B&B in 3 farmhouse rooms and a camping barn (BYO sleeping bag). Breakfast (£8) and suppers (from £14) are available with notice. Dogs need prior permission.

DETAILS
■ **Open** - All year. 24 hours.
■ **Beds** - Camping Barn 14: 1x6, 1x4 + 4 mattresses. B&B 8: 1x4(family), 1x2 (double), 1x2 (twin).
■ **Price/night** - Barn: Mid week £12pp or £120 sole use. Friday and Saturday night must be sole use: £240/two nights or £180/one night. B&B: £30-£35pp

CONTACT: Christine Hevey
Tel: 01539 821689
c.hevey@btinternet.com
Kentmere, Kendal, Cumbria, LA8 9JP

DACRES STABLE
CAMPING BARN
210r

A short drive from Kendal, Dacres Stable Camping Barn is on the Eastern edge of the Lake District National Park. On a gated road away from the main A6 it is a perfect base for exploring the Yorkshire Dales, the Lake District and the Eden Valley. Great too for mountain biking, walking, & cycling on quiet tracks and lanes. The camping barn comfortably sleeps 8 on a sole use, self-catering basis. A separate big barn provides play space for children and extra storage.

DETAILS
■ **Open** - All year.
■ **Beds** - 8: 1x2 1x6.
■ **Price/night** - Sole use only - from £55pn (min 2 nights). Discounts for midweek/longer stays.

CONTACT: Hilary Fell
Tel: 01539 823208 Mob: 07788 633936
dacresstablecampingbarn.blogspot.
co.uk
Grisedale Farm, Whinfell, Kendal,
Cumbria, LA8 9EN

ELTERWATER
HOSTEL
211

Located in the peaceful village of Elterwater, in the Langdale Valley, 15 mins' drive from Ambleside. The area has many walks for people of all abilities, from gentle riverside meanders to the challenge presented by the Langdale Pikes, Bowfell and Scafell. Pubs, shops and other amenities are nearby. The area is popular for both on and off-road cycling, rock climbing and other outdoor activities. An ideal overnight stop on the Cumbria Way.

DETAILS

■ **Open** - All year (Nov-Feb groups only). Access 7.30am-11.30pm. Reception open 7.30am to 10am and 5pm to 10.30pm.
■ **Beds** - 38 : 6x2, 1x4, 1x4 en suite, 3x6
■ **Price/night** - From £25pp, £21 in low season. For exclusive hire please call.

CONTACT: Nick Owen
Tel: 015394 37245
enquiries@elterwaterhostel.co.uk
www.elterwaterhostel.co.uk
Elterwater, Ambleside LA22 9HX

THORNEY HOW

212

Thorney How offers clean, comfortable accommodation in Grasmere. Family-run and welcoming it provides en suite, B&B and self-catering accommodation. Close to the Coast to Coast path, local village and lake, it is your perfect Lake District base. A bar, restaurant and spacious grounds complete the experience.

DETAILS

■ **Open** - All year. Closed 10.30am to 3.30pm – check in 3.30pm to 10.30pm.
■ **Beds** - 42: Main House 26: 2xdbl, 1xtwin, 2x4, 2x6. Bunkhouse 16
■ **Price/night** - B/house from £20. Main House B&B from £25.50. Dble en suite from £77.00. 4 person rooms from £76.00. Larger groups please enquire.

CONTACT: Taylor Nuttall
Tel: 01539 435597
enquiries@thorneyhow.co.uk
www.thorneyhow.co.uk
Thorney How, Off Helm Close &
Easedale Rd, Grasmere, Cumbria,
LA22 9QW

GRASMERE
HOSTEL

213

This small, deluxe 4* hostel is situated on a farm in the heart of the Lake District National Park and a short stroll from the idyllic village of Grasmere. It is ideal for individuals, couples, families and groups, especially if you want sole use for a club, school or special event. For groups requiring more space, 4 luxury cottages and a Micro Lodge Pod are also available. The hostel, recommended by the Guardian and the Rough Guide, has first class facilities including a sauna.

DETAILS

■ **Open** - All year. Reception open until 9pm. 24hr access once checked in.
■ **Beds** - 24: 1x3, 1x4, 1x5, 2x6.
■ **Price/night** - From £20 pppn. Sole use from £475 per night.

CONTACT: Dave Keighley
Tel: 015394 35055
dave@grasmerehostel.co.uk
www.grasmerehostel.co.uk
Broadrayne Farm, Keswick Road,
Grasmere, Cumbria, LA22 9RU

GREAT LANGDALE
BUNKHOUSE
214l

Great value accommodation for groups, families and individuals amidst some of the finest mountain scenery in England. Immediate access to world class mountain biking, road cycling, walking, fell running and climbing. Biomass central heating throughout, separate male and female shower and toilet facilities - always warm with hot showers! No cooking/dining facilities but Sticklebarn Tavern is right next door. Hearty breakfasts at New Dungeon Ghyll Hotel. Well behaved dogs allowed in private rooms.

DETAILS
- **Open** - All year. All day.
- **Beds** - 21: 3x2, 1x7, 1x8 all bunkbeds.
- **Price/night** - From £15pn.

CONTACT: Ben or Sabrina
Tel: Please contact via e-mail
langdale.bunkhouse@gmail.com
www.greatlangdalebunkhouse.co.uk
Great Langdale, Ambleside, Cumbria,
LA22 9JU

RYDAL HALL
YOUTH CENTRE
214r

Situated next to Rydal Beck in the heart of the Lake District, Rydal Hall Youth Centre provides accommodation for groups of up to 29 in four dormitories plus a large common room with wood-burning stove, drying room and a fully-equipped stainless steel kitchen. There is also a quiet campsite for individuals and families, eco-pods in the grounds and en suite accommodation for up to 50 in the main Hall.

DETAILS
- **Open** - All year. All day.
- **Beds** - Dormitories for 29: 1x10, 1x9, 1x6, 1x4.
- **Price/night** - £315. Discounts and late deals possible. Pods £47.50 for 1 night, £42pn 2+ nights, £37pn 4+ nights.

CONTACT: Bookings Office
Tel: 01539 432050
groupbookings@rydalhall.org
www.rydalhall.org
Rydal Hall, Ambleside, Cumbria,
LA22 9LX

SHEPHERDS
CROOK

215

Noran Bank Farm is near Ullswater just through Patterdale in Cumbria, just 5 minutes' walk away from the Coast to Coast route and The Westmorland Way. Shepherd's Crook Bunkhouse is a barn converted to a very high standard and sleeps 8. Duvets, linen and towels are provided. DIY breakfast and packed lunches can be pre-booked. It is very popular with Coast to Coasters, walkers, cyclists and for family/friends get-togethers.

DETAILS

- **Open** - All year.
- **Beds** - 8: 1x6, 1x2 + B&B.
- **Price/night** - £15pp (6 bed room), £20pp (double room). Sole use £120. Farmhouse B&B £30pp.

CONTACT: Mrs Heather Jackson
Tel: 017684 82327 Mob: 07833 981504
heathernoranbank@gmail.com
www.noranbankfarm.co.uk
Noran Bank Farm, Patterdale, Penrith, Cumbria, CA11 0NR

FISHER-GILL
CAMPING BARN
216

Situated in Thirlmere at the foot of the Helvellyn mountains, close to Sticks Pass and the spectacular Fisher-Gill waterfall, the camping barn offers direct access to numerous walks, hill and rock climbing. It is just off the A591, with local and national bus stops at the end of the lane. Accommodation consists of two rooms: a kitchen/diner with all the basic equipment and 10 bed bunkroom (sleeping bags/liners are required). A pub serving meals is within walking distance. Perfect for quite country retreats, but not suitable for late night drinking parties.

DETAILS
- **Open** - All year. Check in by 9pm.
- **Beds** - 10
- **Price/night** - £16pp. Sole use £160.

CONTACT: Mrs Jean Hodgson
Tel: 017687 74391 or 73232
stybeckfarm@btconnect.com
www.stybeckfarm.co.uk
Stybeck Farm, Thirlmere, Keswick,
Cumbria CA12 4TN

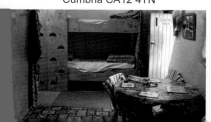

ST JOHNS IN THE VALE
CAMPING BARN
217

St John's-in-the-Vale Camping Barn, a renovated 18th century stable on a peaceful hill farm, has stunning views to Blencathra, Helvellyn and Castle Rock. The Barn has a sleeping area upstairs (mattress provided) and a sitting/dining area below. A separate toilet, shower and cooking area (BYO equipment) are within the building. A wood-burning stove makes it nice and cosy. Outside there is a BBQ area. As there is no light pollution, the star-filled night skies are magical. Northern Lights have been seen too!

DETAILS

- **Open** - All year. All day.
- **Beds** - 8 : 1x8
- **Price/night** - £11.00 per person.

CONTACT: Graham or Sarah
Tel: 017687 79242 (Bookings 017687 74301)
info@campingbarn.com
www.campingbarn.com
Low Bridge End Farm, St John's-in-the-Vale, Keswick, CA12 4TS

CARLISLE DIOCESAN
YOUTH CENTRE
218l

ROOKIN HOUSE
CAMPING BARN
218r

Near St John's-in-the-Vale and just four miles from Keswick. The centre offers flexible accommodation for groups in modern en suite bunkrooms. With fell walking, climbing, orienteering, geo-caching and cycling on the doorstep and amazing views from the two buildings. Perfect for a group retreat, large family get-together or field trips. The buildings can be hire separately or together. BYO sleeping bag, pillowcase and towel.

Rookin House Farm Camping Barn sleeps up to 24 with central heating, fully equipped kitchen and inside toilets & showers (BYO bedding). The centre also has luxury self-catering group accommodation and provides outdoor activities. At the heart of the Lake District surrounded by some of the best walking country and close to C2C cycle route.

 GROUPS ONLY

DETAILS

- **Open** - All year. 24 hours.
- **Beds** - 39: School 25: 1x6,1x5,3x4,1x2. Chapel 14: 3x4,1x2.
- **Price/night** - Mixed aged groups £12pp from Cumbria, £13.50 from elsewhere. Adult only groups £17pp

DETAILS

- **Open** - All year. All day
- **Beds** - 65: Camping Barn 24: 2x6, 1x12. Barn 23. Blencathra View 18.
- **Price/night** - Camping Barn mid week £17.50pp (min of 4 people), weekends £400 for 2 night stay for 12 people plus £12.50pp for extra people. Additional nights £150 per night for up to 12 people.

CONTACT: Warden
Tel: 0753 0968 219
carlisledyc@gmail.com
www.cdyc.org.uk/
St John's-in-the-Vale, Keswick,
Cumbria,CA12 4UB

CONTACT: Deb and Emma
Tel: 017684 83561
deborah@rookinhouse.co.uk
www.rookinhouse.co.uk
Rookin House Farm, Troutbeck,
Ullswater,Penrith,Cumbria, CA11 0SS

THE WHITE HORSE
INN BUNKHOUSE

The White Horse Inn has 2 bunkhouses, the former stables of this traditional Lake District inn, at the foot of Blencathra. Guests are welcome to socialise in the Inn which has great pub food, open fires, local ales and is open from 11am to 11pm. Each bunkhouse has a basic kitchen, dining area and bunkrooms sleeping 4 to 6. Right on the C2C, with paths to the mountains from the garden.

DETAILS

- **Open** - All year. All day access.
- **Beds** - 50:1x8,3x6,6x4 (2 bunkhouses)
- **Price/night** - £12pp. Private rooms: 4 bed £48, 6 bed £72, 8 bed £96. Sole use of 24 bed bunkhouse £260. 26 bed bunkhouse £280. Bedding £5/stay. Enquire for Xmas/New Year.

CONTACT: Phil or Cozmin
Tel: 017687 79883
info@thewhitehorse-blencathra.co.uk
www.thewhitehorse-blencathra.co.uk
The White Horse Inn, Scales, Nr Threlkeld, Keswick, CA12 4SY

BLAKEBECK FARM
CAMPING BARN
220l

At the foot of Souther Fell, within easy reach of Blencathra, Blakebeck Farm is set amidst the wildflower meadows of Mungrisdale. On the C2C cycle route and the Cumbria Way. Perfect as an overnight stop for cyclists or weekend break for walkers and families. The large upstairs room has mattresses provided (BYO sleeping bags). The kitchen has basic equipment and utensils. Towels, bedding, DIY breakfast & pack lunches can be pre-booked. One dog welcome with sole use. Not suitable for parties.

DETAILS
- **Open** - All year. All day
- **Beds** - 10: 1x10 + holiday cottages
- **Price/night** - £11 per person. Sole use £100. Dog £10 per stay.

CONTACT: Judith
Tel: 017687 79957 Mob: 07789287121
j.egan001@btinternet.com
blakebeckfarm.co.uk/camping-barn/
Blakebeck, Mungrisdale, Penrith,
CA11 0SZ

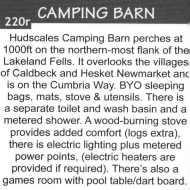

HUDSCALES
CAMPING BARN
220r

Hudscales Camping Barn perches at 1000ft on the northern-most flank of the Lakeland Fells. It overlooks the villages of Caldbeck and Hesket Newmarket and is on the Cumbria Way. BYO sleeping bags, mats, stove & utensils. There is a separate toilet and wash basin and a metered shower. A wood-burning stove provides added comfort (logs extra), there is electric lighting plus metered power points, (electric heaters are provided if required). There's also a games room with pool table/dart board.

DETAILS
- **Open** - All year. All day.
- **Beds** - 12: 1x12
- **Price/night** - £11 per person.

CONTACT: Office/William/Judith
Tel: Booking office: 017687 74301/Farm: 016974 77199
wrcowx@gmail.com
www.lakelandcampingbarns.co.uk
Hudscales, Hesket Newmarket, Wigton, Cumbria, CA7 8JZ

SKIDDAW
HOUSE

221l

DENTON
HOUSE

221r

The highest hostel in Britain! Escape the crowds at this remote mountain hostel. No roads, no other buildings, and no phone signal; just uninterrupted views of beautiful mountain wilderness. But there's no need to compromise on comfort, with wood-burning stoves, hot showers, a well-stocked bar and your bed made up for you. It's half way up Skiddaw but an easy walk or mountain bike ride from Keswick or Threlkeld.

Denton House is a purpose built hostel and outdoor centre in the Lake District offering bunkhouse accommodation. Warm and well equipped for self-catering, the centre was designed for groups with parking for 40 cars. A variety of outdoor activities can be arranged on site. There is equipment storage and access to the River Greta across the road.

DETAILS

■ **Open** - March-Oct. Winter: Group only. Check in from 5pm, check out by 10am.
■ **Beds** - 22 : 1 x 8, 2 x 5, 1 x 4
■ **Price/night** - From £18 (adult), £11.50 (U18). YHA members £1.50 - £3 discount. Camping £8. Cards not accepted.

DETAILS

■ **Open** - All year (including Christmas). Office hours 9am - 8pm.
■ **Beds** - 56: 1x4, 2x6, 1x8, 2x10, 1x12.
■ **Price/night** - £17 midweek, £19 weekend. Sole use £900 (midweek) £999 (weekend). Breakfast £6. Pack lunch £6. Dinner £10. Activities £30/half day.

CONTACT: Martin or Suzy
Tel: 07747 174293
info@skiddawhouse.co.uk
www.skiddawhouse.co.uk
Bassenthwaite, Keswick, Cumbria,
CA12 4QX

CONTACT: Libby Scott
Tel: 01768 775351
keswickhostel@hotmail.co.uk
www.dentonhouse-keswick.co.uk
Penrith Road, Keswick, Cumbria,
CA12 4JW

DERWENTWATER
INDEPENDENT HOSTEL 222

Family run and friendly, Derwentwater Independent Hostel is a Georgian mansion in 17 acres of grounds with stunning mountain views. Just 2 miles from Keswick, close to the Coast to Coast route and the delights of Borrowdale it makes a great base for individuals, families, groups and conferences. The hostel has plenty of space in and out for you to use and relax. Home-made food is available.

DETAILS

■ **Open** - All Year. 7am - 11pm.
■ **Beds** - 88: 1x4, 2x5, 3x6, 3x8, 1x10, 1x22
■ **Price/night** - From £21 (adult), £16.50 (child). Family rooms from £72 (for 4). Ask if you want a room for 2 or 3.

CONTACT:
Tel: 01768 777246
reception@derwentwater.org
www.derwentwater.org
Barrow House, Borrowdale, Keswick, Cumbria, CA12 5UR

HAWSE END
CENTRE

223

Hawse End Centre sits at the head of the magnificent Borrowdale Valley on the shores of Derwentwater with easy access to Keswick via launch or lakeside walk. The house is a large, comfortable, country mansion, ideal for large groups, while the Cottage is more suited to smaller group, families and individuals. For the more adventurous there are two yurts with stunning views and transparent domes for star gazing.

Catering & outdoor activities with instruction can be booked in advance.

DETAILS

■ **Open** - All year.
■ **Beds** - House 49: (9 rooms). Cottage 24: (6 rooms). Yurts: 24 (2x12)
■ **Price/night** - Enquire for prices.

CONTACT:
Tel: 01768 812280
cumbriaoutdoors.enquiries@cumbria.gov.uk
www.cumbria.gov.uk/childrensservices/
Hawse End Centre, Portinscale,
Keswick, Cumbria, CA12 5UE

CATBELLS
CAMPING BARN
224l

Catbells Camping Barn sits on the slopes of Catbells in the tranquil Newlands Valley, with magnificent views over the Lake District. The Cumberland Way passes through the farmyard. Keswick is only 4 miles away and both Borrowdale and Buttermere are within walking distance. The camping barn has mattresses (BYO sleeping bag) and is heated with a multi-fuel stove (not suitable for cooking). In the adjacent building is a toilet and a cooking area (BYO stove & equipment). It is possible to walk to a pub which serves food.

DETAILS
- **Open** - All year. All day.
- **Beds** - 10: 1x10
- **Price/night** - £11.00 per person

CONTACT: Mrs Grave
Tel: 01768 774301
info@lakelandcampingbarns.co.uk
www.lakelandcampingbarns.co.uk
Low Skelgill Farm, Newlands, Keswick, Cumbria, CA12 5UE

DINAH HOGGUS
CAMPING BARN
224r

Dinah Hoggus Camping Barn lies on the old Packhorse route to lath on the edge of the village of Rosthwaite in the Borrowdale valley. For walkers it is perfectly located right on the Cumbria Way and the Coast to Coast walk. It sleeps 12 on mattresses (BYO sleeping bag) & has a cooking/dining area. Basic cooking equipment is provided and there's an electric shower. The pub and village shop are just 300m away.

DETAILS
- **Open** - All year.
- **Beds** - 12 : 1 x12
- **Price/night** - £11 pp. Electricity is charged extra by meter reading.

CONTACT:
Tel: Booking office 01946 758198, Farm 01768 777689
info@lakelandcampingbarns.co.uk
www.lakelandcampingbarns.co.uk/barns/dinah-hoggus-camping-barn
Stonecroft, Borrowdale, Keswick, Cumbria, CA12 5XB

LATH
BOTHY

225

lath Bothy sits next to the tarn in the quiet, picturesque hamlet that shares its name. High in a beautiful valley, it offers superb access to the surrounding fells. Visitors should treat the Bothy as a 'stone tent', BYO equipment as for camping such as cutlery, plates, sleeping bags & mats, matches, etc.

The perfect choice for people looking to escape to one of the most remote-feeling places in the Lake District.

DETAILS

- **Open** - Mid March- Mid October
- **Beds** - 6: BYO mats and sleeping bags
- **Price/night** - Low season: £60/night High season: £70/night. Minimum booking of 3 nights.

CONTACT: National Trust Holidays
Tel: 01539 432733
campsite.bookings@nationaltrust.org.uk
www.nationaltrust.org.uk
lath, Borrowdale, Cumbria,
CA12 5UW

HIGH HOUSE

226l

MURT
CAMPING BARN

226r

High House in Seathwaite, at the head of the beautiful valley of Borrowdale, offers comfortable bunkhouse/hostel self-catering accommodation. Popular with walking and climbing clubs, outdoor education and corporate groups, early booking is advised. The building is only let to one group at a time. Two dorms are available each with toilet, washbasin and shower. There is a third dorm reserved for K Fellfarers members, and club members may use this room during your stay. If you wish to have sole use, including this Members Room, there's a £25 supplement per night.

Nestling in the wild and remote Wasdale valley, Murt Camping Barn is ideally situated for high fell walks including Scafell Pike, Mosedale Horseshoe, Great Gable and Screes Tops. Converted from a hay loft and byre, it sleeps 8, with WC, shower & hot water in the same building. Pubs in the village of Nether Wasdale are just a 10 minute walk away and nearest shops are within 5 miles. Waswater is half mile down road, towards the Scafell range of mountains.

      GROUPS ONLY

DETAILS

- **Open** - All year. All day.
- **Beds** - 26: 1x18, 1x8
- **Price/night** - £155

DETAILS

- **Open** - All year
- **Beds** - 8: 1x8
- **Price/night** - £11.00 per person. Sole use bookings only at week ends

CONTACT: Hugh Taylor
Tel: 01524 762067
jhugh.taylor@btinternet.com
www.kfellfarers.co.uk
Seathwaite, Borrowdale, Keswick.

CONTACT:
Tel: Booking office 01768 774301
info@lakelandcampingbarns.co.uk
www.murtbarn.co.uk
Murt, Nether Wasdale, Seascale,
Cumbria, CA20 1ET

CRAGG
CAMPING BARN

227

Cragg Camping Barn, with its stunning views of Buttermere fell is a great base for all outdoor enthusiasts, with great walking, climbing and mountain biking close by. The simple accommodation has mattresses for 8, a kitchen and seating area, a hot shower on a meter, and a toilet/ washbasin with hot & cold water. BYO sleeping bag and stove/ eating utensils if you wish to self-cater. Sole occupancy only. Cragg House Farm also has a holiday cottage sleeping two, enquire for details (017687 70204).

DETAILS

■ **Open** - All year. Arrival from 4pm, late arrivals by arrangement.
■ **Beds** - 8: 1 x 8
■ **Price/night** - £11 per person.

CONTACT: John and Vicki Temple
Tel: Camping Barn 01768 774301.
info@lakelandcampingbarns.co.uk
www.buttermerecottage.co.uk
Cragg House Farm, Buttermere,
Cockermouth, Cumbria, CA13 9XA

LOW GILLERTHWAITE
FIELD CENTRE
228l

In the Ennerdale valley, one of the most beautiful, least spoiled and quietest in the Lake District, Low GIllerthwaite Field Centre sits at the foot of Pillar and Red Pike. Well equipped for groups it is the perfect base for fell walking, rock climbing, bird and wildlife watching, mountain biking, orienteering & canoeing. The centre generates its own hydro-electricity. Vehicle access is by forest track and a BT payphone is on-site as most mobiles do not work here.

DETAILS
- **Open** - All year (except Christmas and Boxing Day). 24 hours.
- **Beds** - 40: 2x4, 1x8, 1x10, 1x14.
- **Price/night** - From £11.50 per person (children and students), £15.50 (adults), camping is £5 per person.

CONTACT: Ellen or Walter
Tel: 01946 861229
Warden@lgfc.org.uk
www.lgfc.org.uk
Ennerdale, Cleator, CA23 3AX

THE WILD WOOL
BARN
228r

Nestled in the peace of the Ennerdale Valley, overlooking Ennerdale Water, The Wild Wool Barn provides luxury bunkhouse accommodation for 6 (plus up to 4 camping). Traditional wood-burning stove, electric heating, cooker and shower marry tradition with luxury. With no mobile signal or WiFi The Wild Wool Barn is a true chance to get away from it all and explore the rarely visited Western Lake District.

    GROUPS ONLY

DETAILS
- **Open** - All year. Easter to October: Groups only.
- **Beds** - 6: 1x6 + 4 camping
- **Price/night** - £30pp. Sole use: from 1 night £120 to 7 nights £380. Bank holidays min 3 nights. Camping £10pp

CONTACT: Susan Denham-Smith
Tel: 01946 861270
susan@wildwoolworkshop.co.uk
www.wildwoolworkshop.co.uk
Routen Farm Cottage, Ennerdale, CA23 3AU

SUMMERGROVE
HALLS
229

Close to the start of the Coast to Coast Walk at Whitehaven and within easy access to the Cumbrian Coast and Lake District, Summergrove Halls offers en suite self-catering accommodation in rooms with small double (3/4 size) beds. Bed linen and towels are provided along with basic toiletries. Self-cater or choose from the popular dinner menu in Terrace Bar and Grill. Breakfast is available and communal areas include a TV room. Nestled in attractive grounds there are nature and cycle trails from the door, as well as an on-site gym.

DETAILS

- **Open** - All Year. All day
- **Beds** - 131
- **Price/night** - from £27.60

CONTACT: Reception
Tel: 01946 813328
info@summergrovehalls.co.uk
www.summergrovehalls.co.uk
Hensingham, Whitehaven, Cumbria,
CA28 8XZ

HOLME WOOD
BOTHY

230

Holme Wood Bothy offers basic accommodation in a spectacular secluded location, right on the shore of Loweswater. This "stone tent" provides a roof, kitchen area and sleeping platform. Visitors must bring all camping equipment including plates, matches, sleeping mats, sleeping bags, food and water. If you are looking for a remote and basic getaway with easy access to the lake, this bothy is your perfect choice. Great for accessing the lakes and canoeing on Loweswater.

 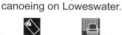

DETAILS
- **Open** - All year. All day.
- **Beds** - 6- BYO mats and sleeping bag.
- **Price/night** - Low season: £60/night
High season: £70/night

CONTACT:National Trust Holidays
Tel: 015394 32733
campsite.bookings@nationaltrust.org.uk
www.nationaltrust.org.uk
Watergate Farm, Loweswater,
Cockermouth, Cumbria, CA13 0RU

SWALLOW BARN
CAMPING BARN
231l

In the picturesque Loweswater Valley, Swallow Barn is part of a set of buildings dating back to 1670 on a working beef and sheep farm. Sleeping 18 on mattresses (BYO sleeping bags), there is a cooking and eating area, metered showers & plug socket and 2 toilets. Perfect for exploring the Western Fells on both high and low level walks with spectacular views, or enjoying the peace and tranquillity of the valley. On the C2C Cycle Route. The Kirkstyle pub (1 mi) serves food, Cockermouth (8 mi).

HILLSIDE FARM
BUNKBARN
231r

A Georgian farmstead, still a working farm, right on Hadrian's Wall National Trail and Cycleway near the Solway Coast AONB. Stunning views over the Solway Firth marshes towards Scotland. Bunkbarn or B&B rooms available. The bunkbarn, in a converted stable block, has cooking facilities & hot showers. Towels and sleeping bags can be hired. Communal (but not sleeping) areas are heated. Breakfast or bacon sandwiches available with notice. Walking, cycling and family groups are most welcome.

DETAILS

- **Open** - All year. All day.
- **Beds** - 18: 1x9, 3x3
- **Price/night** - £11 per person.

CONTACT: Kath Leck
Tel: Booking office: 017687 74301, Farm: 01946 861465
info@lakelandcampingbarns.co.uk
www.lakelandcampingbarns.co.uk
Waterend Farm, Loweswater, Cockermouth, Cumbria, CA13 0SU

DETAILS

- **Open** - All year. 10am to 9pm.
- **Beds** - 12
- **Price/night** - £12pp inc shower. £4 Full English, £2 bacon/sausage sandwiches.

CONTACT: Mrs Sandra Rudd
Tel: 01228 576398
ruddshillside1@btinternet.com
www.hadrianswalkbnb.co.uk
Hillside Farm, Boustead Hill, Burgh-by-Sands, Carlisle, Cumbria, CA5 6AA

WAYFARERS
INDEPENDENT HOSTEL 232l

232r
CARLISLE
CITY HOSTEL

Close to Penrith town centre and perfect for those on the C2C Cycle Route. Excellent value accommodation to those visiting Penrith, the Eden Valley and the North Lake District National Park. Bike cleaning and maintenance facilities and bike hire on-site. Full kitchen and dining facilities, en suite rooms with made up beds, lockers, bedside lights. Individuals, small parties and groups of up to 18 are welcome.

DETAILS
- **Open** - Feb-Dec. Reception open 8am-11am, 4pm-9pm.
- **Beds** - 18: 2x2 (twin), 1x6, 2x4.
- **Price/night** - From £23pp (dorm room bed). Sole use from £370pn. Family room: Sun-Thurs from £60. B/fast: £4. Towel: £1.

CONTACT: Mark Rhodes
Tel: 01768 866011
guests@wayfarershostel.com
www.wayfarershostel.com
19 Brunswick Square, Penrith, Cumbria, CA11 7LR

Carlisle's only independent hostel. Located on picturesque Abbey Street, the building is an old Georgian terrace accommodating up to 20 guests. There is a communal kitchen, lounge with TV, DVDs & book swap and a dining room. Free tea, coffee and WiFi in communal areas. Prices include basic breakfast.

A great place from which to explore Carlisle, The Tuille House Museum, The Eden Valley, Hadrian's Wall and more. The staff look forward to welcoming you as their guest to the hostel and the city.

DETAILS
- **Open** - All year. Check in is between 3pm – 8pm ONLY (Sunday 4pm-8pm).
- **Beds** - 20 : 2x6, 2x4.
- **Price/night** - £18 to £25 pp. Groups of over 8 by pre-arrangement only.

CONTACT: Jonathan Quinlan
Tel: 07914 720821
info@carlislecityhostel.com
www.carlislecityhostel.com
36 Abbey Street, Carlisle, CA3 8TX

HAGGS BANK
BUNKHOUSE
233l

In the stunning North Pennines AONB, "England's last wilderness," perfect for lovers of the great outdoors especially walkers & cyclists. Isaac's Tea Trail passes through the site, which is also directly on the C2C with bicycle hire (inc. electric bikes) available nearby. Pre booked breakfast and evening meals can be provided for larger groups. The campsite has tiered pitches to enhance the views across the Nent valley. Electric hook-ups available in the car park.

DETAILS
■ **Open** - All year. All day access.
■ **Beds** - 24: 1x4/5, 1x9, 1x10.
■ **Price/night** - £20pp,Sole use: £380, £1080/3 nights. Camping: £10, U15, £5. Motorhomes/caravans £20 up to 2 people

CONTACT: Danny Taylor
Tel: 07919 092403/ 01434 382486
info@haggsbank.com
haggsbank.com
Haggs Bank Bunkhouse, Nentsbury, Alston, Cumbria, CA9 3LH

ALSTON
YOUTH HOSTEL
233r

On the very eastern edge of Cumbria, nestled in the North Pennines and within the historic town of Alston, is Alston Youth Hostel. Not only is the hostel about halfway on the very popular C2C Cycle Route but it is also located directly on the Pennine Way! You'll receive a wonderfully warm welcome (as warm as our large drying room!!) and hopefully see the resident red squirrels!

DETAILS
■ **Open** - All year. 8am - 10am, 5pm - 10pm
■ **Beds** - 30: 2x2, 2x4, 3x6
■ **Price/night** - From £20.50pp, discount for YHA. Private rms from £36 or family rms from £34. Sole use from £380 for 2 nghts midweek, £590 for 2 nights Fri-Sat

CONTACT: Linda, Neil or Jenny
Tel: 01434 381509
alston@yha.org.uk
alstonyouthhostel.co.uk/
Firs Edge, The Firs, Alston, Cumbria, CA9 3RW

NINEBANKS
YOUTH HOSTEL
234

Book a bed, a room, or the whole hostel! Ninebanks 4* hostel, an 18th century cottage, has en suite bedrooms, a sitting room with log-burner, a spacious dining room and a stunning rural location. There are now two new self-catering high quality chalets; 1 double & 1 family/double, fully self-contained and separate from the hostel. Dogs welcome with prior notice on sole use or in the chalets.

CONTACT: Pauline or Ian
Tel: 01434 345228
contact@ninebanks.com
www.ninebanks.org.uk
Orchard House, Mohope, Hexham, Northumberland NE47 8DQ

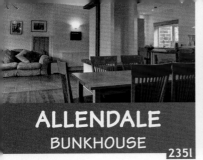

ALLENDALE
BUNKHOUSE
235l

BARRINGTON
BUNKHOUSE
235r

The Allendale Bunkhouse was completely refurbished and thoroughly modernised in 2014. It sits on the Market Square overlooking the hustle and bustle of this small country town and the fells and river beyond. An oasis for walkers, cyclists, horse riders, families, groups of friends and youth & school groups alike. Book a bunk, a room, a floor (up to 18) or the whole bunkhouse (up to 38). Allendale is well served with tea rooms, the Forge art gallery & café, a quirky gift shop, pharmacy, and three wonderful country pubs, all serving food.

Situated in the peaceful village of Rookhope, Weardale, Barrington Bunkhouse accommodates 15 people. There's room for 13 in the bunkhouse, whilst the adjacent caravan sleeps two. Camping space is also available. The kitchen is equipped with two toasters, a kettle, a microwave, and a fridge, whilst The Rookhope Inn serves fine food and good drinks and is located just next door. Everyone is welcome; cyclists, walkers and family groups.

DETAILS

- **Open** - All year. All day.
- **Beds** - 12 (+1): 1 x 12 + 1 fold up bed
- **Price/night** - £24pp incl. snack b/fast. Camping £14 with b/fast, £10 without. Sole use rates negotiable.

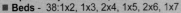

DETAILS

- **Open** - All year. 8am-8pm.
- **Beds** - 38:1x2, 1x3, 2x4, 1x5, 2x6, 1x7
- **Price/night** - From £14 - £40pp.

CONTACT: Valerie Livingston
Tel: 01388 517656
barrington_bunkhouse@hotmail.co.uk
www.barrington-bunkhouse-rookhope.com
Barrington Cottage, Rookhope,
Weardale, Co. Durham, DL13 2BG

CONTACT: Linda Beck
Tel: 01434 618579
info@allendalebunkhouse.co.uk
www.allendalebunkhouse.co.uk
Market Place, Allendale, Hexham,
NE47 9BD

EDMUNDBYERS YHA
HOSTEL
236l

Edmunbyers hostel lies in moorland, close to the Northumberland/County Durham boundary, with fine views and just two miles from Derwent Reservoir, for sailing and fishing. Ideal for walking holidays, it's also on the C2C Cycle Route and is close to Hadrians Wall and the Beamish outdoor museum. Cosy and comfortable with optional home cooked evening meals and breakfasts.

DETAILS

■ **Open** - All year (camping Apr-Oct). Check in 5-10pm, check out 8-10am.
■ **Beds** - 28: 2x6, 2x5,1x4,1x3. 8 pitches for camping.
■ **Price/night** - From £23 (adult), £19 (under 18). Discounts for YHA members: Room for 3 £60, 4 £70, 5 £80, 6 £90.

CONTACT: Debbie Clarke
Tel: 01207 255651
info@lowhousehaven.co.uk
www.lowhousehaven.co.uk
Low House, Edmundbyers, Consett, Durham, DH8 9NL

DEMESNE FARM
BUNKHOUSE
236r

This bunkhouse is on a working hill farm in the centre of Bellingham and near to Northumberland National Park. Situated on the Pennine Way, Route 68, and the Reivers & Sandstone Way cycle routes, it is an ideal base for exploring Northumberland, Hadrian's Wall, Kielder Water and many climbing crags. The bunkhouse is very well appointed with quality bunks, a well equipped kitchen, a farmhouse table to seat 15 and a large comfortable communal area.

DETAILS

■ **Open** - All year. Flexible but no check in after 9pm.
■ **Beds** - 15: 1x8, 1x4, 1x3.
■ **Price/night** - £21 per person, £16 under 18's (including linen).

CONTACT: Robert Telfer
Tel: 01434 220258 Mobile 07967 396345
stay@demesnefarmcampsite.co.uk
www.demesnefarmcampsite.co.uk
Demesne Farm, Bellingham, Hexham, Northumberland, NE48 2BS

SLACK HOUSE
FARM

Slack House Farm is an organic dairy farm overlooking Birdoswald Roman Fort on Hadrian's Wall. It is on the NCN 72 cycle route and is only 0.5km from the Hadrian's Wall National Trail. The bunkbarn is next to Gladje in the Scypen café and farm shop (Birdoswald cheese is made on-site). The bunkbarn is warm and cosy and has basic self-catering facilities. Breakfasts, farmhouse suppers and packed lunches can be provided.

DETAILS

■ **Open** - All year. Check in from 5pm, check out by 10am.
■ **Beds** - 18: 1x10, 1x5, 1x3 (family)
■ **Price/night** - Beds £15pp. Camp-bed Loft £12pp. Sole use: 5 bed room £60, family £45, private 10 bed dorm £80.

CONTACT: Dianne Horn
Tel: 01697 747351 Mob: 07900 472342
slackhouseorganicfarm@gmail.com
www.slackhousefarm.co.uk
Slack House Farm, Gilsland Brampton, Cumbria, CA8 7DB

GIBBS HILL
FARM HOSTEL
238

Gibbs Hill Farm Hostel is on a working hill farm near Once Brewed on Hadrian's Wall and close to the Pennine Way. Designed to reduce energy consumption, it is centrally heated throughout. Comprising 3 bunkrooms, 2 shower rooms, 2 toilets, a well equipped kitchen, a comfortable communal area and a large deck where you can enjoy the evening sun. Ideal for families who can book a whole room with private facilities. Study groups welcome.

DETAILS

■ **Open** - All year. Hours flexible but no check in after 9pm.
■ **Beds** - 18: 3x6
■ **Price/night** - £18 adult, £12 child (under 12), including bedding.

CONTACT: Valerie Gibson
Tel: 01434 344030
val@gibbshillfarm.co.uk
www.gibbshillfarm.co.uk
Gibbs Hill Farm, Bardon Mill, Nr Hexham, Northumberland, NE47 7AP

TARSET TOR
BUNKHOUSE

In the heart of the Northumberland International Dark Sky Park and close to the Pennine Way. These striking timber eco-buildings integrate into their natural surroundings making the most of this remarkable location and providing the perfect base for outdoor adventures. The bunkhouse and bothies provide stylish, modern, versatile & comfortable self-catering accommodation which can be used for events, conferences & parties.

DETAILS

■ **Open** - Mid January - December.
■ **Beds** - 44: Bunkhouse:16-20. Bothies: 4x8. 3 campervan bays.
■ **Price/night** - Bunkhouse: £352 to £400. Bothies: £176 to £200.

CONTACT: Robert and Claire Cocker
Tel: 01434 240980
info@tarset-tor.co.uk
www.tarset-tor.co.uk
Greystones, Lanehead, Tarset, Hexham,
NE48 1NT

WALLINGTON
BUNKHOUSE

240

Situated in the heart of the National Trust Wallington Estate visitors to the bunkhouse will have free access to the mansion, it's shops and café and everything the estate has to offer. Perfect for groups of families with lots of on-site activities including cycling and play areas or for walkers wanting a base from which to visit the Cheviots and Hadrian's Wall, both within an hour's drive. The bunkhouse is perfect for self-catering groups with a large well equipped kitchen a large living/dining area and sleeping 20 in four rooms.

DETAILS

- **Open** - All year. All day.
- **Beds** - 20: 2x8, 2x2
- **Price/night** - From £320 for two nights.

CONTACT: National Trust Holidays
Tel: 0344 335 1296
bunkhouses@nationaltrust.org.uk
www.nationaltrust.org.uk
Wallington, Cambo, Morpeth,
Northumberland, NE61 4AR

TOMLINSONS
BUNKHOUSE
241

Located in the historic town of Rothbury overlooking the River Coquet, Tomlinson's is a one-stop shop for low-cost accommodation, homemade meals and cycle hire. There's also a function room for hire. Rothbury is becoming the Northumberland National Park's cycling hub and the bunkhouse is just metres from a string of off-road cycle tracks and public footpaths. The bunkhouse has a fleet of mountain bikes available to hire and instructors to lead cycle groups of all ages. Perfect for families and groups.

DETAILS

- **Open** - All year. All day.
- **Beds** - 21: 1x8, 1x6 1x6 x 1 double
- **Price/night** - Dorms £25pp. Double room £60. Whole bunkhouse from £400.

CONTACT: Jackie
Tel: 01669 621979
info@tomlinsonsrothbury.co.uk
www.tomlinsonsrothbury.co.uk
Bridge Street, Rothbury,
Northumberland, NE65 7SE

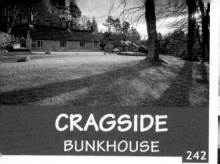

CRAGSIDE
BUNKHOUSE
242

A traditional conversion of a Victorian worker's cottage in the centre of the National Trust's Cragside Estate with fabulous views overlooking the lake and surrounding hills. Cragside bunkhouse sleeps 16 in 4 rooms with a well equipped. self-catering kitchen making it the perfect base for families or other groups wanting to explore this stunning part of the UK. Located in the heart of Northumberland within an hour's drive of the coast, the Cheviots and Hadrian's Wall.

      GROUPS ONLY

DETAILS

■ **Open** - All Year. All day
■ **Beds** - 16: 1x6, 1x4, 3x2
■ **Price/night** - 2 nights sole use from: £320

CONTACT: National Trust Holidays
Tel: 0344 335 1296
bunkhouses@nationaltrust.org.uk
www.nationaltrust.org.uk
Cragside, Rothbury, Morpeth,
Northumberland, NE65 7PX

ALNWICK
YOUTH HOSTEL
243

This family friendly 4* hostel has en suite rooms, cosy lounge, games room and a spacious dining room. Located in the centre of town, it is ideal for Alnwick Castle, of Downton Abbey and Harry Potter fame and Alnwick Garden. The coast, with castles at Dunstanburgh and Bamburgh, Farne Isles, magical Holy Island and glorious sandy beaches is just a 15 min drive. While inland there's the Cheviot Hills & Hadrian's Wall.

DETAILS

- **Open** - All year. 8-10am, 4-9pm
- **Beds** - 56: 1xdbl, 2x2, 1x3, 6x4,1x5, 3x6
- **Price/night** - Dorm from £20, under 18 from £15. 2 bedded rooms from £49.00. 4 bedded rooms from £69.00

CONTACT: Andrew Clarkson
Tel: 01665 660800
info@alnwickyouthhostel.co.uk
www.alnwickyouthhostel.co.uk
34 - 38 Green Batt, Alnwick,
Northumberland, NE66 1TU

CALICO BARN
BUNKBARN
244

On the Northumberland Coast, close to Amble and Warkworth, Calico Barn is perfect for walkers and cyclists on NCN1 and Coast & Castles routes. The bunkhouse has a log burner and is designed to be a home from home. Fully equipped kitchen and dining area, private and shared rooms with comfortable bunk beds. Cereal breakfast included and self-cook breakfast packs available. Veranda and paddock with BBQ and fire pit.

DETAILS

- **Open** - All year. All day.
- **Beds** - 18: 2x2, 1x6, 2x4
- **Price/night** - Twin: £50 Quad: £100 6-Bed £150. Beds in shared room £25. Whole Barn £450. Self-catering with cereals, tea & coffee provided

CONTACT: Alison
Tel: 01670 458118
hello@hemscotthill.com
www.tractorsandtents.com/bunkbarn/
Hemscott Hill Farm, Widdrington,
Morpeth, Northumberland, NE61 5EQ

ALBATROSS

245

Fly high with the award winning "Albatross"! This clean and modern hostel is located in Newcastle's city centre. Providing rooms from 2 bed to 12 beds and anything in between for as little as £16.50. The overnight price includes; linen, 24hr reception, fully fitted self-catering kitchen with free tea, coffee and toast, free WiFi access and computer terminals, pool table, satellite TV, free baggage storage and laundry facilities.

The Albatross offers the perfect city centre base for international travellers, walkers, cyclists, and bikers.

DETAILS

- **Open** - All year. All day.
- **Beds** - 176
- **Price/night** - From £16.50pp (dorm).

CONTACT: Reception
Tel: 0191 2331330
info@albatrossnewcastle.co.uk
albatrossnewcastle.co.uk
51 Grainger Street, Newcastle upon Tyne, NE1 5JE

HOUGHTON NORTH FARM
246l

SPRUCE COTTAGE
246r
BUNKHOUSE

Houghton North Farm, partly built with stones from Hadrian's Wall is in the beautiful Northumberland countryside 15 miles from the start of the Hadrian's Wall Trail. This spacious new build is perfect for groups, individuals or families. The bunkrooms are located around the central courtyard. There is a self-catering kitchen (continental breakfast included). The TV lounge has a log fire and WiFi. Long-term parking, baggage transfer and packed lunches are available on request.

A former forestry worker's cottage in the centre of Byrness on the Pennine Way and on the edge of Northumberland National Park. Ideal for exploring Northumberland, Kielder Forest and the Scottish Borders. It is perfect for groups, individuals and families with in full sized single beds (not bunks) plus a Z bed. Both the large living and dining (seating for 10) rooms have open fires. The kitchen is well equipped. The multi award winning Forest View Inn is opposite with real ale & food if booked in advance.

DETAILS

- **Open** - All year. Arrive after 3.30pm depart by 10am.
- **Beds** - 22: 1x5, 3x4, 1x3, 1x2.
- **Price/night** - B&B from £25-£35 (adult) Group discounts.

DETAILS

- **Open** - April to Oct. Nov to March group only. Opens 4pm checkout 9.30am.
- **Beds** - 10: 1x2, 1x3, 1x4 plus a Z bed.
- **Price/night** - From £21. U16s £18.

CONTACT: Mrs Paula Laws
Tel: 01661 854364
wjlaws@btconnect.com
www.houghtonnorthfarm.co.uk
Houghton North Farm, Heddon-on-the-Wall, Northumberland, NE15 0EZ

CONTACT: Colin or Joyce
Tel: 07880 711807
joycetaylor1703@hotmail.co.uk
www.forestviewbyrness.co.uk/
2 Otterburn Green, Byrness Village, Northumberland, NE19 1TS

MOUNTHOOLY
BUNKHOUSE
247l

Nestled in the beautiful College Valley, North Northumberland, Mounthooly Bunkhouse is a perfect stop off on the Pennine Way and St Cuthbert's Way. With bunkrooms, a well equipped kitchen and living area with log burner. Bedding is supplied. Cars need a permit to access the private valley which is provided on arrival. A haven for wildlife with red squirrels, otters and a thriving population of feral goats in the valley. The perfect wild get away from it all.

DETAILS
- **Open** - All Year. All day.
- **Beds** - 24: 2x9 1x2 1x4
- **Price/night** - £17pp. Discount for concessions and sole use

CONTACT: Charlene Drysdale
Tel: 01668 216 210
mounthooly@college-valley.co.uk
www.college-valley.co.uk/Mounthooly.htm
Mount Hooley, College Valley, Wooler, Northumberland, NE71 6TU

247r

WOOLER
YOUTH HOSTEL

Wooler Youth Hostel & Shepherd's Huts, on the edge of the town offer an ideal base for exploring the Northumberland National Park, the Cheviot Hills, local castles and fine sandy beaches. For walkers there's St Cuthbert's Way and for cyclists, Wooler Cycle Hub routes, Pennine Cycleway and the Sandstone Way. There are bridleways perfect for mountain biking and some of the best bouldering in the UK.

DETAILS
- **Open** - April-Oct. (open for group bookings Nov to March). 7am-11pm.
- **Beds** - 54: 1x2, 2x4, 4x4, 1x6, 1x8. Shepherd's huts 3x2, 1x3 (family).
- **Price/night** - From £18, £12.50 child. Group discounts available.

CONTACT: Hostel Manager
Tel: 01668 281365
info@woolerhostel.co.uk
www.woolerhostel.co.uk
30 Cheviot Street, Wooler, Northumberland, NE71 6LW

CHATTON PARK
BUNKHOUSE
248l

BLUEBELL
FARM BUNKBARN
248r

A former smithy converted into a self-catering bunkhouse on a mixed working farm, 1/2 mile from Chatton. 8 miles from Northumberland's vast empty beaches and historic castles and 5 miles from the heather clad Cheviot Hills. Walking, water sports, climbing, fishing, golf and cycling are all nearby. The 2 dorms can be rented separately. There is a fully equipped kitchen & seating around the original blacksmith's fire + hot showers.

Bluebell Farm Bunkbarn is within walking distance of shops and pubs. It is ideally located for exploring Nothumberland's Heritage Coast, the Cheviot Hills and the Scottish Borders. The Bunkbarn sleeps 14, the Studio 4, plus 2 studio apartments and 5 self-catering cottages There is a shared modern toilet block. BYO sleeping bags/towels or hire. Studio apartments & cottages have bed linen.

DETAILS

- **Open** - All year. Flexible times but no check in after 9pm.
- **Beds** - 12: 2x6.
- **Price/night** - From £15.00. Group rates available. Teens must be with a responsible adult. Dogs: £10/dog/stay

DETAILS

- **Open** - All year. Check in by 9 pm, departure by 10 am.
- **Beds** - Bunkbarn 14: 1x8, 1x6. Studio 4: 1x4.
- **Price/night** - Bunkbarn: £15, U16s £8. Studio: £20, U16s £10. Linen and towel hire £8pp. Sole use rates available.

CONTACT: Jane or Duncan
Tel: 01668 215247
jaord@btinternet.com
www.chattonparkfarm.co.uk
Chatton Park Farm, Chatton, Alnwick, Northumberland, NE66 5RA

CONTACT: Phyl
Tel: 01668 213362
corillas@icloud.com
www.bluebellfarmbelford.com
Bluebell Farm Caravan Park, Belford, Northumberland, NE70 7QE

THE HIDES

Located in Seahouses within easy walking distance of the beach. The Hides provide affordable accommodation on the Northumbrian Coast ,perfect for groups, families or independent travellers. Each "Hide" is an en suite room sleeping 4 in beds and bunks. The rooms open onto a communal courtyard with access to the well equipped kitchen, bike storage and laundry room.

DETAILS

- **Open** - All year. 9am - 6pm.
- **Beds** - 20: 5x4
- **Price/night** - £20, U14 £16,(U1 free). Min charge 2 adults/night (£40). Christmas & New Year £25/adult & £22/child - min stay 3 nights. £5 pets/night. Duvet hire £5.00/night

CONTACT: Kerry
Tel: 01665 720645
info@the-hides.co.uk
www.the-hides.co.uk
146 Main Street Seahouses
Northumberland NE68 7UA

SEAHOUSES
HOSTEL

250

Within easy walking distance of Seahouses, this recently refurbished hostel offers affordable, spacious & comfortable accommodation. A perfect base for visiting the beaches and castles of the Northumbrian Coast. Popular with divers, families, cyclists, walkers, school, church and youth groups. Parties of all sizes welcome. Sole use also available. Booking is essential.

DETAILS

■ **Open** - All year. Arrive after 4pm, depart by 10am unless otherwise agreed.
■ **Beds** - 42: 1×8, 2×2 (en-suite), 1×6 (en-suite wet room), 2×4, 1×6, 1×10
■ **Price/night** - £19-£25pp. Children, recognised youth groups & leaders: £16pp. Under 5s free. Min 2 night booking

CONTACT: Karen Leadbitter
Tel: 07531 305206
seahouseshostel@outlook.com
www.seahouseshostel.org.uk
157 Main Street, North Sunderland,
Seahouses, Northumberland NE68 7TU

SPRINGHILL
BUNKHOUSE

251

Springhill's Lookout & Wigwams offer great value, comfortable accommodation which can be booked as a whole or on a per bed/night basis. Ideal for groups, families and independent travellers. Superbly located on the Northumberland Heritage Coastline there are stunning views towards the Farne Islands and Cheviot Hills while Seahouses and Bamburgh are within very easy reach.

EAT & SLEEP
LINDISFARNE

252

Perfectly located for visiting Lindisfarne and the castles and beaches of the North Northumberland coast.

Eat & Sleep Lindisfarne has a wheelchair accessible room as well 6 bed dorms. Eat in the on-site bistro or self-cater in the bunkhouse kitchen. A perfect stop-off on the St Cuthberts Way and St Oswalds Way walking routes or the Sandstone Way and Coast and Castle cycle routes, Cyclists are well catered for with cycle storage.

DETAILS
- **Open** - All year. All day.
- **Beds** - 27: 4x6, 1x3(wheelchair accessible)
- **Price/night** - from £20pp

CONTACT: Shaun Dixon
Tel: 01289 381827
hello@eatandsleeplindisfarne.co.uk
eatandsleeplindisfarne.co.uk
West Mains House, Beal, Berwick upon Tweed, TD15 2PD

MAUGHOLD
VENTURE CENTRE
253l

Maughold Venture Centre Bunkhouse overlooks farmland with views out to sea. The popular beach of Port e Vullen is just 10 min's walk away. Enjoy self-catering accommodation, with en suite, centrally heated rooms. Tasty meals are available from the neighbouring Venture Centre, where you can also book kayaking, abseiling, air rifle shooting, archery, gorge walking, dinghy sailing & team events. With its own stop, Lewaigue Halt, on the Manx Electric Railway you have easy access to Douglas, Ramsey, mountains & tranquil glens.

DETAILS

- **Open** - January - December. 24 hours.
- **Beds** - 52: 2x2, 1x5, 4x8, 2x10.
- **Price/night** - £12-£15 per person.

CONTACT: Simon Read
Tel: 01624 814240
contact@adventure-centre.co.uk
www.adventure-centre.co.uk
The Venture Centre, Maughold, Isle of Man, IM7 1AW

KNOCKALOE BEG
FARM BUNKHOUSE
253r

A working farm nestled under Peel Hill, Isle of Man, Knockaloe Beg offers B&B, cottages, bunkhouse and glamping. The bunkhouse sleeps 8; with beds at one end of the room, dining and seating at the other. The Bothy is a cosy twin bed room. Washing facilities are a short step outside, below the rooms. In the orchard there are two deluxe, en suite glamping cabins each sleeping four.

DETAILS

- **Open** - Bunkhouse: 1 April-30 September. Bothy: All year.
- **Beds** - 18: Bunkhouse 8, Bothy 2. Cabins 8: 2x4
- **Price/night** - Bunkhouse: £15pp; min 2 people. TT/Classic TT fortnight: £120pn sole use (max 8). Bothy: £20 pp, min 2 people. Breakfast (when available): £10pp

CONTACT: Fiona and John Anderson
Tel: 01624 844279
info@knockaloebegfarm.com
www.knockaloebegfarm.com/
Patrick, Isle of Man, IM5 3AQ

Northen Ireland

Castle Ward Estate © National Trust, John Millar

CASTLE WARD
BUNKHOUSE

255

In the heart of the National Trust's Castle Ward Estate in Northern Ireland, this bunkhouse is the perfect base to explore the park and gardens or visit the beautiful shores of Stangford Lough.

The bunkhouse sleeps up to 14 in three rooms making it a great choice for groups or family get-togethers. The estate is criss-crossed with footpaths and cycle trails and has a number of play areas making this a particularly family friendly location. The bunkhouse and estate are also great for team building weekends or groups holidaying together.

     GROUPS ONLY

DETAILS

Open - All Year. All day
Beds - 14: 2x6, 1x2
Price/night - 2 nights from £320

CONTACT: National Trust Holidays
Tel: 0344 335 1296
bunkhouses@nationaltrust.org.uk
www.nationaltrust.org.uk
Castle Ward, Strangford, Down,
BT30 7LS

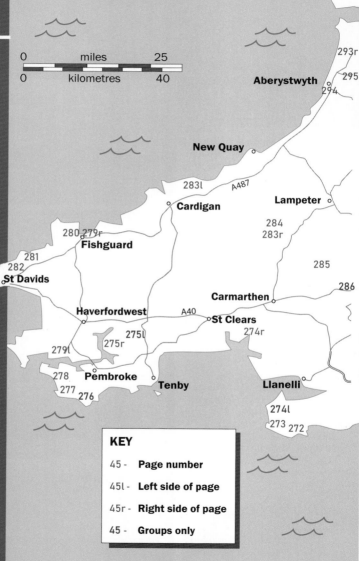

South Wales

0 | miles | 25
0 | kilometres | 40

293r

295

Aberystwyth

294

New Quay

283l   A487

Cardigan

Lampeter

284
283r

280 279r

Fishguard

285

281

282

286

St Davids

Carmarthen

Haverfordwest   A40   St Clears

274r

279l

275l

275r

278

Pembroke   Tenby

Llanelli

277 276

274l

273 272

KEY

45 -   **Page number**

45l -   **Left side of page**

45r -   **Right side of page**

45 -   **Groups only**

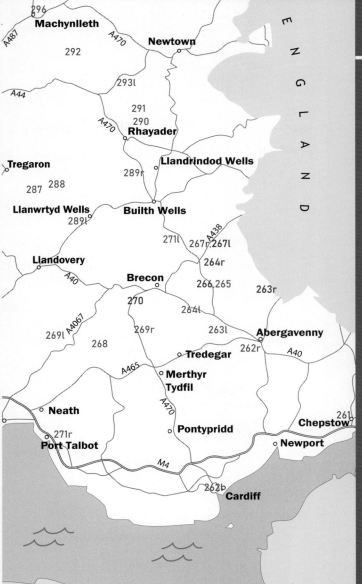

296

Machynlleth

A487

A470

Newtown

292

A44

293l

291

290

A470

Rhayader

Tregaron

Llandrindod Wells

289r

287 288

Llanwrtyd Wells

289l

Builth Wells

271l

267r, 267l

A438

Llandovery

A40

264r

Brecon

266, 265

263r

270

264l

269l

A4067

269r

263l

Abergavenny

268

262r

A40

Tredegar

A465

Merthyr Tydfil

A470

Neath

271r

Pontypridd

Port Talbot

M4

261

Chepstow

Newport

262b

Cardiff

ENGLAND

South Wales

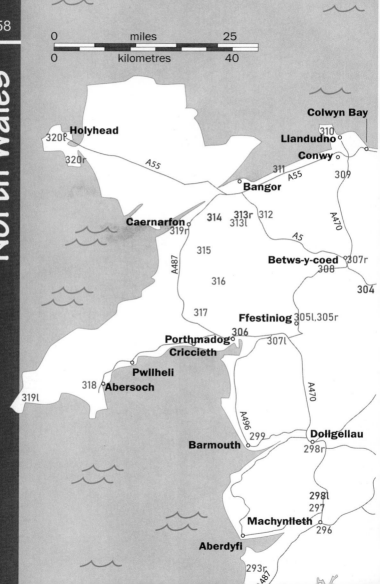

North Wales

0   miles   25
0   kilometres   40

Colwyn Bay

Holyhead

320l

320r

A55

310

Llandudno

Conwy

311

A55

309

Bangor

A470

314

313r

312

313l

Caernarfon

319r

A5

315

Betws-y-coed

307r

A487

316

308

304

317

Ffestiniog

305l, 305r

Porthmadog

306

307l

Criccieth

Pwllheli

318

Abersoch

319l

A470

A496

Barmouth

299

Dolgellau

298r

298l

297

Machynlleth

296

Aberdyfi

293r

487

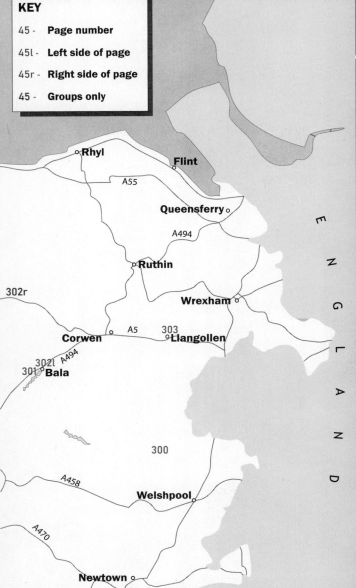

KEY

45 -   Page number

45l -   Left side of page

45r -   Right side of page

45 -   Groups only

Rhyl

Flint

A55

Queensferry

A494

Ruthin

302r

Wrexham

Corwen   A5   303
Llangollen

302l   A494

301   Bala

300

A458

Welshpool

A470

Newtown

ENGLAND

North Wales

Wales

GREEN MAN
BACKPACKERS

Situated in the heart of Chepstow, Green Man Backpackers offers inspired accommodation in a Grade 2 historic building. Chepstow is the starting/finishing point for Offa's Dyke path, the Wales Coast Path, Gloucester Way, the Wye Valley Walk, The Forest of Dean, and the Wye Valley AONB. Just 1 mile from Land's End/John O'Groats route.

DETAILS

■ **Open** - All year. All day. Except New Year's Eve/Day.
■ **Beds** - 49: 28 in dorms of 6 or 4 beds, 5 en suite family/twin rooms.
■ **Price/night** - Dorms from £22pp, family/4 bed rooms from £65 (en suite from £75), 5 bed from £75, family/double en suite (sleeps 3) from £55.

CONTACT: Mick and Ness
Tel: 01291 626773 Mob: 07870611979
info@greenmanbackpackers.co.uk
www.chepstowgreenman.co.uk
13 Beaufort Square, Chepstow, NP16 5EP (Car park NP16 5LL)

RIVER HOUSE
HOSTEL
262l

This family run 4* hostel in the heart of Cardiff was voted number 1 in Hostelworld's list of best hostels. Opened in 2007 to rave reviews, the brother and sister team have made sure this will be the best hostel experience you will come across on your travels. With fabulous views of the world famous Millennium Stadium and River Taff and the central train and bus stations just 5 mins' walk away. What's stopping you?

DETAILS
- **Open** - All year. 24 hours.
- **Beds** - 50: 2 bed private rooms, 4 bed dorms and 6 bed dorms.
- **Price/night** - From £16pp. Private (twin) rooms from £36 for two people. All prices include breakfast.

CONTACT: Reception
Tel: 02920 399810
info@riverhousebackpackers.com
www.riverhousebackpackers.com
59 Fitzhamon Embankment, Riverside, Cardiff, CF11 6AN

MIDDLE NINFA
BUNKHOUSE
262r

Middle Ninfa Farm, on the edge of the Blaenavon Industrial Landscape World Heritage Site in the Brecon Beacons, offers bunkhouse/cottage accommodation, camping and hands-on training in coracle making and willow sculpture. Sympathetically renovated to retain the rustic charm with fine views over the Usk Valley, the bunkhouse provides comfortable self-catering accommodation for up to 6 people. BYO food, sleeping bags, & pillowcases.

DETAILS
- **Open** - All year.
- **Beds** - 6: 1x4, 1x2 (dbl) plus camping.
- **Price/night** - From £10 per person. Weekly rate for 6 persons £300-360. Camping £5 pp + pitch fee of £5/£10.

CONTACT: Richard and Rohan Lewis
Tel: 01873 854662
bookings@middleninfa.co.uk
www.middleninfa.co.uk
Middle Ninfa Farm, Llanellen, Abergavenny, NP7 9LE

WERN WATKIN
BUNKHOUSE
263l

Wern Watkin Bunkhouse (also known as YHA Llangattock) sits high up on Mynnedd Llangattock in the Brecon Beacons National Park. There is direct access on foot to the mountainside and a flat mountain road to a National Cycle Route. The Llangattock Cave complex is within easy walking distance and the scenic Wye and Usk river valleys are just a short drive away. Instruction in a range of outdoor activities can be arranged.

DETAILS

■ **Open** - All year. All day.
■ **Beds** - 30: 4x6, 1x4, 2x2. All rooms except one are en suite
■ **Price/night** - Sole use £450 week nights, £630 w/ends. Smaller groups by negotiation £16- £18.50pp.

CONTACT: Andrew Fryer
Tel: 01873 812307
enquiries@wernwatkin.co.uk
www.wernwatkin.co.uk
Wern Watkin, Hillside, Llangattock,
Crickhowell, NP8 1LG

THE WAIN HOUSE
263r

This old stone barn continues the tradition of 900 years when Llanthony Priory next door provided accommodation. Surrounded by the Black Mountains in the Brecon Beacons National Park, it is your ideal base for all mountain activities. There is a fully equipped kitchen, hot showers, heating throughout and a wood burning stove. Small or large groups are welcome with sole use and a minimum charge. Two pubs nearby offer real ale and bar food.

GROUPS ONLY

DETAILS

■ **Open** - All year. All day. No restrictions.
■ **Beds** - 16: 1 x 8; 1 x 4; 1 x 6.
■ **Price/night** - £30 per person for a two-night weekend, with a minimum charge of £300. Reduction for mid-week bookings.

CONTACT: Cordelia Passmore
Tel: 01873 890359
courtfarm@llanthony.co.uk
www.llanthonybunkbarn.co.uk
Court Farm, Llanthony, Abergavenny,
Monmouthshire, NP7 7NN

THE STAR
BUNKHOUSE

264l

An ideal base for exploring the beautiful Brecon Beacons National Park. The bunkhouse is situated in the village of Bwlch alongside the Beacons Way long distance path. Expect a warm & comfortable stay in this dog friendly bunkhouse with spacious bedrooms, cosy lounge/dining area, fully-equipped kitchen, outside BBQ area, hot showers, drying room and car park. Accommodation for up to 20 people in bunkbeds in 6 bedrooms. Private bedrooms or sole use available. Individuals, couples & groups welcome.

DETAILS
- **Open** - All year. All day
- **Beds** - 20: 1×4 (en-suite), 3×4, 2×2
- **Price/night** - Standard rate £19pp

CONTACT: Emma or Pete Harrison
Tel: 01874 730080 Mobile:07341 906937
info@starbunkhouse.com
www.starbunkhouse.com
Brecon Road (A40), Bwlch, Brecon, Powys, LD3 7RQ

CADARN
BUNKHOUSE

264r

On a small hill farm in the Brecon Beacons National Park, Cadarn Bunkhouse is surrounded by views of the Black Mountains and the Wye Valley With easy access to the mountains it is perfect for walking, mountain biking and horse riding whist the River Glasbury is great for canoeing. Self-cater, B&B, half/ full board or eat at the pub in Felindre half a mile away. Close to Hay on Wye and Brecon. Pony trekking available on-site, plus bike and canoe hire.

DETAILS
- **Open** - All year.
- **Beds** - 57: Large Bunkhouse 47 in 7 rooms, Small Bunkhouse 9: 3x3
- **Price/night** - From £16 pppn.

CONTACT: Haydn Jones
Tel: 01497 847351
info@tregoydriding.co.uk
www.tregoydriding.co.uk
Tregoyd Mountain Riders, Lower Cwmcadarn Farm, Felindre, Three Cocks, Brecon, Powys, Wales LD3 0TB

BRECON
BUNKHOUSE

265

Brecon Bunkhouse is a spacious, comfortable, clean bunkhouse in the Brecon Beacons, offering great value self-catering accommodation. Sitting in the Black Mountains, with mountain walks from the door, the ideal base for horse riding, mountain biking and canoeing. There is a riding centre on the farm and the bunkhouse has a drying room and storage/cleaning facilities for bikes and canoes. Camping available.

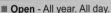

DETAILS

- **Open** - All year. All day.
- **Beds** - 28+3: 1x10,1x2,1x2,1x6,1x8. Plus extra 3 bed room available.
- **Price/night** - £15 pp, min of 4 people. £250 for sole use plus £45 for extra en suite family room with 3 single beds.

CONTACT: Paul and Emily Turner
Tel: 01874 711500
breconbunkhouse@gmail.com
www.brecon-bunkhouse.co.uk
Brecon Bunkhouse, Cwmfforest Farm,
Pengenfford, Talgarth, Brecon, LD3 0EU

THE DRAGONS
BACK

266

The Dragons Back (formerly The Castle Inn) is a pub with B&B, camping & bunkrooms in the Brecon Beacons National Park. The bunkrooms are fully carpeted and centrally heated with en suite wet rooms, self-catering, drying facilities and secure storage. Stag/hens welcome. Dogs £5 pn in the bunkhouse. Meals in the pub. Glamping is available in our Shepherds hut and the Tardis !

DETAILS

■ **Open** - All year. Arrive after 2pm, depart before 11 am.
■ **Beds** - 44: Bunkhouse 28: 1x6, 1x10, 1x12. B&B: 10: 4 rooms
■ **Price/night** - £16pp, £22pp with b/fast. Min of 5 people required for 6 bunk room, 7 for 10 b/room, or 9 for 12 b/room. Sole use £375, or £550 with breakfast

CONTACT: Jill Deakin
Tel: 01874711353
info@thedragonsback.co.uk
www.thedragonsback.co.uk
Pengenffordd, LD3 0EP

WYE VALLEY CANOES
BUNKHOUSE
267l

WOODLANDS
BUNKHOUSE
267r

n a converted Welsh Chapel, Wye Valley Canoes 5* award-winning Bunkhouse is a warm, modern space with huge sofas and a slide to reach the ground floor!

There is a small kitchen area but the River Café next door can cater for you. Enjoy the swanky bathrooms, power showers and designer furniture. Canoes, kayaks, mountain bikes and Vespa scooters can be hired and activities arranged. The beautiful market town of Hay on Wye is just 4 miles away.

Woodlands Bunkhouse is a converted stable set in the 10 acre grounds of Woodlands Centre. It overlooks the River Wye and has wonderful views of the Black Mountains. The historic town of Hay on Wye is near by.

The Bunkhouse provides comfortable, modern accommodation for families and groups. There's a well equipped kitchen and dining room and 22 beds in 9 rooms. The bunkhouse can arrange courses in a variety of outdoor activities.

DETAILS

- **Open** - All year. All day
- **Beds** - 14: 12x1 (pods), 1 x double
- **Price/night** - From £1370 for a 2 night weekend.

DETAILS

- **Open** - All year. 24 hours.
- **Beds** - 22 in rooms of 1 to 6 plus camping in the grounds.
- **Price/night** - £16 pp + VAT. Reduction for children and large group bookings.

CONTACT: Jane Hughes
Tel: 01497 847213
info@wyevalleycanoes.co.uk
www.wyevalleycanoes.co.uk
The Boat House, Glasbury-On-Wye,
Herefordshire, HR3 5NP

CONTACT: Annie Clipson
Tel: 01497 847272
annie.clipson@oxfordshireoutdoors.co.uk
www.woodlandsoec.org
Glasbury on Wye, Powys, HR3 5LP

CLYNGWYN
BUNKHOUSE
268

Clyngwyn 4* Bunkhouse sits in the Brecon Beacons, only minutes away from the waterfalls and caves of Ystradfellte and Sgwd Yr Eira. Your ideal base for a wide range of outdoor activities. The bunkhouse sleeps up to 19, plus camping, three double B&B rooms and a romantic shepherd's hut in it's own private meadow.

DETAILS

■ **Open** - All year. All day.
■ **Beds** - Bunkhouse 19, B&B 6, Shepherds Hut 2
■ **Price/night** - Sun-Thurs: up to 19 people £285, up to 15 £230 or £18pp. Fri/Sat: up to 19 people £325, up to 15 £260. B&B £30pp. Shepherds Hut £75 (sleeps 2).

CONTACT: Julie Hurst
Tel: 01639 722930
enquiries@bunkhouse-south-wales.co.uk
www.bunkhouse-south-wales.co.uk
Clyngwyn Farm, Ystradfellte Rd,
Pontneddfechan, Powys, SA11 5US

CRAIG Y NOS
CASTLE

269l

Craig Y Nos Castle sits in the Brecon Beacons. The Nurses Block can be booked on a daily or a room basis, and also sole use as group accommodation. Offering B&B or self- catering, the choice is yours. The Castle provides hearty meals, cosy evenings by the wood burning stoves and a free history tour. See website for best rates and deals.

DETAILS

■ **Open** - All year
■ **Beds** - Nurses Block: 21: 10x2, 1x1. Castle: 67 rooms: (64 en suite)
■ **Price/night** - Nurses Block sole use:- 1 night £350, 2 nights £500, 3 nights £600, 5 nights £700. B&B in Nurses Block per twin room: £67.50pn midweek, £87.50pn weekend. Breakfast for groups £6.50pp.

CONTACT: Reception
Tel: 01639 730725
info@craigynoscastle.com
www.craigynoscastle.com
Craig Y Nos Castle, Brecon Road, Penycae, Powys, SA9 1GL

COED OWEN
BUNKHOUSE

269r

Set on a hill farm in the heart of the Brecon Beacons, 2 hours' walk from Pen Y Fan. This Bunkhouse provides well appointed self-catering accommodation; ideal for stag, hen and family parties. Outdoor activities can be organised or there's direct access onto the mountains and waterfalls close by. Bike Park Wales, Merthyr Tydfil, Penderyn Whiskey and Brecon are all within easy reach. The pub, at the bottom of the drive, serves great food and fine ales.

DETAILS

■ **Open** - All year round 8am - 10pm
■ **Beds** - 26: 2x6, 1x10, 1 dbl, 1 twin.
■ **Price/night** - From £22pp with bed linen. Min of two nights at weekends.

CONTACT: Molly or Netty Rees
Tel: 07508544044 (anytime)
07984316050
info@breconbeaconsbunkhouse.co.uk
www.breconbeaconsbunkhouse.co.uk
Coed Owen Farm, Cwmtaff, Merthyr Tydfil , CF48 2HY

DAN Y GYRN
BUNKHOUSE

270

Dan Y Gyrn Bunkhouse is the perfect base for walkers, cyclists, families or groups. Located in the heart of the Brecon Beacons it provides the ideal base from which to explore this National Park. This comfortable, modern bunkhouse with amazing views is close to the main access route to Pen Y Fan so great for walking groups. The bunkhouse is also a hit with families with a large garden for children to play in. Sleeping 15 in 3 rooms and very well equipped for self-catering this bunkhouse is perfect accommodation for groups.

DETAILS

- **Open** - All year. All day
- **Beds** - 15: 2x6, 1x3 campbeds
- **Price/night** - From £336 for two nights

CONTACT: National Trust Holidays
Tel: 0344 335 1296
bunkhouses@nationaltrust.org.uk
www.nationaltrust.org.uk/holidays
Blaenglyn Farm, Libanus, Brecon,
Powys, LD3 8NF

RIVER CABIN

271l

River Cabin is set in an old cider orchard overlooking the mill stream. It sleeps up to 4 in a cosy bunkroom with bunk beds & a double futon. There is a kitchen/lounge area, sunny dining porch, patio & private garden with picnic table, fire pit and BBQ. The price includes heating, hot water, showers, WiFi & use of bike store. From Easter - October a small campsite is operated alongside the cabin. Located on the Wye Valley Walk & National Cycle Route 8, it's a fantastic exploration base for walkers & cyclists. Canoeing, pony trekking, gliding, bike hire, rope and climbing centre all close by.

DETAILS

- **Open** - All year, 24 hour access.
- **Beds** - 4: 1 x 4 plus camping
- **Price/night** - From £25 pp.

CONTACT: Alistair / Nicky Legge
Tel: 01982 560312 Mob: 07720 717124
info@rivercabin.co.uk
www.rivercabin.co.uk
Erwood, Builth Wells, Powys, LD2 3TQ

L&A
OUTDOOR CENTRE

271r

Accommodation for up to 290 people in self-catering cabins (3 recently upgraded to include hot tubs) & bunkhouses in the Swansea Bay area. A large activity hall, meeting rooms, cafe/bar & 300 seat dining hall are available, a commercial kitchen can be hired. Set in 50+ acres of woodland/pasture with open air pool, pets' corner, kennels, BBQs & bike wash. Ideal for the Afan Aergoed & Glyncorrwg mountain bike trails.

DETAILS

- **Open** - All day.
- **Beds** - Cabin: 117: 6/8 bed units. Bunkhouse: 175:10,16,24,30,40 bed.
- **Price/night** - Bunkhouses: £12pp, £15 with bedding. Cabins: 6 bed £90 to £150, 8 bed £100 to £180, depending on length of stay. Groups please enquire.

CONTACT: Nigel
Tel: 01639 885 509
info@landaoutdoorcentre.co.uk
www.landaoutdoorcentre.co.uk
Goytre, West Glamorgan SA13 2YP

EASTERN SLADE
BARN

272

Eastern Slade Barn is a luxury farmhouse conversion on a working farm pn the Gower Peninsula. The Gower has glorious beaches, castles & a network of traffic free lanes, ideal for mountain bikes. The Coastal Path passes through the farm. Port Eynon seaside village is a 30 mins' walk, while Oxwich Bay with its castle, beach & hotel serving tasty meals is just a 20 min walk. Camping is also available and weddings/birthdays can be accommodated.

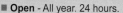
DETAILS

- **Open** - All year. 24 hours.
- **Beds** - 15: 1x5, 2x2/3 (double with bunk above), 1x2, 2 in lounge
- **Price/night** - £15pp, £180 sole use. High season £20pp, £240 sole use.

CONTACT: Kate
Tel: 07970 969814
tynrheol@hotmail.com
www.easternsladebarngower.co.uk
Eastern Slade Farm, Oxwich, Gower, Swansea, SA3 1NA

RHOSSILI
BUNKHOUSE

Rhossili 4* Bunkhouse is situated at the end of the Gower Peninsula, in an Area of Outstanding Natural Beauty. It is within easy walking distance of three glorious beaches, (including Rhossili Bay voted the best beach in Europe and in the top ten in the World 2017). Ideal for families and groups and perfectly located for a wide range of outdoor activities including walking, surfing, cycling & climbing.

DETAILS

- **Open** - All year except January. Check in 4-9pm; check out by 10:30am.
- **Beds** - 18: 1x4, 2x3, 4x2. 4 sofa-beds in lounge (sole use).
- **Price/night** - Shared (small groups) £16-£20. Full (group of 18) £340. Sole (group of 22) £390.

CONTACT: Josephine Higgins
Tel: 01792 391509
bookings@rhossili.org
www.rhossilibunkhouse.com
Rhossili Bunkhouse, Rhossili, Swansea,
SA3 1PL

HARDINGSDOWN
BUNKHOUSE
274l

Hardingsdown Bunkhouse provides accommodation for families or groups. Comfortable and well appointed it is perfect for exploring The Gower with its nature reserves, family beaches and castles. Llangennith beach is renowned for its surfing while Mewslade Bay and Fall Bay are popular with climbers. The Chaffhouse sleeping 12 is also available.

 GROUPS ONLY

DETAILS
- **Open** - All year. 24 hours.
- **Beds** - 26: Bunkhouse 14: 1x5, 1x3, 3x2. Chaffhouse: 12
- **Price/night** - SOLE USE £220pn (w/ends, b/hols & school hols), £200pn (midweek). Weekly rates available. INDIVIDUALS mid week, shared use, £20 pppn. Enquire for rates in the Chaffhouse.

CONTACT: Allison Tyrrell
Tel: 01792 386222
bunkhousegower@btconnect.com
www.bunkhousegower.co.uk
Lower Hardingsdown Farm, Llangennith,
Gower, Swansea, SA3 1HT

PANTYRATHRO
HOSTEL
274r

Llansteffan is a beautiful, quaint village at the tip of the Towi River and Carmarthen Bay. The sandy beaches below the castle offer swimming and relaxation. The virtually traffic free country lanes make the area ideal for cycling. The Wales Coastal Path is on the doorstep and the city of Carmarthen offers most social and cultural activities. The Pantyrathro International Hostel provides dorm accommodation, private rooms, and also has 3 new en suite units of 6, 9 and 12 beds.

DETAILS
- **Open** - February to January. 24 hours.
- **Beds** - 50: 1x10, 1x9, 2x6, 4x4, 1x3
- **Price/night** - £17pp dorm. Group discounts.

CONTACT: Ken Knuckles
Tel: 01267 241014
kenknuckles@hotmail.com
www.backpackershostelwales.com
Pantyrathro International Hostel,
Llansteffan, Carmarthen, SA33 5AJ

PENQUOIT
CENTRE
275l

The Penquoit Centre, a converted courtyard of historic longhouses, provides hostel accommodation for groups of 10-25. The grounds comprising fields & ancient woodland give direct access to the Cresswell River and the Pembrokeshire National Park. The area is rich in bird life and is within easy reach of over 20 beautiful beaches, the Preseli Hills, castles, Tenby, Caldy, riding and canoeing. The Centre is ideal for family and friend get-togethers, art, yoga, drama, healing and dancing, with a long room ideal for group activities.

DETAILS

■ **Open** - All year.
■ **Beds** - 25+: 1x10, 1x15, + 2 private rooms.
■ **Price/night** - £16 per person.

CONTACT: Joan Carlisle
Tel: 01646 651666
lee@penquoitcentre.co.uk
Lawrenny, Kilgetty, Pembrokeshire,
SA68 0PL

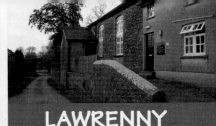

LAWRENNY
HOSTEL
275r

Once a Victorian village school, the Lawrenny Hostel is superbly placed for exploring South Pembrokeshire. Warm, clean and comfortable, with modern facilities, the accommodation is ideal for individuals or groups, training courses or events. The adjoining village hall is also available to rent and there is a community shop, pub and an award-winning tearoom nearby.

DETAILS

■ **Open** - All year. Arrange check in with warden/all day access.
■ **Beds** - 22: 2 x 4 (bunks), 2 x 4 (dbl + bunks), 1 x 6 (dbl/sgl + bunks)
■ **Price/night** - Adults £16, children (4-17) £10. Dbl rooms £37 (couple), £50 (with children). Sole use £250 per night.

CONTACT: Laura Lort-Phillips
Tel: 01646 651270
hostel@lawrennyvillage.co.uk
www.lawrennyhostel.com
Lawrenny Millennium Hostel, Lawrenny,
Pembrokeshire, SA68 0PW

STACKPOLE
OUTDOOR CENTRE
276

The 147-bed, platinum eco-award-winning, Stackpole Centre is the perfect venue for large families/groups, special interest breaks and outdoor activities. It comprises four large houses, three cottages and a manor house. Close to wild woodlands and stunning beaches.

DETAILS

■ **Open** - All year. All day. Reception 9-5.
■ **Beds** - Swan House: 13 bedrooms (24 guests). Shearwater House; 7 bedrooms (17 guests). Kestrel House: 12 b/rooms (35 guests). Kingfisher: 10 b/rooms (44 guests). Manor House: 3 b/rooms (9 guests). 3 cottages: 9 b/rooms (18 guests)
■ **Price/night** - Whole site £1900, Kingfisher £650, Kestrel £395 Shearwater £295, Swan £550. Min stay 2 nights.

CONTACT: Stackpole Reception
Tel: 01646 623 110
Stackpole.bookings@nationaltrust.org.uk
www.nationaltrust.org.uk/holidays
The Old Home Farm Yard, Stackpole, nr
Pembroke, Pembrokeshire, SA71 5DQ

WARREN FARM
GLAMPING
277

A cosy bunkhouse & beautiful big bell tents, right on the Pembrokeshire Coast Path with fantastic views out to sea. The closest you can stay to excellent climbing at Castlemartin Range, plus brilliant surfing at Freshwater West & Broadhaven South and within striking distance of many of Pembrokeshire's fabulous tourist attractions. All the accommodation is comfortable and well equipped. Don't delay, come glamping!

DETAILS

■ **Open** - All year. Check in 5-6pm, flexible by arrangement.
■ **Beds** - Bunkhouse: 12. Bell Tents: 6x8. Camping, plus an expanding range of pods for couples & individuals
■ **Price/night** - Check website for latest accommodation & prices. From £12ppn

CONTACT: Jane or Hannah, via email
stay@warrenfarm.wales
www.warrenfarm.wales
Warren Farm, Warren, near
Castlemartin, SA71 5HS

GUPTON FARM

278

Gupton Farm is the National Trust's new visitor base at Freshwater West, with camping, farmhouse accommodation and community facilities on-site.
You can be assured of a warm welcome and a relaxed and informal atmosphere. There are great facilities including a heated shower block, a wet weather barn, and loads of outdoor space.
Gupton Farm is your ideal base for exploring the beaches and countryside of Pembrokeshire. The Pembrokeshire Coast Path is close by.

DETAILS

■ **Open** - Farmhouse & camper van parking all year. Camping seasonal.
■ **Beds** - 10 +camping
■ **Price/night** - From £8.50pp

CONTACT: Campsite Manager
Tel: 01646 623110
guptonfarm@nationaltrust.org.uk
www.nationaltrust.org.uk/holidays
Gupton, Castlemartin, Penfro,
Pembrokeshire, SA71 5HW

UPPER NEESTON
LODGES
279l

Environmentally sensitive barn conversions close to the Milford Haven Waterway in the Pembrokeshire Coast National Park. Ideal for divers, climbers, walkers or get-togethers. The four independent 5* lodges have fully fitted kitchens and have access to garden/patio, laundry/drying room, secure storage and ample parking.

DETAILS

■ **Open** - All year. Check in from 4pm. Check out before 10.30am.
■ **Beds** - Cowshed 10: 1x6,1x4. Barn 8: 1x6,1x2, Granary 1x3. Dairy 1x3
■ **Price/night** - From £17.50 (inc linen). Min 2 nights at w/ends (3 nights b/h). Sole use: min 6 Barn, 8 Cowshed. Smaller groups/individuals by agreement.

CONTACT: Sean or Mandy Tilling
Tel: 01646 690750
mail@upperneeston.co.uk
www.upperneeston.co.uk
Upper Neeston Farm, Dale Road, Herbrandston, Milford Haven, SA73 3RY

JAMES JOHN
HAMILTON HOUSE
279r

James John Hamilton House is a new conversion of the first free school in Fishguard, built in 1850 by James John Hamilton. The house provides comfortable, characterful self-catering accommodation for 10 people in four private rooms. Across the garden is Hamilton House Backpackers (see p280) with an extra 9 beds. It's close to the centre of Fishguard with pubs & cafes. The Pembrokeshire Coastal Path passes through the town and communities of grey seals and dolphins are regularly seen in the local harbours.

DETAILS

■ **Open** - All year.
■ **Beds** - 10 (+9): 1 x twin, 2 x dbl, 1 x 4 (dbl & bunk) plus 9 beds next door.
■ **Price/night** - From £20-£28 pp.

CONTACT: Steve Roberts
Tel: 01348 874288
stephenism@hotmail.com
www.jamesjohnhamilton.co.uk
19a Hamilton St, Fishguard SA65 9HL

HAMILTON
BACKPACKERS

280

Hamilton Lodge is just one minute's walk from the centre of Fishguard and close to the Pembrokeshire Coast Path. Comfortable and friendly, sleeping nine in total – with an en suite double and two dormitories. Fully equipped kitchen, dining area and lounge. Charming, private garden and covered patio with seating. Free light breakfast included.

Groups of up to 18 are welcome in collaboration with James John Hamilton House hostel next door (see p279r).

DETAILS

■ **Open** - All year.
■ **Beds** - 9 (+10): 1 x 4, 1 x 3 and 1 x 2. (Plus 10 next door)
■ **Price/night** - From £20 to £21 pp in dorms, from £24.50 pp in double en suite.

CONTACT: Quentin Maclaurin
Tel: 01348 874797 / 07505562939
hamiltonbackpackers@hotmail.com
www.hamiltonbackpackers.co.uk
23 Hamilton Street, Fishguard,
Pembrokeshire, SA65 9HL

OLD SCHOOL
HOSTEL

Escape to this wonderful rugged corner of the Pembrokeshire Coast National Park. Old School Hostel is in Trefin, a pretty village which has a pub and a café, just a quarter of a mile from the world famous coast path. Circular walks from the door take you to stunning wild beaches & harbours. The cathedral city of St. Davids and the popular Whitesands Bay are 20 minutes by car.

DETAILS

■ **Open** - All year, but we strongly advise you check availability first.
■ **Beds** - 22: 1x6, 3x2, 2x2/3 (bunk with dbl lower bed), 1×4 (1 dbl + 1 bunk). Single occupancy available.
■ **Price/night** - From £16. Kids £10. Single occ from £30. Sole use from £230.

CONTACT: Sue or Chris
Tel: 01348 831800
oldschoolhostel@btconnect.com
www.oldschoolhostel.com
Ffordd-yr-Afon, Trefin, Haverfordwest, Pembrokeshire, SA62 5AU

CAERHAFOD
LODGE
282

Ideally situated between the famous cathedral city of St Davids and the Irish ferry port of Fishguard, the 4* Lodge overlooks the spectacular Pembrokeshire coastline. Within walking distance of the well known Sloop Inn at Porthgain and the internationally renowned Coastal Path. An ideal stopover for cyclists with The Celtic Trail cycle route passing the bottom of the drive. The lodge sleeps 23 in 5 separate rooms, all en suite with great showers.

DETAILS

■ **Open** - All year. Check in from 4pm, check out 10.30 am. All day access.
■ **Beds** - 23: 3x4, 1x5, 1x6.
■ **Price/night** - Adult £20. U16 £15 when booking 2+ nights. Group rates available

CONTACT: Carolyn Rees
Tel: 01348 837859
Caerhafod@aol.com
www.caerhafod.co.uk
Llanrhian, St Davids, Haverfordwest,
Pembrokeshire, SA62 5BD

PIGGERY POKE
4 STAR HOSTEL

SHAGGY
SHEEP

283l 283r

Piggery Poke is a 16 bed, 4 star hostel on the public footpath that loops from the Wales Coast Path between Mwnt and Aberporth. Newly converted to provide self-catering hostel accommodation, it has 3 dormitories sleeping up to 8, 5 and 3, each with en suite facilities. Local cycle routes include Lôn Teifi (within 4 miles) and the Celtic Trail, Sustrans Route 82. A courtesy collection/delivery service is usually available from points within 15 miles along the coast for walkers/cyclists and their luggage/cycles.

Shaggy Sheep offers budget bunkhouse accommodation in the stunning surroundings of Carmarthenshire, just 25 mins' drive from the Ceredigion coastline and its amazing beaches. Perfect for activity, stag and hen parties. Nestled in the Teifi valley with village pubs and restaurants within walking distance. Bedding is included and facilities include a self-catering kitchen and a lounge, with garden and BBQ area. Shaggy Sheep are experts at organising adventure activity holidays.

DETAILS

- **Open** - All year. 7.30am to 10am and 4pm to 10pm, at the latest
- **Beds** - 16: 1 x 8, 1 x 5, 1 x 3
- **Price/night** - £25 per person.

CONTACT: Paul or Angela
Tel: 01239 811777
hostel@piggerypoke.co.uk
www.piggerypoke.co.uk
Ffrwdwenith Isaf, Felinwynt, Cardigan,
SA43 1RW

DETAILS

- **Open** - Jan-Dec. All day.
- **Beds** - 22: 5x4, 1x2
- **Price/night** - Email with numbers and length of stay for a quote

CONTACT: Chris
Tel: 01559 363911
bookings@shaggysheepwales.co.uk
www.shaggysheepwales.com
Old Commerce House, Pontwelly,
Llandysul, Carmarthen SA44 4AJ

THE LONG BARN

Penrhiw is an organic farm with views over the Teifi Valley. The stunning Ceredigion Coast and the Cambrian Mountains are an easy drive away and the busy small town of Llandysul (1.5 miles) has all essential supplies. The farm's location is ideal for exploring, studying or simply admiring the Welsh countryside. Local activities include fishing, swimming, climbing, abseiling, canoeing, farm walks and cycling.

DETAILS

- **Open** - All year. All day.
- **Beds** - 43: Long Barn 31: 1x15, 1x14, 1x2. Cowshed: 6:1x6. Annex 3: 1x3 (dbl+sgl). Cwtsh 3: 1x3 (dbl+sofa bed)
- **Price/night** - £15pp. Discount for groups and mid week bookings.

CONTACT: Tom or Eva
Tel: 01559 363200 Mob 07733 026874
cowcher@thelongbarn.co.uk
www.thelongbarn.co.uk
Penrhiw, Capel Dewi, Llandysul,
Ceredigion, SA44 4PG

GILFACH WEN
BARN

285

Gilfach Wen Barn provides homely self-catering 4* bunkhouse accommodation for individuals, extended families or groups on a working farm. It is ideally located for exploring Carmarthenshire, Pembrokeshire, Brecon Beacons and the Gower. There is a downstairs bedroom and shower room for disabled. Walker, cyclist and equestrian friendly.

DETAILS

- **Open** - All year. All day.
- **Beds** - 32: 3x6, 1x5, 1x4,1x3,1x2. Total 10 dble beds & 12 singles in 7 bedrooms
- **Price/night** - From £17.50pp. During school holidays and at weekends minimum numbers apply for advance bookings. Last minute bookings at weekend may be available at £20pp.

CONTACT: Jillie
Tel: 07780 476737
info@brechfa-bunkhouse.com
www.brechfa-bunkhouse.com
Gilfach Wen, Brechfa, Carmarthenshire,
SA32 7QL

DINEFWR
BUNKHOUSE
286

On a National Trust estate one mile from Llandeilo, Dinefwr Bunkhouse sits in the heart of an 18th century park enclosing a medieval deer park, next to the historic Newton House. Quite the perfect holiday location for groups or families who enjoy walking or other outdoor activities.

This beautifully presented, characterful bunkhouse sleeps up to 16 in an 8 bed dorm and 2 & 3 bedded rooms and has a well equipped kitchen for self-catering.

DETAILS

- **Open** - All year. All day
- **Beds** - 16: 1x8, 1x2, 2x3
- **Price/night** - For groups of 8 or less from £160 per night. Extra £20 per person per night for parties with over 8 people.

CONTACT: National Trust Holidays
Tel: 0344 335 1296
bunkhouses@nationaltrust.org.uk
www.nationaltrust.org.uk/holidays
Dinefwr Park, Llandeilo,
Carmarthenshire, SA19 6RT

TYNCORNEL
HOSTEL
287

Tyncornel is a former farmhouse set in stunning Cambrian mountain scenery at the head of the beautiful Doethie Valley. It is one of the most remote hostels in Wales, favoured by walkers, cyclists, and bird watchers. It is on the Cambrian Way long distance footpath. The hostel has 16 places. There is a cosy common room with wood-burning stove, two dormitories with built-in bunk beds and a self-catering kitchen.

DETAILS

■ **Open** - All year. Reception 5pm -11pm, 7am -10am.
■ **Beds** - 16: 2x8.
■ **Price/night** - £14 per adult, £10 (under 18s). Whole hostel bookings £200 and private rooms available. Campers £8.

CONTACT: Janet or Richard
Tel: 01980 629259
Tyncornel.bookings@btinternet.com
www.elenydd-hostels.co.uk
Llanddewi Brefi, Tregaron, Ceredigion, SY25 6PH

DOLGOCH
HOSTEL
288

Experience the peace of the remote Tywi valley in an era before electricity at this 17th century farmhouse. Dolgoch is a traditional simple hostel owned by the Elenydd Wilderness Trust. It has hot showers, log burner, self-catering kitchen, dormitories & private rooms. The Lôn Las Cymru and the Cambrian Way pass nearby and there are many mountain tracks to explore. Ideal for bird-watchers and lovers of the solitude of the scenic Cambrian mountains.

DETAILS

- **Open** - All year. 24 hours. Reception 5pm -11pm, 8am -10am.
- **Beds** - 20: 3 rooms inc private rooms.
- **Price/night** - £14 per adult, £10 (under 18). Campers £8

CONTACT: Gillian Keen
Tel: 01440 730 226
gill.keen@dolgoch.org
www.elenydd-hostels.co.uk
Dolgoch, Tregaron, Ceredigion,
SY25 6NR

STONECROFT
LODGE
289l

Stonecroft Lodge self-catering guest house is in Llanwrtyd Wells, 'the smallest town in Britain'. Surrounded by the green fields and mountains of mid Wales, Llanwrtyd is in renowned red kite country and is a great base for mountain biking, walking & pony trekking. The hostel has private and shared rooms with made-up beds, a fully equipped kitchen, lounge with TV, free laundry and drying, central heating, a large riverside garden and ample parking. The hostel adjoins the Stonecroft Inn for great beer and food.

DETAILS
■ **Open** - All year. All day. Call on arrival.
■ **Beds** - 27: 1x1, 3x4, 1x6, 4x(dbl+sgl)
■ **Price/night** - £16. Discounts for 3+ nights. Phone for sole use rates.

CONTACT: Jane Brown
Tel: 01591 610332
party@stonecroft.co.uk
www.stonecroft.co.uk
Dolecoed Road, Llanwrtyd Wells, Powys, LD5 4RA

NEW INN
BUNKHOUSE
289r

The 16th century New Inn on the River Wye is ideal for exploring mid Wales. The bunkhouse is great for parties of walkers and cyclists, plus there are double, twin and family B&B rooms. The bunkhouse is self-contained with toilets and showers. There are no self-catering facilities but the Inn serves delicious home-cooked locally grown food. There is ample parking.

DETAILS
■ **Open** - All year. All day.
■ **Beds** - Bunkhouse 10: 1x6, 1x4; B&B 11: family rooms, double & twin
■ **Price/night** - £12 pp (B/house), 6 bed room £60, 4 bed room £40. Breakfast £5.50pp. En suite B&B in the Inn £70 double/twin. Family rooms from £100.

CONTACT: Debbie and Dave
Tel: 01597 860211
newinn1960@gmail.com
www.pigsfolly.co.uk/bunkhouse.htm
New Inn, Newbridge-on-Wye, Llandrindod Wells, Powys, LD1 6HY

BEILI NEUADD
BUNKHOUSE
290

A converted 18th century stone barn in stunning countryside just 2 miles from the small market town of Rhayader - the gateway to the Elan Valley and Cambrian Mountains. On three National Cycle routes and the Trans Cambrian Route, Beili Neuadd offers lovely gardens, ponds and stunning scenery. The centrally heated barn sleeps 16 in 3 en suite rooms and includes a fully equipped kitchen/dining room and drying room. B& B accommodation is also available in the main house and there is space to camp in the paddock.

DETAILS

- **Open** - All year. All day access.
- **Beds** - 16: 2x6,1x4. B&B: 3 x double.
- **Price/night** - £19 per person, sole occupancy £275. B&B £50pp, £80 for two.

CONTACT: David and Alison Parker
Tel: 01597 810211
info@beilineuadd.co.uk
www.beilineuadd.co.uk
Beili Neuadd, Rhayader, LD6 5NS

MID WALES
BUNKHOUSE

291

Mid Wales Bunkhouse has a superb unspoilt rural location, close to the Elan Valley, for any activity or occasion with a stunning natural garden. Explore or swim in the river. There's walking and biking from the door, even accommodation for your horse. Fully equipped for self catering or meals provided. Authentic tipi and camping. Available for groups of up to 26 or individuals.

DETAILS

■ **Open** - All year. 24 hours. Arrive after 3pm (advise if after 7pm), leave by 11am.
■ **Beds** - 20
■ **Price/night** - £16pp, £80 for private 6-bed room. Sole use of dormitory area (sleeps 14) £190 per night. Sole use of bunkhouse (20 people) £250 per night

CONTACT: John or Steph
Tel: 01597 870081 Mob: 07507 343262
enquiries@bunkhousemidwales.co.uk
www.bunkhousemidwales.co.uk
Woodhouse Farm, St Harmon,
Rhayader, LD6 5LY

HAFREN FOREST
BUNKHOUSE
292

This former weather station has been converted into a comfortable bunkhouse located on the edge of the Hafren Forest. It is close to Plumlimon, in a quiet rural location between Llanidloes and Machynlleth in the Cambrian Mountains. A great base for walking, running, cycling (both on and off road), kayaking, wildlife watching, fly fishing, family groups and parties. Fully central heated the bunkhouse has a large dining room, well equipped kitchen and comfortable lounge with TV, DVD and playstation.

DETAILS

■ **Open** - All year.
■ **Beds** - 21: 2x4, 1x5, 1x8
■ **Price/night** - From £17pp midweek, £20pp weekends

CONTACT: Darren and Sarah
Tel: 07871 740514
mrsh66@btinternet.com
www.fb.com/hafrenbunkhouse/
Staylittle, nr Llanidloes, Powys,
SY19 7DB

PLASNEWYDD
BUNKHOUSE
293l

BORTH
YOUTH HOSTEL
293r

Set in the beautiful Mid Wales countryside on the Glyndwrs Way the 4* bunkhouse is an ideal location for exploring or unwinding. Built to the highest standards it provides high quality accommodation for groups or individuals. It can also be booked for conferences and seminars. Attractions close by include sailing, golf course, outdoor pursuit centre, shooting range, motorbike school and the picturesque market town of Llanidloes (0.5 mile) with many places to eat and drink.

DETAILS
- **Open** - All year. 24 hours. Arrival and departure times by arrangement.
- **Beds** - 27 in 2 dorms + 1 family room.
- **Price/night** - Sole use £403 per night. Individuals £20 pp.

CONTACT: Susan
Tel: 01686 412431 / 07975 913049
susanvaughan67@aol.co.uk
www.plasnewyddbunkhouse.co.uk
Gorn Rd, Llanidloes, Powys, SY18 6LA

With 4 miles of stunning beach just 20 metres from the front door, Borth Youth Hostel is the perfect location for a beach holiday. This Edwardian house has 9 bedrooms with sea views and is a great base for visits to the Centre for Alternative Technology, Aberystwyth or the beautiful Dyfi Biosphere. Snowdonia National Park is just a short drive away Making Borth perfect for both mountain biking & surfing. With two classrooms, Borth YHA is idea for school trips too. The hostel has free WiFi, a games and TV room, bike storage and drying room. Meals and a licensed bar are available.

DETAILS
- **Open** - All year. Check in 5 - 10.30pm. Check out 8am - 10am
- **Beds** - 60
- **Price/night** - from £18 pp

CONTACT: John Taylor
Tel: 01970 871498
john@borthyouthhostel.co.uk
Ceredigion, Wales, SY24 5JS

MAES-Y-MOR

Maes-y-Mor offers superior self-catering accommodation at budget prices. With 7 twin & 1 double room plus 1 en suite family room it is ideally situated near the town centre, around the corner from the beach and 5 mins' walk to train/bus stations. Accommodation at the hostel is room-only with self-catering facilities. All rooms have TVs & tea/coffee making facilities. Car parking and secure bike storage. A 4* double room apartment and a new 4* boutique self-catering house sleeping 7 are also available

DETAILS

■ **Open** - All year. 8am to 9.30pm
■ **Beds** - 19 : 7 x 2 (twin), 1 x 2 (double), 1 x 3 (family en-suite)
■ **Price/night** - Twin/doubles from £50. Single rooms from £30. Group discounts.

CONTACT: Mererid or Alaw
Tel: 01970 639270.
maesymor@hotmail.co.uk
www.maesymor.co.uk
25 Bath Street, Aberystwyth, SY23 2NN

PLAS DOLAU
COUNTRY HOUSE
295

Plas Dolau is set in 25 acres just 3 miles from Aberystwyth. Ideal for exploring West Wales, walking, cycling, riding, fishing and golf. The warm country mansion has mainly dormitory style accommodation for up to 45 people.

An adjoining Swedish style farmhouse can take another 15. Plas Dolau includes meeting rooms, dining rooms, games room & outdoor areas. Ideally suited for youth groups, field courses, retreats, house parties or individuals.

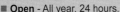
DETAILS

- **Open** - All year. 24 hours.
- **Beds** - 45:+cots. Plus 16 in farmhouse
- **Price/night** - From £20 (inc breakfast) to £35 (private, en suite, full breakfast). From £650 for the whole mansion.

CONTACT: Pat Twigg
Tel: 01970 617834
pat@plasdolau.co.uk
www.plasdolau.co.uk
Lovesgrove, Aberystwyth, SY23 3HP

TOAD HALL

Toad Hall sits beside the River Dovey, close to Snowdonia National Park and Machynlleth. NCN Cycle route 8 and Glyndwrs Way pass near by.

The hostel accommodation comprises a four bed-roomed self contained unit above the family home. A flat garden is ideal for camping or bike/canoe storage.

DETAILS

■ **Open** - Not always open, please phone to find out and always pre-book. Please vacate rooms from 12 -3 pm for cleaning. No arrivals after 11pm.
■ **Beds** - 10: 1x4 (family), 1x2 (twin), 1x2 (dbl), 1x2
■ **Price/night** - £16 pp + £2 per stay for bedding. Reductions for groups.

CONTACT: Will
Tel: 01654 700597 Mob: 07866 362507
or 07807 849216
willcoyn@hotmail.com
Toad Hall, Doll St, Machynlleth, Powys, SY20 8BH

CORRIS
HOSTEL

Perfect for group and family gatherings, Corris hostel is a renowned haven from the stresses of the outside world; with its homely atmosphere, friendly staff and cosy wood fires. Outside there are landscaped hill gardens with barbecue and campfire areas. Situated in the Dyfi Biosphere and southern Snowdonia National Park, the hostel is close to Cadair Idris and Centre for Alternative Technology. A walkers and cyclists paradise in addition to many other attractions.

DETAILS

- **Open** - Most of year. All day access.
- **Beds** - 42/44
- **Price/night** - Adult £18, child £13. Breakfast £4.25. Private rooms extra.

CONTACT: Michael or Debbie or Kevin
Tel: 01654 761686
mail@corrishostel.co.uk
www.corrishostel.co.uk
Old School, Corris, Machynlleth, Powys, SY20 9TQ

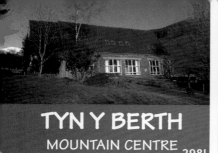

TYN Y BERTH
MOUNTAIN CENTRE
298l

Ty'n y Berth sits at the foot of Cadair Idris on the southern edge of the Snowdonia National Park. Surrounded by mountains, valleys and crystal clear rivers, yet only 12 miles from the coast, it's a great location for outdoor activities and family holidays. The spacious accommodation sleeps up to 43 including a separate unit for 8 which can also be hired on its own. Corris is within walking distance and has a CAMRA pub. Courses are available in a wide range of outdoor activities.

        GROUPS ONLY

DETAILS

■ **Open** - All year. All day.
■ **Beds** - 43: 35:1x8,1x9 3x6, 2x2, 2x1 + 2 occasional beds. Rugog:8
■ **Price/night** - £378+vat, sole use self catering. Rugog unit £110+vat.

CONTACT: Jane
Tel: 01654 761678
info@corris-bunkhouse.co.uk
www.corris-bunkhouse.co.uk
Corris Uchaf, Machynlleth, Powys,
SY20 9RH

HYB BUNKHOUSE
DOLGELLAU
298r

HyB Bunkhouse is in Dolgellau (Lon Las, Sustrans 82), mid Wales, at the foot of Cader Idris. Centrally located above Medi Gifts, with free parking at rear for up to four cars, there are shops, pubs and restaurants on the doorstep.

HyB backs onto the Mawddach trail near the river Wnion and it is 10 minutes' drive to Coed y Brenin mountain biking centre. This quirky listed building has original features such as oak floors, beams and panelling and offers a good night's sleep.

DETAILS

■ **Open** - All year except Xmas and New Year.
■ **Beds** - 16: 4 x 4.
■ **Price/night** - £20 per person. Limited bedding sets available @£5.

CONTACT: Nia
Tel: 01341 421755
post@medi-gifts.com
2-3 Heol y Bont (Bridge St), Dolgellau,
Gwynedd, LL40 1AU

BUNKORAMA

Whether you're a lone cyclist or a group of walkers you will love discovering this cosy clean and comfortable accommodation with breathtaking views of Cader Idris and Cardigan Bay. Handy for Cycle Route 8, the Cambrian Way & Mawddach Trail and at only £15 per night Bunkorama is an ideal place to make a stopover or spend a few days exploring the mountains, rivers and beaches of the Cambrian Coast.

DETAILS

■ **Open** - All year round.
■ **Beds** - 2 rooms each sleeping 4. Plus sofa bed in lounge
■ **Price/night** - £15 pp + £5 per stay if bedding needed and towel available £2 per stay

CONTACT: Graham
Tel: 01341 281134 or 07738467196
thebunkorama@gmail.com
www.bunkorama.co.uk
Gwastad Agnes Off Panorama Road,
Barmouth, Gwynedd, LL42 1DX

Green Hub
Organic Garden

This garden is loved by the st...
organic gardening course. T...
will be used in our kitchen...
we well be running more
...

BUNKHOUSE
AT THE WORKHOUSE
300

The well equipped, community run bunkhouse at Y Dolydd Llanfyllin Workhouse offers a unique opportunity to stay in one of the last remaining Victorian workhouses still open to the public. Handy for Welshpool, Oswestry & Shrewsbury and close to the Berwyn Mountains National Nature Reserve it has access to a wide range of outdoor and adventure activities. Nearby attractions include Lake Vyrnwy and Pistyll Rhaeadr waterfall, the tallest single drop waterfall in the UK.

DETAILS

■ **Open** - March - October inclusive.
■ **Beds** - 24: 1x4, 1x8, 1x12
■ **Price/night** - £15 incl. linen, duvets & pillows. Group discounts may apply.

CONTACT: Tree Marshall
Tel: 07534 354 082
bunkhouse@the-workhouse.com
www.the-workhouse.org.uk/
Y Dolydd, Workhouse, Llanfyllin,
SY22 5LD

BALA
BACKPACKERS
301

For outdoor adventures within the Snowdonia National Park, Bala Backpackers offers great value 'hostel-style' accommodation, including; 30+ comfy SINGLE BEDS in bedrooms of 3,4 or 5, 3 private TWIN ROOMS and 3 new EN SUITES. Located in a quiet, sunny, chapel square, in the bustling market town of Bala with its five-mile-long lake and white-water river for raft rides.

DETAILS

■ **Open** - All year by arrangement. 8.30-20.30. Front door locked 00.30 – 6.00am.
■ **Beds** - 45: 2x3, 3x4, 3x5 + 3 twin rooms + 3 en suites
■ **Price/night** - 1 night £21, 2 nights £39, 3 nights £49, weekly £89. Twin room: £49 or en suites from £59. Double holiday-let: £220/4 nights. Sheet-bag hire £3/week.

CONTACT: Stella Shaw
Tel: 01678 521700
info@Bala-Backpackers.co.uk
www.Bala-Backpackers.co.uk
32 Tegid Street, Bala, LL23 7EL

BALA
BUNK HOUSE
302l

TYDDYN BYCHAN
302r

Being a converted 200 year old Welsh stone building, Bala Bunk House is full of character, set back from the road in over an acre of picturesque grounds with private parking and splendid views of the Berwyn Hills. Ideal for all types of groups, family parties and individuals. Close to many outdoor activity centres and all amenities, it is the perfect base for walkers and watersport enthusiasts with Bala Lake and the National White Water Centre on the doorstep.

DETAILS
- **Open** - All year. No restrictions.
- **Beds** - 26: 1x2, 1x4, 1x6, 1x8, 1x6 self-contained.
- **Price/night** - Single night from £17 pp, two or more nights from £16pp per night

CONTACT: Guy and Jane Williams
Tel: 01678 520738
thehappyunion@btinternet.com
www.balabunkhouse.co.uk
Tomen Y Castell, Llanfor, Bala,
Gwynedd, LL23 7HD

Tyddyn Bychan is an 18th century Welsh farm surrounded by fields. It is an excellent self-catering base for mountain biking, road cycling, canoeing, walking, climbing, fishing and numerous watersports including white water rafting. The main bunkhouse sleeps 18 in two en suite rooms. All bunks are handmade to a very high standard. The smaller bunkhouse sleeps 9 in two en suite rooms. All bedding is included. Delicious homemade food is available if booked in advance. There is a good parking area well away from the road.

GROUPS ONLY

DETAILS
- **Open** - All year All day.
- **Beds** - 28: 1x10; 1x8; 1x6; 1x3
- **Price/night** - £15 pp including bedding.

CONTACT: Lynda
Tel: 01490 420680 Mob: 07523 995741
lynda@tyddynbychan.co.uk
www.tyddynbychan.co.uk
Cefn Brith, Cerrigydrudion, Conwy,
LL21 9TS

LLANGOLLEN
HOSTEL
303

Llangollen Hostel, in the Dee Valley is your perfect location for walking, cycling, canoeing and white water rafting. Families will love visiting the steam railway, horse drawn canal boats and Pontcysyllte Aqueduct - a World Heritage Site. The town offers a great choice of restaurants/pubs and is home to a fringe music and arts festival and the International Eisteddfod. Llandegla, Chester, Wrexham and Offa's Dyke Path are all nearby. A warm welcome awaits!

DETAILS

- **Open** - All year. All day.
- **Beds** - 32.
- **Price/night** - From £19pp dorm. £20pp for 3,4,5 or 6 bed room. £45 twin/double or £50 en suite. Family of 4 £60, £10 per extra child. Book direct for the best prices.

CONTACT: Arlo Dennis
Tel: 01978 861773
info@llangollenhostel.co.uk
www.llangollenhostel.co.uk
Berwyn Street, Llangollen, LL20 8NB

HENDRE ISAF
BASECAMP
304

This converted Grade 2 stone farm building is the perfect base for enjoying the Snowdonia National Park. Part of the 8,000 hectare Ysbyty Estate, it offers spacious, well appointed group accommodation. Local attractions include the Tree Top Adventure Course at Betws-y-Coed, Zip World at Penrhyn Quarry, Bethesda, Zip World and Bounce Below at Llechwedd Slate Caverns, Blaenau Ffestiniog and the Plas y Brenin National Mountain Centre.

GROUPS ONLY

DETAILS
- **Open** - All year. 24 hours.
- **Beds** - 18: 2 x dormitories + 1x1 single
- **Price/night** - 2 nights from £380.

CONTACT: Hendre Isaf Basecamp at
National Trust Holidays
Tel: 0344 335 1296
bunkhouses@nationaltrust.org.uk
www.nationaltrust.org.uk/holidays/
hendre-isaf-bunkhouse-wales
National Trust Ysbyty Estate Office,
Dinas, Betws-y-Coed, Conwy, LL24 0HF

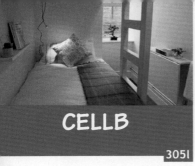

CELLB

305l

After a long day of adventures, why not rest your weary head in an Edwardian police house hostel? Conveniently located in the centre of Blaenau Ffestiniog. There is a self-catering kitchen, a drying room and secure bike storage. Need a break from cooking? There's a restaurant upstairs, or just enjoy a cheeky drink in the bar. What's more there's a cinema too! CellB is the perfect place to recover, recuperate, and soak up the vibrant landscape.

DETAILS

- **Open** - All year. All day
- **Beds** - 11: 1x6, 1x3, 1x2
- **Price/night** - From £20. Sole use from £396 for the weekend (Friday – Sunday) £1,386 for the week.

CONTACT: Reception
Tel: 01766 832001
prisoner@cellb.org
cellb.org
Park Square, Blaenau Ffestiniog
LL41 3AD

TREKS
BUNKHOUSE

305r

Treks 4* Bunkhouse perches in the mountains on the outskirts of the village of Blaenau Ffestiniog. Ideal for those who enjoy the rugged beauty of Snowdonia, it is a former golf club recently converted to provide self-catering accommodation for individuals and groups. There are many attractions nearby including, Llechwedd Slate Caverns, Bounce Below, Zip World Titan, Antur Stiniog, Ffestiniog Railway, Go Below Adventures, Coed y Brenin Mountain Bike Centre, Portmeirion Italian Village, Bala White Water Rafting and Harlech Castle.

DETAILS

- **Open** - All year. Check in 14:00 - 20:00
- **Beds** - 16: 1x6, 1x4, 1x3, 1x2, 1x1
- **Price/night** - £20 per person

CONTACT: Dyfed
Tel: 07796 172 318
treksbunkhouse@gmail.com
www.treksbunkhouse.co.uk
Y Cefn, Ffestiniog, Gwynedd, LL41 4PS

SNOWDON LODGE
GROUP HOSTEL
306

Stay in the birthplace of Lawrence of Arabia! Snowdon Lodge provides self-catering group accommodation. Located in the village of Tremadog, Snowdon Lodge is perfect for family reunions or groups wanting to explore Snowdonia and the Llyn Peninsula. It has 10 rooms (twins, doubles and small dormitories), an additional lecture room and a large car park leading to woodland walks.

       GROUPS ONLY

DETAILS

■ **Open** - January – December. All day.
■ **Beds** - 35: 2 x 6 (family), 1 x 5, 1 x 6 , 3 x twin, 3 x double
■ **Price/night** - Sole use £600 per night. Min of 2 nights, 3 on bank holidays. Discounts for longer stays.

CONTACT: Carl or Anja
Tel: 01766 515354
info@snowdonlodge.co.uk
www.snowdonlodge.co.uk
Lawrence House, Church Street,
Tremadog, Nr Porthmadog, Gwynedd,
Snowdonia, LL49 9PS

MAENTWROG
BUNKHOUSE
307l

VAGABOND
307r
BUNKHOUSE

Maentwrog Bunkhouse is a newly cowshed on a working farm. It has a fully equipped kitchen, underfloor heating, TV/DVD BBQ area, laundry, power washer and bike lockup. Local activities include hill walking (Moelwyn and Cnicht 10 mins away), white water rafting, Coed y Brenin cycling centre, Blaenau Ffestiniog down hill cycle track, RopeWorks & canyoning. Ffestiniog railway and several beautiful beaches are within 15-20 mins' drive. The Welsh costal path passes the end of the lane.

The Vagabond Bunkhouse/Hostel is in the village of Betws-y-Coed, in the heart of the Snowdonia National Park.

This unique bunkhouse is very well designed and appointed, with ready made up beds, free hot drinks, seriously hot showers, a well equipped kitchen & a bar. Catering is available. Outside there's a climbing wall & power wash.

DETAILS

- **Open** - All year. Reception open 7.30am-10am and 4.30pm-7.30pm
- **Beds** - 36: 2x8, 2x6,2x4
- **Price/night** - £19.00pp. B&B (obligatory at weekends) £24.00, B&B and evening meal £31.00. Heated dog kennel £3.00 per night

DETAILS

- **Open** - All Year.
- **Beds** - 4
- **Price/night** - £18pp bring sleeping bags or hire bed linen @£5/person/stay

CONTACT: Mrs Eurliw M Jones
Tel: 01766 590231
emj2@hotmail.co.uk
www.bunkhousesnowdonia.com
Felen Rhyd Fach, Maentwrog, Blaenau Ffestiniog, Gwynedd, LL41 4HY

CONTACT: Neil Cawthra
Tel: 01690710850 mobile: 07816 076546
neilcawthra@mail.com
www.thevagabond.co.uk
Craiglan, Betws-y-Coed, Conway, LL24 0AW

LLEDR HOUSE

308

Lledr House nestles in Snowdonia National Park. Once a YHA and now newly refurbished, guests delight in the luxury mattresses, modern bathrooms, well equipped kitchen and extended car park. Individuals, groups and families. enjoy the clean, cheap, comfortable accommodation. Betws-y-Coed, Llyn Elsi and Tree Tops high rope course close by.

DETAILS

■ **Open** - Open March to November incl. Check in from 5pm till 10.30pm.
■ **Beds** - 36: House 31: 1x9, 2x4,1x6, 3x2, 2x1. Cabin 5: 1x5
■ **Price/night** - From £18pp. Single rooms £22.50. Sole use £550 (min of 3 nights BH). Cabin £120 (min of 2 nights).

CONTACT: Brian or Melanie Quilter
Tel: 01690 750202 Mobile: 07915 397705 or 07915 397660
Lledrhouse@aol.com
www.ukyh.com
Pont-y-Pant, Dolwyddelan, North Wales, LL25 0DQ

CONWY VALLEY
BACKPACKERS BARN 309

Conwy Valley Backpackers is situated on a peaceful organic farm in the heart of the beautiful Conwy Valley, with excellent access to Snowdonia. Centrally heated with a fully equipped self-catering kitchen, log fires and hot showers. Secure bike/canoe storage. Grazing for horses and tourist information are available. Local activities range from fishing and hiking to white water rafting and mountain biking. Surf Snowdonia is within walking distance and Zip World is a short drive away.

DETAILS

- **Open** - All year. All day.
- **Beds** - 20: 1x4, 1x6 & 1x10
- **Price/night** - From £20pp. Sole use from £275. £3pp bed linen hire.

CONTACT: Claudia
Tel: 01492 660504 Mob: 07956 851425
info@conwyvalleybarn.com
www.conwyvalleybarn.com
Pyllau Gloewon Farm, Tal-y-Bont,
Conwy, Gwynedd, LL32 8YX

LLANDUDNO
HOSTEL

310

Llandudno Hostel is a Victorian 4* boutique hostel where individuals, families and groups (including schools) are welcome all year. Set in the heart of the Victorian seaside town of Llandudno, it's your perfect base for shopping & exploring the many local attractions, including blue flag beaches, dry slope skiing, ten pin bowling, bronze age copper mine, traditional pier, museums and fishing trips.

DETAILS

■ **Open** - All year (telephone in winter prior to arrival). All day.
■ **Beds** - 46: 2x8, 2x6, 4x2, 1x4, 1xfamily
■ **Price/night** - From £23 per person, £55 per private twin room, £60 per private twin en suite. Group and family rates on request. Special offers autumn/winter.

CONTACT: James or Melissa
Tel: 01492 877430
info@llandudnohostel.co.uk
www.llandudnohostel.co.uk
14 Charlton Street, Llandudno, LL30 2AA

PLATTS FARM
BUNKHOUSE
311

Platt's Farm Campsite and 3* Bunkhouse is situated in a range of Victorian farm buildings, in the charming village of Llanfairfechan. Close to the A55, the Bunkhouse lies at the start/end of the 14 Welsh 3000 peaks walks in the Snowdonia National Park, within a 10 min walk of the Wales coastal path and on the No.5 cycle route. Shops, pubs and cafés are within 5 mins' walk. Just 15 mins from Zipworld, Bethesda & 20 mins from Surf Snowdonia.

DETAILS

■ **Open** - All year. Check out before 11am, check in after 2pm.
■ **Beds** - 10
■ **Price/night** - £15.50 pppn. Sole use £155 per night.

CONTACT: Sam Davies
Tel: 01248 680105
sam@plattsfarm.com
www.plattsfarm.com
Platts Farm Bunkhouse, Aber Road,
Llanfairfechan, Conwy, LL33 0HL

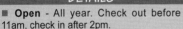

CABAN CYSGU
BUNKHOUSE

Caban Cysgu, run by the community of Gerlan, offers purpose-built accommodation at the foot of the Carneddau. Perfect for walking in Snowdonia, it's a great base for the 'Fourteen 3000ft Peaks' long-distance challenge. It's just a 5 minute drive to Zip World; the longest and fastest zip line in Europe. There are also plenty of mountain bike trails on the doorstep while road cyclists have the Sustrans route 'Lôn Las Ogwen' just a mile away. For climbers, Idwal is close by, while Afon Ogwen is popular with canoeists.

DETAILS

- **Open** - All year. All day.
- **Beds** - 16 : 1x5, 1x2, 1x1, 1x8
- **Price/night** - From £14 - £16

CONTACT: Dewi Emyln, Manager
Tel: 01248 605573 Mob: 07464676753
dewi@cabancysgu-gerlan.co.uk
www.cabancysgu-gerlan.co.uk
Fford Gerlan, Gerlan, Bethesda,
Bangor, LL57 3ST

LODGE DINORWIG

313l

OLD SCHOOL
LODGE

313r

On the edge of Snowdonia National Park, Lodge Dinorwig, a former school, has a 14 bed bunkroom. Breakfast is included and evening meals can be booked but there is no self-catering.

Perfectly located for all the high adrenaline activities Snowdonia has to offer and with easy access to attractions such as Bounce Below as well as Snowdon and Llanberis. The on-site café will provide tea and cake after a day in the mountains.

In the small mountain village of Deiniolen, in the heart of Snowdonia not far from Llanberis, The Old School Lodge is the perfect base for groups of all kinds wishing to explore the rugged splendour of North Wales. Perfect for groups of walkers or climbers, the Lodge provides high quality accommodation for those looking for a warm comfortable base to come home to after a day out on the Welsh Mountains. Facilities include a well equipped self-catering kitchen, lounge, games room & resources room.

DETAILS

- **Open** - All year. Check in from 3pm, check out by 11am.
- **Beds** - 14: 1x14
- **Price/night** - From £25-£29. Sole use from £300-£350 including breakfast

DETAILS

- **Open** - All year. All day.
- **Beds** - 38: 1x6,7x4,2x2
- **Price/night** - £19.00pp, Scouts and Guides £14.25 Minimum stay 2 nights, minimum charge based on 12 people.

CONTACT: Simon and Sonni
Tel: 01286 871632
info@lodge-dinorwig.co.uk
www.lodge-dinorwig.co.uk/
Dinorwig, Caernarfon, Gwynedd,
LL55 3EY

CONTACT: Booking Secretary
Tel: 0151 632 4943
activities@oldschoollodge.org.uk
www.oldschoollodge.org.uk
Deiniolen, Caernarfon LL55 3HH

ARETE
OUTDOOR CENTRE
314

The Arete Outdoor Centre, in Snowdonia National Park, offers excellent access to the stunning coastline, mountains & lakes of North Wales and Anglesey. With comfortable, affordable, bunkhouse accommodation and large kitchens this is a great base for groups of friends or family. The team can advise on how best to spend your stay and a range of exciting outdoor activities are available through the centre's well qualified staff.

    GROUPS ONLY

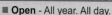

DETAILS

■ **Open** - All year. All day.
■ **Beds** - 100+ in 22 rooms split into three blocks of 20, 58 and 30+
■ **Price/night** - Catered from £30pp, self-catering from £15 pp. Sole use deals.

CONTACT: Gareth Davies
Tel: 01286 672136
info@aretecentre.co.uk
www.aretecentre.co.uk
Arete Outdoor Education Centre,
Llanrug, Caernarfon, Gwynedd,
LL55 4AP

PENTRE BACH
BUNKHOUSE

Situated between Waunfawr and Betws Garmon, Pentre Bach Bunkhouse provides dog friendly accommodation, outdoor activities and a campsite. The ground floor of the bunkhouse has a dining/cooking area while upstairs there are alpine sleeping platforms with mattresses for 16. Showers, toilets and washing/drying facilities, shared with the campsite, are just across the yard.

DETAILS

■ **Open** - 9am-10pm for enquiries. Arrive from 4pm, leave by 11am.
■ **Beds** - 16: 1x16.
■ **Price/night** - £12 per person (inc gas / electric / showers). Sole use bookings negotiable according to group size.

CONTACT: Karen Neil
Tel: 01286 650643(5-10pm) or
07798733939(9-5pm)
info@bachventures.co.uk
www.pentrebachbunkhouse.co.uk
Pentre Bach, Waunfawr, Caernarfon,
Gwynedd, LL54 7AJ

RHYD DDU
OUTDOOR CENTRE
316

The Rhyd Ddu Bunkhouse provides group accommodation at the foot of Snowdon and the Nantlle Ridge. Sleeping 31 in 6 bedrooms, it has a fully equipped kitchen and a large communal/dining room with a big screen - great for movie nights! Boasting glorious views, central heating, fibre Wifi, parking, bike storage, drying room and a large garden. Bring your own sleeping bag, pillow case and towel. A pub, cafe, and steam train station are all within 2 minutes walk.

DETAILS

■ **Open** - All year. All day. Check in from 4pm, check out by 11am.
■ **Beds** - 31: 1x12, 1x5, 3x4, 1x2
■ **Price/night** - Sole use from £250 per night. Minimum stay of 2 nights.

CONTACT: Robat
Tel: 01286 882688
stay@canolfan-rhyd-ddu.cymru
www.snowdonia-bunkhouse.wales
Rhyd Ddu Outdoor Centre, Rhyd Ddu, Snowdonia, Wales LL54 6TL

CWM PENNANT
TRAINING CENTRE
317

Cwm Pennant Hostel is a welcoming 56 bed hostel offering relaxed accommodation for individuals, families and groups. We offer breakfast, dinner and packed lunches. Set within stunning grounds in the Snowdonia National Park it has fantastic views of the Cwm Pennant valley and Moel Hebog.

DETAILS

■ **Open** - All year (Dec to Feb advance bookings only). 7:30-12noon; 4.30-10pm.
■ **Beds** - 56: 4x4, 1x6, 1x8, 1x10, 1x16.
■ **Price/night** - £19.50 (adult), £16.50 (under 16), under 3's free. From £1,295 sole use two night weekend. Breakfast from £4. Discounts for advanced booking. Packed lunches from £6. Evening meals on request from £7.

CONTACT:
Tel: 01766 530888
bookings@cwmpennanthostel.com
www.cwmpennanthostel.com
Golan, Garndolbenmaen, Gwynedd,
LL51 9AQ

ABERSOCH
SGUBOR UNNOS

Luxury bunkhouse accommodation on a family farm in the village of Llangian. Just one mile from Abersoch which is famed for watersports, the bunkhouse is an ideal base for walking the newly opened Llyn Coast Path, surfing, cycling, golf, fishing and sailing. Spinning and knitting courses using the farm's own wool available. The three modern bunkrooms are ideal for individuals or groups with a fully equipped kitchen/lounge, disabled facilities, secure storage and parking.

DETAILS

- **Open** - All year. All day.
- **Beds** - 14: 2 x 4, 1 x 6
- **Price/night** - £20 (adult), £10 (under 10 years), including a light breakfast and bed linen. Discount for 3+ nights.

CONTACT: Phil or Meinir
Tel: 01758 713527
enquiries@tanrallt.com
www.tanrallt.com
Fferm Tanrallt Farm, Llangian, Abersoch, Gwynedd, LL53 7LN

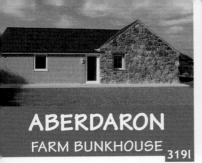

ABERDARON
FARM BUNKHOUSE
319l

Aberdaron Farm Bunkhouse is two miles from Aberdaron village, it has underfloor heating and a large comfortable social room. Bring sleeping bags or hire duvet sets for £3. Whistling Sands is close by and Bardsey Island lies across The Sound off the tip of the Llyn Peninsula. Pets allowed (with notice). Holiday cottages/camping available.

DETAILS
- **Open** - All year. All day (arrive after 4pm and leave by 11am).
- **Beds** - 15: 1x8, 1x4 (en suite), 1x3 (en suite)
- **Price/night** - £16pp, £18 pp (en suite) inc breakfast. Enquire for sole use of room/bunkhouse/family room prices. Minimum of 3 days on bank holidays.

CONTACT: Gillian Jones
Tel: 01758 760345 Mob: 0779 414 7195
enquiries@aberdaronfarmholidays.co.uk
www.aberdaronfarmholidays.co.uk
Y Gweithdy, Anelog, Aberdaron, Pwllheli, LL53 8BT

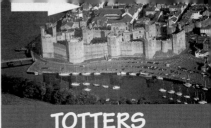

TOTTERS
319r

Totters sits in the heart of the historic castle town of Caernarfon just 30m from the Menai Straits. Close to many pubs and restaurants but with good public transport to the Snowdonia National Park. The hostel is a 200 year old, five floored town house with five bedrooms sleeping either 4 or 6 and a huge double/family en suite. Opposite there is a self-catering town house sleeping 6.

DETAILS
- **Open** - All year. All day. Check in by 10 pm.
- **Beds** - 28: 3x6, 2x4, 1x2 (en suite), 1x2 (twin)
- **Price/night** - £18.50pp in a dorm. £50 for a double/twin en suite. £44 for a twin. Discounts for groups.

CONTACT: Bob/Henryette
Tel: 01286 672963 Mob: 07979 830470
totters.hostel@googlemail.com
www.totters.co.uk
Plas Porth Yr Aur, 2 High Street, Caernarfon, Gwynedd, LL55 1RN

ANGLESEY
OUTDOOR CENTRE
320l

Anglesey Outdoor Centre is an ideal base for groups, individuals or families. It is just a mile from Porthdafarch Beach & the coast path, and only 2km from Sustrans Cycle Route 8. It has four self contained areas each with their own self-catering and bathroom facilities. These can be hired individually or together. Full catering an option and an on-site bar/bistro. Yurts and Cabans also available.

DETAILS
- **Open** - All year, 24 hour access.
- **Beds** - 68; Main Centre 33:1x7,4x5,1x4,1x2. Maris Annexe 10:5x2. Ty Pen Annexe 8:1x4,2x2. Gogarth Dorms 16:1x7,1x7,1x2.
- **Price/night** - £10pp (Gogarth Dorms) to £24pp (en suite twin). Ask for sole use.

CONTACT: Penny Hurndall
Tel: 01407 769351
angleseyoutdoors@gmail.com
www.angleseyoutdoors.com
Porthdafarch Road, Holyhead, Anglesey,
LL65 2LP

OUTDOOR
ALTERNATIVE
320r

This purpose built 4* centre is quietly tucked away in Rhoscolyn, an Area of Outstanding Natural Beauty on the Anglesey Coast. Just 5 mins' walk to the sandy beach at Borthwen and a stone's throw from the Anglesey Coastal Path. Perfect for friends & families, outdoor groups, schools and universities. Your ideal base for kayaking, climbing, sailing walking, bird watching or beach holidays Careful energy use is encouraged, with composting and recycling. Nearby Holyhead has ferry links to Ireland.

DETAILS
- **Open** - All year. 24 hour access.
- **Beds** - 20: 2x2, 1x4, 2x6. 20: 1x3, 3x4, 1x5.
- **Price/night** - £22pp. £385 for sole use.

CONTACT: Jacqui Short
Tel: 01407 860469
enquiries@outdooralternative.co.uk
www.outdooralternative.co.uk
Cerrig-yr-Adar, Rhoscolyn, Holyhead,
Anglesey, LL65 2NQ

Hostel yr Hen Ysgol
Trefin 1⁄2 m
The Old School Hostel

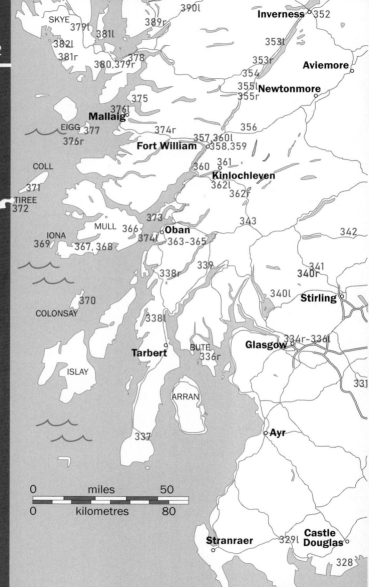

South Scotland

SKYE
379l
381l
389r
390l
Inverness o 352
382l
381r
378
380, 379r
353l
353r
354
Aviemore o
355l
355r
Newtonmore o
375
376l
Mallaig o
EIGG 377
376r
374r
356
357, 360l
358, 359
Fort William o
COLL
360
361
Kinlochleven
371
362l
362r
TIREE
372
343
342
373
366
IONA 367, 368
374l
Oban o
363–365
369
370
338r
339
341
340r
COLONSAY
340l
Stirling o
338l
334r–336l
Glasgow o
Tarbert o
BUTE
336r
331
ISLAY
ARRAN
337
Ayr o

0   miles   50
0   kilometres   80

Stranraer o
329l
Castle Douglas o
328

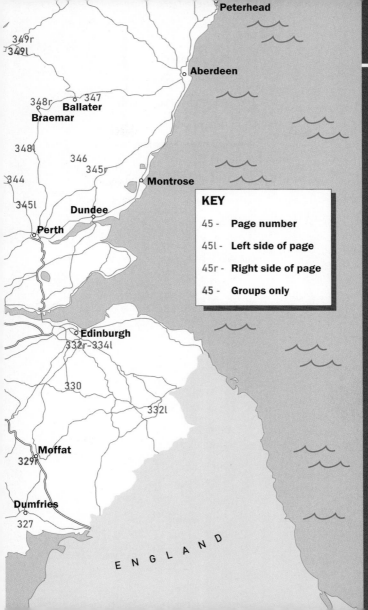

South Scotland

Peterhead

Aberdeen

349r
349l

348r   347
Ballater
Braemar

348l
346
345r
344
Montrose
345l
Dundee
Perth

KEY

45 -   Page number

45l -   Left side of page

45r -   Right side of page

45 -   Groups only

Edinburgh
332r-334l

330

332l

Moffat
329r

Dumfries
327

E N G L A N D

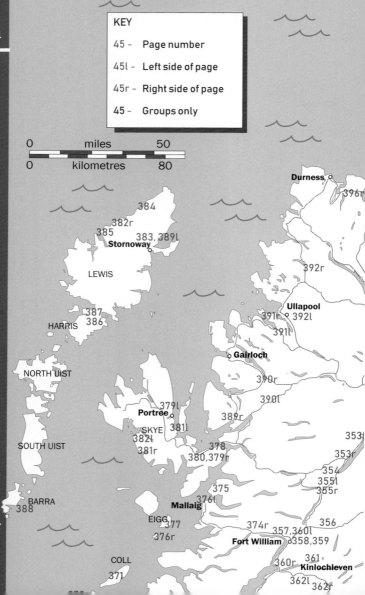

KEY

45 –   Page number

45l –   Left side of page

45r –   Right side of page

45 –   Groups only

0   miles   50

0   kilometres   80

Durness 396r

384

382r

385   383, 389l

Stornoway

392r

LEWIS

387   **Ullapool**

386   391r   392l

HARRIS   391l

Gairloch

NORTH UIST   390r

390l

379l

Portree

389r

SKYE   381

382l   378   353l

381r   380, 379r

SOUTH UIST   353r

354

375   355l

376l   355r

BARRA

388   **Mallaig**

EIGG   356

377   374r   357, 360l

376r   **Fort William**   358, 359

361

COLL   360r   **Kinlochleven**

371   362l   362r

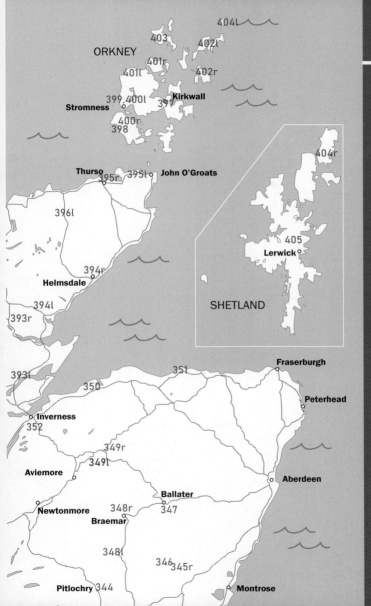

ORKNEY

404l

403

402l

401r

402r

401l

399 400l

Stromness

Kirkwall

397

400r

398

Thurso

395r 395l John O'Groats

396l

394r

Helmsdale

394l

393r

404r

Lerwick

405

SHETLAND

393l

351

350

Fraserburgh

Peterhead

Inverness

352

349r

349l

Aviemore

Newtonmore

348r

Ballater

347

Braemar

Aberdeen

348l

346 345r

Pitlochry 344

Montrose

North Scotland

Scotland

Isle of Eigg © Glebe Barn pg 377

MARTHROWN
OF MABIE

Marthrown is set in the heart of Mabie Forest, 6 miles south of Dumfries. It has a sauna, a wood burning spring water hot tub, a large BBQ, garden areas, a challenge course and plenty of room for groups. There are a variety of mountain bike routes and the 7Stanes mountain bike trails are nearby. Catered meals available for groups. As well as the bunkhouse, there are also Mongolian yurts an American style tipi and the jewel in the crown is the iron age roundhouse for parties or weddings.

DETAILS

■ **Open** - All year. 24 hours - late arrival by arrangement.
■ **Beds** - 26: 1x8:1x7:1x6:1x5 + Roundhouse, 2 Yurts, Tipi and camping.
■ **Price/night** - £16 to £19.50.

CONTACT: Mike or Pam Hazlehurst
Tel: 01387 247900
pamhazlehurst@hotmail.com
www.marthrownofmabie.co.uk
Mabie Forest, Dumfries, DG2 8HB

CASTLE CREAVIE
HAY BARN HOSTEL
328

This comfortable family friendly hostel sleeps 4, is set on a working farm and is surrounded by spectacular Galloway countryside. The hugely spacious open plan design has oak floors, comfy beds, dining area, wood burning stove, separate kitchen with basic cooking facilities, washroom & W.C. There are also: hot showers, washing/drying facilities, bike wash and store. Breakfast and farm produce available. The ideal base for walkers and cyclists with 7Stanes and NCN Route 7 close by.

DETAILS

- **Open** - All year. All day.
- **Beds** - 4: 1x4.
- **Price/night** - £20pp bed linen provided & beds made up. £80.00 for sole use. Electricity included.

CONTACT: Charlie and Elaine Wannop
Tel: 01557 500238
elaine@castlecreavie.co.uk
www.castlecreavie.co.uk
Castle Creavie, Kirkcudbright, DG6 4QE

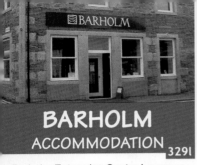

BARHOLM
ACCOMMODATION

329l

Barholm Enterprise Centre houses a variety of businesses including an Arts and Crafts Co-operative and Barholm Accommodation which has en suite shared and private rooms. Perfect for cyclists, walkers, fishermen or those who generally enjoy the outdoors. Facilites include a communal kitchenette (fridge/freezer, kettle, toaster and microwave), sitting room with TV, on-site cycle hire and bike repair facilities & electric car charging.

DETAILS

- **Open** - All year. All Day.
- **Beds** - 25: 1x6, 1x5, 1x4, 1x1, 2x1+ camp-bed, 1x2+ camp-bed
- **Price/night** - from £16.50

CONTACT: Jenny Adams
Tel: 01671 820810
jenny.barholm@gmail.com
barholm-centre.co.uk/barholm-accommodation/
St Johns Street, Creetown, Dumfries and Galloway, DG8 7JE

WELL ROAD
CENTRE

329r

The Well Road Centre sits in its own grounds in the charming town of Moffat. It is ideal for all types of groups, conferences, residential workshops, sports events and outdoor activity clubs. The Centre has two spacious meeting rooms, a large bright self-catering kitchen fully equipped for 65, a games hall for indoor activities, a table tennis room and a snooker room. Bring your own sleeping bags or duvets. Ample parking for cars & minibuses.

DETAILS

- **Open** - All year. All day.
- **Beds** - 70: in 13 rooms (2 en suite).
- **Price/night** - From £830 for two nights mid week for up to 30 people. £25 pp for 31+ . From £955 for two nights weekend for up to 35 people. £25 pp for 31+.

CONTACT: Ben Larmour
Tel: 01683 221040
Ben8363@aol.com
www.wellroadcentre.com
Well Road Centre, Moffat, DG10 9BT

CLEIKUM MILL
LODGE
330

Cleikum Mill Lodge is a renovated characterful building in the heart of the Tweed Valley. The Mill sleeps 12 in total: 8 on the ground floor, the Lower Mill and 4 on the first floor, the Upper Mill. Book individual rooms, a floor or the whole Mill. Innerleithen a 7Stanes trail centre, is on the NCR1 and Southern Upland Way. It has a shop, pubs and cafés.

DETAILS

■ **Open** - All year. All day. Check in after 4pm, check out before 10am.
■ **Beds** - 12: Lower Mill: 1x2, 2x3. Upper Mill: 2x2
■ **Price/night** - Lower Mill: £50 per room + £15 for 3rd person. Sole use 3 nights or more from £459. Upper Mill £100, discounts for 3 nights or more.

CONTACT: Graham and Miriam
Tel: 07790 592747
hello@cleikum-mill-lodge.co.uk
www.cleikum-mill-lodge.co.uk
7 Cleikum Mill, High St, Innerleithen, Scottish Borders EH44 6QT

WEE ROW
HOSTEL

331

Located in the heart of New Lanark World Heritage Site and just one hour's drive from either Glasgow or Edinburgh 'Wee Row' is the perfect base for your holiday. The award winning New Lanark Visitor Centre is on the doorstep; step back in time and rediscover life in this working mill village. The hostel sleeps 62 in 18 private rooms (all en suite) and has terrific views over the River Clyde and surrounding countryside. Facilities include bike storage, laundry and drying room. Cooked breakfasts and evening meals are available.

DETAILS

- **Open** - March- End November
- **Beds** - 62: 6x2, 1x3, 3x3, 8x4 +Studio
- **Price/night** - From £19.50 per person

CONTACT: Reception
Tel: 01555 666 710
weerowhostel@newlanark.org
www.newlanarkhostel.co.uk
Wee Row Hostel, Wee Row, New Lanark, Lanark, Lanarkshire, ML11 9DJ

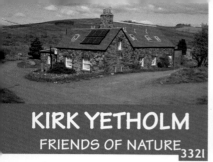

KIRK YETHOLM
FRIENDS OF NATURE 332l

Kirk Yetholm Friends of Nature House is perfectly located at the start/end of the Pennine Way. It is also close to St. Cuthbert's Way, the Borderloop Cycle Route and Sustrans Route 84. It's a great base too for local day hikes, ideal for individuals, families and small groups. Recently upgraded, the house offers a comfortable, friendly and peaceful retreat. Evening meals and breakfast are available in the adjacent hotel.

DETAILS
■ **Open** - All year (Nov-Feb groups only). Reception 5pm-11pm & 8am-10am.
■ **Beds** - 22: 1x7, 1x5, 1x4, 2x2 (twin), 1x2 (bunk).
■ **Price/night** - From £18, under 18's from £15. Discounts for IFN / SYHA / HI.

CONTACT: Manager
Tel: 01573 420639
kirkyetholm@thefriendsofnature.org.uk
www.thefriendsofnature.org.uk
Friends of Nature House, Waukford, Kirk Yetholm, Kelso, Roxburghshire, TD5 8PG

EURO HOSTEL
332r EDINBURGH HALLS

Euro Hostel Edinburgh Halls is the perfect place to base your summer visit to Edinburgh. Available from 4th June to 31st August you can have an apartment to yourself or share with others for a great budget stay. Located in the heart of the Old Town close to the Royal Mile, Euro Hostel Edinburgh Halls is perfect for backpackers, shoppers, groups or those visiting the famous Edinburgh Festival. Single or twin private bedrooms are available or you can rent a whole apartment for up to 12.

DETAILS
■ **Open** - Check-in from 3pm and check-out by 11am
■ **Beds** - 338:
■ **Price/night** - From £20

CONTACT: Reception
Tel: +44 (0) 8454 900 461
edinburgh@eurohostels.co.uk
www.eurohostels.co.uk/edinburgh/
Kincaids Court, Guthrie Street Edinburgh
EH1 1JT

ROYAL MILE
BACKPACKERS
333l

CASTLE ROCK
HOSTEL
333r

Royal Mile Backpackers is a small and lively hostel with its own special character! Perfectly located on the Royal Mile, the most famous street in Edinburgh, Royal Mile Backpackers is the ideal place to stay for the independent traveller.

The comfortable beds and cosy common areas will make you feel at home and the friendly staff are always on hand to help you make the most of your time in Edinburgh.

In a wonderful location, facing south with a sunny aspect and panoramic views over the city, Castle Rock Hostel is just steps away from the city centre with the historic Royal Mile, the busy pubs and late-late nightlife of the Grassmarket and Cowgate. Then of course there is the famous Edinburgh Castle. Most of the rooms have no traffic noise and there are loads of great facilities, 24 hour reception and no curfew. With its beautiful and dramatic skyline Edinburgh is truly one of the world's great cities.

DETAILS

- **Open** - All year, all day. Reception 6.30am - 3am (24hrs during August).
- **Beds** - 46
- **Price/night** - From £11 per person. ID required for check in.

CONTACT: Receptionist
Tel: 0131 557 6120
royalmile@scotlandstophostels.com
www.royalmilebackpackers.com
105 High Street, Edinburgh, EH1 1SG

DETAILS

- **Open** - All year. Reception 24 hours.
- **Beds** - 302
- **Price/night** - From £14 per person. ID required for check in.

CONTACT: Receptionist
Tel: 0131 225 9666
castlerock@scotlandstophostels.com
www.castlerockedinburgh.com
15 Johnston Terrace, Edinburgh, EH1 2PW

HIGH STREET
HOSTEL
334l

The High Street Hostel has become a hugely popular destination for world travellers since opening in 1985 and is one of Europe's best regarded and most atmospheric hostels. Located just off the historic Royal Mile in a 400 year old building, it is your perfect base for exploring all the city's many attractions – and of course its wonderful nightlife. Providing excellence in location, ambience and facilities, the hostel is highly recommended by more than ten of the world's top backpacker travel guides. Come along and see for yourself!

DETAILS
- **Open** - All year. All day.
- **Beds** - 156.
- **Price/night** - From £14 per person. ID required for check in.

CONTACT: Reception
Tel: 0131 557 3984
highstreet@scotlandstophostels.com
www.highstreethostel.com
8 Blackfriars St., Edinburgh, EH1 1NE

EURO HOSTEL
GLASGOW
334r

Your smarter alternative to a hotel in the city, just five mins' walk from Central Station, with friendly staff, a lively bar and clean comfortable private & shared en suite rooms. Perfect for clubbing, shopping and discovering the city's cultural heritage and live music scene. Or for visiting family, coast to coast cycle rides, attending sporting events or just a good sleep to break a long journey. The VIP suites are ideal for groups.

DETAILS
- **Open** - All year. Late and early check outs available.
- **Beds** - 444 rooms: single, doubles, 2, 4, 8 and 14 person all en suite
- **Price/night** - Beds from £10, Rooms from £20. VIP suites from £14pp. Ask about group discounts and special offers.

CONTACT: Reception
Tel: 0141 222 2828
glasgow@euro-hostels.co.uk
www.eurohostels.co.uk/glasgow/
318 Clyde Street, Glasgow, G1 4NR

BLYTHSWOOD
HOUSE
335

In the heart of Glasgow city centre.
Blythswood House is the perfect base
from which to explore everything the
city has to offer. The single rooms are
grouped in flats of 2,6,7 or 8 so perfect
for individuals or groups wanting to visit
Glasgow in the summer. All rooms
are en suite and each flat has self-catering
facilities. Easily accessible from the city's
train and bus stations Blythswood House
welcomes walkers and cyclists.

DETAILS

■ **Open** - Mid June - Early September
■ **Beds** - 170 single rooms within flats 2,
6, 7, or 8 some doubles available.
■ **Price/night** - Individual £38 , £230pp/
week, Student discounts available. 15%
reduction for 6+ people

CONTACT: Rebecca Forsyth
Tel: 0141 566 1121
accommodation@gsa.ac.uk
www.gsa.ac.uk/summervacation
200 West Regent Street, Glasgow,
G2 4DQ

TARTAN
LODGE
336l

Within walking distance of Glasgow city centre, Tartan Lodge, offers contemporary elegance with a smattering of old world charm. Set within a former 19th century church and Masonic Lodge you will find affordable accommodation for budget and business travellers with a selection of double and twin en suite bedrooms and shared dormitories with family facilities. Towels can be hired.

DETAILS
- **Open** - All year. Check in from 2pm. Check out by 11am
- **Beds** - 93: 5xdouble, 2xtwin, 1xtriple. Dorms: 2x3, 8x4, 1x4 female, 2x6, 1x6 female, 2x8
- **Price/night** - Dorms from £10pp. Private rooms from £50 per room

CONTACT: Reception
Tel: 0141 554 5970
info@tartanlodge.co.uk
www.tartanlodge.co.uk
235 Alexandra Parade, Glasgow, G31 3AW

BUTE
BACKPACKERS
336r

Bute Backpackers is a well established 4* hostel, located on the seafront of Rothesay on the Isle of Bute. It accommodates up to 45 people in 14 bedrooms of single, twin, double & family rooms (some en suite). The main house has a sea front sun lounge with TV and free WiFi, a fully equipped self-catering kitchen and a laundry room. There are regular live music sessions and open mic nights. Plenty of free on street parking and a secure bike shed.

DETAILS
- **Open** - All year. 24hr access, no curfew. Reception 9am - 10pm
- **Beds** - 45 beds: 14 bedrooms; 4 family rooms, 4 twin rooms, 6 bunk rooms.
- **Price/night** - £25pp. £15pp (under 16).

CONTACT: Reception
Tel: 01700 501876
butebackpackers@hotmail.com
www.butebackpackers.co.uk
The Pier View, 36 Argyle Street, Rothesay, Isle of Bute, PA20 0AX

CAMPBELTOWN
BACKPACKERS

337

The Campbeltown Backpackers is housed in the Old Schoolhouse, a Grade B listed building. The hostel offers easy access to the facilities of Campbeltown including swimming pool, gym, cinema and distillery tours. It is a good stop along the Kintyre Way which gives walkers spectacular views of the surrounding islands. The area also enjoys very good windsurfing, surfing, mountain bike routes and other major cycle trails.

DETAILS

■ **Open** - All year. Leave by 10.30am on day of departure.
■ **Beds** - 16: 1x6, 1x10
■ **Price/night** - £18pp pre booked, £20 on the day

CONTACT: Alan
Tel: 01586 551188
info@campbeltownbackpackers.co.uk
www.campbeltownbackpackers.co.uk
Kintyre Amenity Trust, Big Kiln,
Campbeltown, Argyll, PA28 6JF

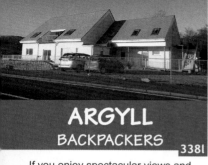

ARGYLL
BACKPACKERS
338l

TORRAN BAY
HOSTEL
338r

If you enjoy spectacular views and watching wildlife in modern comfortable self-catering accommodation then you'll love Argyll Backbackers! Located on the banks of Loch Fyne, just minutes from Cycle Route 78 in the hamlet of Inverneil and perfect for island hopping to/from Arran and Islay. You'll be able to stock up on supplies from Tarbert or Ardrishaig / Lochgilphead, depending on your route.

With 16 en suite rooms, Torran Bay Hostel lies at the southern end of Loch Awe and offers the perfect base for your Highland holiday. Enjoy excellent free fishing or launch your boat from Torran Farm land and spend the day on the 25 mile long Loch. Boats can be hired via the hostel. Other activities include hiking, cycling, bird watching or golf.

DETAILS

■ **Open** - 1st April until 31 October. 1st November - 31 March sole use only
■ **Beds** - 22: 2x2(dbl), 2x2(bunks), 2x4(bunks) en suite, 1x6(bunks) en suite.
■ **Price/night** - £22pp (£20 3 nights or more). Sole use: 1 Nov-31 Mar, £440pn; 20th Dec-6 Jan, £480pn

DETAILS

■ **Open** - All year. All day.
■ **Beds** - 34: 10 x 2 or double, 2 x double and single, 1 x 4 , 2 x 3
■ **Price/night** - From £45 to £72 per room. inc continental breakfast and parking. Group bookings welcome. Please note: prices per room not per person.

CONTACT: Pam Richmond
Tel: 01546 603366 Mobile:07786 157727
argyllbackpackers@sky.com
www.argyllbackpackers.com/
Inverneil Bridge, Inverneil, Lochgilphead,
Argyll, PA30 8ES

CONTACT: Sheila Brolly
Tel: 01546 810 133 or 01546 810 270
sheilabro1@hotmail.co.uk
www.torran-bay.co.uk/accommodation
Torran Farm, Ford, Lochgilphead.
PA31 8RH

INVERARAY
HOSTEL

The historic town of Inveraray, on the western shore of Loch Fyne, is a superb location for exploring Scotland's Southern Highlands and Islands. Inverarary Hostel, a purpose built wooden building, is perfect for independent holidaymakers who enjoy socialising with other guests from many different backgrounds. The hostel offers basic, comfortable accommodation in private rooms & dorms, an excellent self-catering kitchen, dining and sitting areas.

DETAILS

■ **Open** - March to Oct. Sole-use only Nov- Feb. Reception 3.30pm - 9.30pm.
■ **Beds** - 21 in 10 rooms
■ **Price/night** - From £19pp. Breakfast £3.90.

CONTACT: Dawn or Ruben
Tel: 01499 302 454
info@inverarayhostel.co.uk
www.inverarayhostel.co.uk
Dalmally Road, Inveraray, Argyll,
PA32 8XD

BALMAHA
BUNKHOUSE
340l

TROSSACHS
TRYST
340r

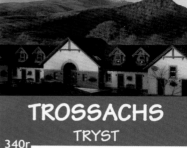

On the banks of Loch Lomond on the West Highland Way, Balmaha Bunkhouse offers quality accommodation. Continental breakfast, bedding, WiFi, tea & coffee are included. The bunkhouse is ideal for hen, stag and family get-togethers. A private self-catering chalet (The Roost) sleeps 4 and there's B&B (en suite) in the main house. Kayaks and Canadian canoes can be hired on site.

Now specialising in group bookings with sole use, the 4* Trossachs Tryst sits amidst beautiful scenery on the edge of the Trossachs National Park and close to the vibrant town of Callender.

The hostel is very well appointed and all rooms are en suite. Use the on-site cycling centre or enjoy the local outdoor activities such as hill walking, pony trekking, Go-ape, Segway treks, water sports and fishing.

DETAILS

- **Open** - Arrive 2pm-7pm, leave by 10am
- **Beds** - Bunkhouse 14: 1x6,1x4 (family),1x2 (double/twin),1x2 (twin); The Roost 4: 1x4; B&B: 1xdbl, 1x2(bunks)
- **Price/night** - £20pp. Sole use: bunkhouse £280, The Roost £80. Dog (bunkhouse only) £5, B&B £35. No cards.

CONTACT: Del and Nikki
Tel: 01360 870343 Mob: 07931217254
enquiries@balmahahouse.co.uk
www.balmahahouse.co.uk
Balmaha, Loch Lomond, G63 0JQ

DETAILS

- **Open** - All year
- **Beds** - Option 1: 32, Option 2: 40, Option 3: 46
- **Price/night** - Option 1: £550 Option 2: £650 Option 3: £750 (approx £16pp). Discounts for longer stays.

CONTACT: Brian Thom
Tel: 07510 765087
bookings@fabb.org.uk
Invertrossachs Road, Callander, Stirling, FK17 8HW

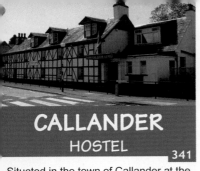

CALLANDER
HOSTEL

341

Situated in the town of Callander at the start of the Loch Lomond and Trossachs National Park, Callander Hostel is a great location for tourists and outdoor enthusiasts alike. With outstanding views over Ben Ledi this Visit Scotland 5* Hostel has comfortable beds, en suite rooms and a fully equipped self-catering kitchen. Everyhting you need for the perfect retreat. The gardens have a children's play area, gas BBQ and seating.

DETAILS

- **Open** - All year. All day. Open 24 hours.
- **Beds** - 28: 2 x 8 bed dorms, 1 x 6, 1 x twin/double, 1 x family room (4)
- **Price/night** - From £18.50 per person in dorm, from £60 per twin/double en suite room.

CONTACT: Patricia
Tel: 01877 331465
bookings@callanderhostel.co.uk
www.callanderhostel.co.uk
6 Bridgend, Callander, FK17 8AH

COMRIE
CROFT

Comrie Croft is a perfect rural retreat for mountain bikers, hikers, families and backpackers, just over an hour from Edinburgh & Glasgow. The 4* hostel offers cosy, home style rooms which are also available for sole group use and weddings. On-site facilities include The Tea Garden cafe, bike shop and lots of grin enducing mountain bike trails, family-friendly valley routes and a well stocked farm shop. A footpath takes you to the vibrant village of Comrie and gives access to stunning glens and mountains.

DETAILS

- **Open** - All year. All day.
- **Beds** - 56 + 46 + 14 (3 units)
- **Price/night** - From £18, U18 free in parent's room. Enquire for sole use.

CONTACT:
Tel: 01764 670140
info@comriecroft.com
www.comriecroft.com
Comrie Croft, By Crieff/Comrie,
Perthshire, PH7 4JZ

BY THE WAY
HOSTEL

343

By The Way Hostel & Campsite lies in the Loch Lomond National Park, halfway between Arrochar's peaks and the grandeur of Glencoe. Perfect for outdoor enthusiasts with excellent walking, climbing and white water rafting. The accommodation ranges from camping, basic trekker huts to a purpose built 4* hostel with twin, double and dormitory rooms, with great self-catering facilities. For more comfort still there are 2 chalets; one with three bedrooms, one with two.

DETAILS

■ **Open** - Hostel/huts closed from end Oct to end March. Camping from April to end Sept. 8am - 10am & 2pm - 8pm.
■ **Beds** - 26 hostel; 36 huts; 50 camping.
■ **Price/night** - Hostel dorms from £20.00pp. Huts vary. Camping £8pp.

CONTACT: Kirsty Burnett
Tel: 01838 400333
info@TyndrumByTheWay.com
www.TyndrumByTheWay.com
Lower Station Rd, Tyndrum, FK20 8RY

PITLOCHRY
BACKPACKERS

344

Located in the centre of beautiful Pitlochry, this friendly, cosy hostel is an old Victorian hotel literally bursting with character and providing dorms and en suite private rooms. Comfy beds come with fitted sheets, duvets and 2 fluffy pillows and private rooms have fresh towels. The bright spacious lounge has comfy sofas and as many free hot drinks as you can drink. There's free WiFi, games, musical instruments and a free pool table. A great place to meet like minded people. You won't want to leave!

DETAILS

- **Open** - March to Nov. 7.30am-1pm and 5pm-10pm (times may vary).
- **Beds** - 79.
- **Price/night** - From £17pp for dorms. Private rooms from £25 pp

CONTACT: Receptionist
Tel: 01796 470044
info@pitlochrybackpackershotel.com
www.pitlochrybackpackershotel.com
134 Atholl Road, Pitlochry, PH16 5AB

JESSIE MACS

345l

n the centre of Birnam just 10 mins' walk from Dunkeld, this refurbished Victorian manse offers a mix of self-catering hostel and B&B accommodation. Your perfect base to discover the mountains, waters, rich culture and heritage of Big Tree Country. Jessie Mac's has doubles, bunk rooms and family rooms, all en suite. One double has wheelchair access.

DETAILS

■ **Open** - Check in: 4pm & 6.30 pm. Check out: by 10.30am.
■ **Beds** - 21: 4x2, 2x4, 1x5
■ **Price/night** - Dorm £20pp +continental breakfast £25 +cooked breakfast £28. Double £28pp (based on 2 sharing) or £33 single occ. Child £10 in shared room. Infants free. Group rates available.

CONTACT: Dot Mechan
Tel: 01350 727 324
info@jessiemacs.co.uk
www.jessiemacs.co.uk
Murthly Terrace, Birnam, Dunkeld
PH8 0BG

AUCHLISHIE
BUNKHOUSE

345r

A brand new (built during winter 2017) family owned bunkhouse situated in Kirriemuir. at the gateway to the Glens of Isla, Prosen and Clova. The Bunkhouse offers excellent facilities to the outdoor enthusiast wanting to experience and enjoy the proximity to the Cairngorms National Park.
This architect designed, purpose built Bunkhouse includes full kitchen, shower and drying room facilities. Cosy duvets, pillows and bed linen are provided. Towels are available at an additional cost.

DETAILS

■ **Open** - All year
■ **Beds** - 24
■ **Price/night** - From £25 per person

CONTACT: James or Nicky
Tel: 07867 476300
yard@auchlishie.co.uk
www.auchlishie-bunkhouse.co.uk
Auchlishie Farm, Kirriemuir, Angus
DD8 4LS

PROSEN
HOSTEL
346

Glenprosen is the most intimate of the Angus Glens on the southernmost edge of the Cairngorms National Park. Two Munros; the Mayar and Driesh link Glenprosen to the Cairngorms plateau. Prosen Hostel is also close to the upgraded East Cairngorms footpath network. Converted to the latest and greenest specification, the 4* hostel offers cosy, quality accommodation for 18. With 4 rooms, sleeping 4, 4 and 6 in bunks and a family room sleeping 4. You can also hire the nearby village hall.

DETAILS

■ **Open** - All year. All day.
■ **Beds** - 18:1x6, 3x4
■ **Price/night** - £18 - £22 pp. Min periods & prices apply for Xmas and New Year.

CONTACT: Hector or Robert
Tel: 01575 540238/302
ihg@prosenhostel.co.uk
www.prosenhostel.co.uk
Prosen Hostel, Balnaboth, Kirriemuir, Angus, DD8 4SA

BALLATER
HOSTEL

347

Ballater Hostel (formerly Habitat @ Ballater) lies in the centre of Ballater, near Balmoral, on the east side of the Cairngorms National Park. Traditional dorms and private rooms, along with large open plan kitchen/dining/communal area. Drying room and cycle storage also available. Either book whole hostel, a room or just a bed - no minimum stay. Excellent facilities, comfortable beds and a warm and friendly welcome awaits you – the kettle is always on!

DETAILS

■ **Open** - All year. Reception open 8-10am & 5-10pm. No access 10am-5pm.
■ **Beds** - 28: 1x8, 1x6, 1x2, 3x4 (family)
■ **Price/night** - Dorm beds from £18.70. Private rooms from £29.50 per room.

CONTACT: Dominique & Daniel
Tel: 01339 753752
info@ballater-hostel.com
www.ballater-hostel.com
Bridge Square, Ballater, AB35 5QJ

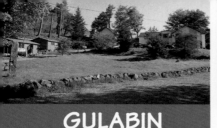

GULABIN
LODGE

348l

Gulabin Lodge nestles in Glenshee at the foot of Beinn Gulabin and is the nearest accommodation to the Glenshee ski slopes. The 4* lodge offers excellent accommodation for individuals, families and groups. On-site there are many outdoor activities including a ski school and equipment hire, mountain bike hire, school residentials and much more. Meals can be provided for groups and also transport to and from airports and stations. In addition to the lodge a separate 12 bed house is also available.

DETAILS
■ **Open** - All year. 24 hours.
■ **Beds** - 37: 9 rooms available.
■ **Price/night** - From £20pp. Contact for fully catered stays and private rooms.

CONTACT: Darren and Tereza
Tel: 01250 885255/ 07799 847014
info@gulabinlodge.co.uk
www.gulabinoutdoors.co.uk
Spittal of Glenshee, By Blairgowrie,
PH10 7QE

BRAEMAR LODGE
BUNKHOUSE

348r

Surrounded by the beauty and tranquillity of Deeside, Braemar Lodge Hotel and Bunkhouse are just a two minute walk from the village. Braemar Lodge Hotel, a former Victorian shooting lodge, is set in extensive grounds. The great value bunkhouse provides comfortable accommodation for up to 12 people within the hotel grounds. The bunkhouse is equipped with two shower rooms, one of which is suitable for wheelchairs. There's a generous, fully equipped, self-catering kitchen, but you are welcome to sample the excellent hotel meals. All bed linen and towels are supplied.

DETAILS
■ **Open** - All year. All day.
■ **Beds** - 12: 3x4
■ **Price/night** - From £17 per person

CONTACT: Reception
Tel: 01339 741627
mail@braemarlodge.co.uk
www.braemarlodge.co.uk
6 Glenshee Rd, Braemar, AB35 5YQ

ABERNETHY
BUNKHOUSE
349l

Sharing a car park with the Speyside Way, the converted Nethy Station offers all that a group of 12-26 could expect from a bunkhouse. It is well equipped and fully central heated. Most rooms have triple bunks and there is a 2 bunk room with unusual access, known as Narnia, as you get there through a wardrobe! Self-catering or catered options. Stag and hen groups welcomed. The bunkhouse is only 200 yards from the local shop, butcher and pub.

 GROUPS ONLY

DETAILS
- **Open** - All year. Anytime.
- **Beds** - 26: 2x9,4x2
- **Price/night** - £16.75 per person. After the minimum of 12 you just pay for those who stay. 10% discount midweek and 20% discount for stays of over 4 nights.

CONTACT: Patricia or Richard
Tel: 01479 821 370
info@nethy.org
www.nethy.org
Station Road, Nethy Bridge, PH25 3DN

ARDENBEG
BUNKHOUSE
349r

Part of the award-winning Craggan Outdoors activity centre, Ardenbeg offers good value, well appointed bunkhouse accommodation with the extra benefit of a large private garden with BBQ, picnic tables & a children's play area. The property is situated on a quiet residential street in Grantown-on-Spey, the historic capital of Strathspey, just a 15 mins' drive from Aviemore and all its amenities. For adventures even closer at hand you can organise a whole host of activities through Craggan Outdoors.

DETAILS
- **Open** - All year. 24 hours access.
- **Beds** - 23: 1x4, 1x5, 1x6, 1x8.
- **Price/night** - £17.25 - £25pp, subject to number of people & duration of stay.

CONTACT: Keith & Jill Ballam
Tel: 01479 873283 / 01479 872824
info@cragganoutdoors.co.uk
www.cragganoutdoors.co.uk
Grant Road, Grantown-on-Spey, Moray
PH26 3LD

FINDHORN
VILLAGE HOSTEL
350

Findhorn Village Hostel is just a stone's throw from the beautiful Moray Coast. Great wildlife sites and the Speyside distilleries are within reach. The hostel provides newly renovated self-catering accommodation for groups or individuals. There are shared bunkrooms, a two person room and an en suite family room. A new annex (6 beds) has a small kitchenette and en suite shower rooms.

DETAILS

- **Open** - All year. Office hours 11am-3pm Mon to Fri.
- **Beds** - 34: 28 in hostel & 6 in Annex; 2x8; 1x2; 1x4/5
- **Price/night** - £19pp. Groups £17pp (min of £170). Bedlinen £3.50. Continental b/fast for groups £4.50.

CONTACT: Justina
Tel: 01309 692339 Mob: 07496 230266
findhornvillagecentre@gmail.com
www.findhornvillagehostel.com
Church Place, Findhorn, Forres, Moray, IV36 3YR

THE SAIL LOFT
BUNKHOUSE
351

Overlooking the beach and the Moray Firth, The Sail Loft bunkhouse has a stunning location. Newly converted from a former sail making loft the bunkhouse is modern and well equipped. It provides self-catering accommodation for 25 in a mixture of single accessible, twin, triple and bunk rooms, with secure cycle storage, cycle wash-down facilities and an outdoor wood fired hot tub. The Sail Loft Bunkhouse is a short easy walk from the historic harbour and town of Portsoy with its wide range of amenities and 10 mins' drive from the eastern end of the Moray Coast Trail at Cullen.

DETAILS

- **Open** - All year.
- **Beds** - 25
- **Price/night** - From £23 per person.

CONTACT: Ian Tillett
Tel: 01261 842695
contact@portsoysailloft.org
www.portsoysailloft.org/
Back Green, Portsoy, AB45 2AF

INVERNESS
STUDENT HOTEL

352

The cosy and friendly Student Hotel enjoys panoramic views of the town and the mountains beyond. Your perfect place to unwind, just yards from the city's varied night-life and a few mins' walk from bus and train stations. Relax in the fabulous lounge with real log fire and drink as much free tea, coffee & hot chocolate as you like. Visit the beautiful ancient pine forest of Glen Affric or the Culloden Battlefield. Famous Loch Ness lies just a few miles upstream and of course has its own special wild animal.

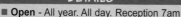

DETAILS

- **Open** - All year. All day. Reception 7am - 10.30pm.
- **Beds** - 57.
- **Price/night** - From £15 per night. ID required for check in.

CONTACT: Receptionist
Tel: 01463 236 556
info@invernessstudenthotel.com
www.invernessstudenthotel.com
8 Culduthel Road, Inverness, IV2 4AB

LOCH NESS
BACKPACKERS

353l

This 18th century Highland farm house provides warm & friendly hostel accommodation. Ideally situated within walking distance of Loch Ness, Urquhart Castle, on the Great Glen Way and with pubs, restaurants and supermarket close by. Residents only bar offers over 70 Scottish beers and 25 Scotch whiskies. Horse riding, fishing, watersports and mountain biking can all be arranged locally. Free parking and free WiFi. Bike storage available except in Jul/Aug.

DETAILS
- **Open** - All year, All day.
- **Beds** - Dorm beds: 32. Family rooms: 2. Private doubles/twins: 3
- **Price/night** - From £17pp. Discounts apply to groups or long term stays

CONTACT: Patrick & Nikki Kipfmiller
Tel: 01456 450807
info@lochness-backpackers.com
www.lochness-backpackers.com
Coiltie Farmhouse, East Lewiston,
Drumnadrochit, Inverness, IV63 6UJ

THE LOCHSIDE
HOSTEL
353r

Perched right on the banks of Loch Ness, the Lochside Hostel has amazing views up and down the loch and can give you direct access to the water's edge. Why not go for a dip in Scotland's largest water body? Take a walk to watch for wildlife? Or even hunt the elusive Nessie!? The Great Glen walking route passes the front door and the End to End cycle route is nearby. Drumnadrochit is just 12 miles away by boat. Recently opened by MacBackpackers, an award winning tour company who also own 3 hostels in Edinburgh, a great stay awaits!

DETAILS
- **Open** - Check in 2pm, check out 10am
- **Beds** - 47: 3x2 (twin), 2x4 (female), 5x4, 1x5, 1x8 all mixed dorms.
- **Price/night** - From £17

CONTACT: Reception
Tel: 01320 351274
lochness@macbackpackers.com
thelochsidehostel.com
Altsigh, Inverness. IV63 7YD

MORAGS LODGE
LOCH NESS

354

A multi-award winning 4* hostel with a range of rooms to meet all needs and budgets in the bustling village of Fort Augustus on the banks of Loch Ness. Your perfect base to explore the Loch Ness area and an ideal stop off on the Great Glen Way. Surrounded by stunning mountain scenery and set in wooded grounds the hostel boasts 24 hour self-catering facilities, excellent home-made cheap meal options, a rustic bar, free WiFi, bike hire and ample car parking.

DETAILS

- **Open** - Open all year. Check in from 4pm (earlier by arrangement).
- **Beds** - 75: 1x7, 6x6, 6x4, 4x2/3
- **Price/night** - From £23pp in dorm beds. Doubles/twins from £29pp. Family rooms from £81.

CONTACT: Claire
Tel: 01320 366289
info@moragslodge.com
www.moragslodge.com
Bunoich Brae, Fort Augustus, PH32 4DG

SADDLE MOUNTAIN
HOSTEL

355l

GREAT GLEN
HOSTEL

355r

Saddle Mountain Hostel is a small and friendly 4* hostel in Invergarry, between Loch Ness and Fort William and at the junction with the road to Skye. The delightful hostel sleeps 24 people in 5 rooms. It has a large kitchen, dining room and lounge, free WiFi, a purpose-built drying room and bike storage. A Great location for Munro bagging, walking, cycling, scenic tours, water sports, fishing, and wildlife watching.

Located between mountains and lochs 20 miles north of Fort William and 10 miles south of Loch Ness, the Great Glen Hostel is your ideal base. Perfect for touring the Highlands, bagging Munros or paddling rivers and lochs. It's only a short walk to the Great Glen Way. The hostel provides comfortable, well appointed accommodation in twin, family and dormitory rooms and has a shop where you can buy your essentials.

DETAILS

- **Open** - All year except Nov. Closed Tues & Wed Dec-Easter. Check-in 4.30-10pm.
- **Beds** - 24: 2 x 6, 1 x 5 (1 dbl, 3 singles), 1 x 4, 1 x 3 (1 dbl, 1 single).
- **Price/night** - From £18pp Whole hostel prices available on request.

CONTACT: Helen or Gregor
Tel: 01809 501412
info@saddlemountainhostel.co.uk
www.saddlemountainhostel.co.uk
Mandally Road, Invergarry, PH35 4HP

DETAILS

- **Open** - All year. All day. Please call first Nov-March.
- **Beds** - 49: 3x2, 1x3, 4x5, 2x6, 1x8
- **Price/night** - Dorm beds from £20. Twin rooms from £24 pppn. Whole hostel for sole use from £450 per night.

CONTACT: The Manager
Tel: 01809 501430
bookings@greatglenhostel.com
www.greatglenhostel.com
South Laggan, Spean Bridge, Invernesshire, PH34 4EA

ÀITE
CRUINNICHIDH

Àite Cruinnichidh, 15 miles northeast of Fort William, occupies a unique sheltered spot adjacent to the Monessie Gorge where you can explore remote glens, mountain passes and lochs. The hostel has a fully equipped kitchen/dining room, sitting room, excellent showers, sauna, seminar room and garden. All bedding is provided. There is a good selection of maps, board games and books. Guests are encouraged to socialise and enjoy the natural environment that the hostel has to offer.

DETAILS

■ **Open** - All year. All day.
■ **Beds** - 28 : 1x6, 4x4, 1x twin, 1x double, 1x family/double en suite.
■ **Price/night** - From £16 per person.

CONTACT: Gavin or Nicola
Tel: 01397 712315
gavin@highland-hostel.co.uk
www.highland-hostel.co.uk
1 Achluachrach, By Roy Bridge, Near Fort William, PH31 4AW

SMIDDY
BUNKHOUSE
357

Find a friendly welcome at this warm & comfortable mountain hostel for your group or family. Enjoy the loch-side location overlooking the Caledonian Canal, 4 miles from Fort William & Ben Nevis with the meeting of the West Highland Way and Great Glen Way on your doorstep. Perfect for the outdoor enthusiast with advice/instruction/guiding from resident instructors for walking/climbing; river, loch and sea kayaking & dinghy sailing. Equipment hire available. AALS licensed & DofE Approved Activity Provider for expeditions.

DETAILS

- **Open** - All year. All day (with key).
- **Beds** - 24: 3x4, 2x6.
- **Price/night** - £16-£22.50(incl bedding).

CONTACT: John or Tina
Tel: 01397 772467
enquiry@highland-mountain-guides.co.uk
www.accommodation-fortwilliam.co.uk
Snowgoose Mountain Centre, Station Road, Corpach, Fort William, PH33 7JH

BANK STREET
LODGE

358

Bank Street Lodge is 100 metres from Fort William High Street which has numerous shops, pubs and restaurants. There is a fully equipped kitchen with cooker, fridge, microwave, cutlery and crockery provided. The common room lounge has a TV, it also provides tables and chairs for meals and a snack vending machine. All bedding is provided. Some rooms are en suite (twins, doubles and family). WiFi is also available in the lounge/TV room.

DETAILS

■ **Open** - All year (closed for 3 days at Xmas). 24 hour reception. Entry from 1.00pm, depart by 10.00am.
■ **Beds** - 43: 6 x 4, 4 x 3, 1 x 7
■ **Price/night** - From £18 to £25.00 per person. Group rates available.

CONTACT: Reception
Tel: 01397 700070
bankstreetlodge@btconnect.com
www.bankstreetlodge.co.uk
Bank Street, Fort William, PH33 6AY

FORT WILLIAM
BACKPACKERS
359

Surrounded by spectacular mountain scenery, Fort William is a mecca for those with a spirit of adventure. You can start (or end) the 'West Highland Way' in Fort William, hike or bike along mountain trails, go for a boat trip on the sea loch or just take it easy amidst the wonderful scenery. Even in winter Fort William stays busy with skiing, snow-boarding, mountaineering and ice-climbing. Set on a hillside above the town, with wonderful views, this cosy hostel provides all you'll need after a day in the hills.

DETAILS

- **Open** - All year. All day. Reception 7am-noon & 5pm-10.30pm
- **Beds** - 38
- **Price/night** - From £17 per person. ID required for check-in.

CONTACT: Receptionist
Tel: 01397 700711
info@fortwilliambackpackers.com
www.fortwilliambackpackers.com
Alma Road, Fort William, PH33 6HB

COORIE DOON
CABIN
360l

Ideally situated next to the road to the Isles, the Caledonian Canal (route of the Great Glen Way) and close to the West Highland Way, Nevis Range and the Glencoe Mountain Resort, this stylish cabin offers easy access to world-class hiking, climbing, skiing, mountain biking, or simply enjoying the amazing view. Es, the owner and a mountaineer, is happy to offer advice. After a day of adventures return to the luxury of a drying room, underfloor heating and sauna!

DETAILS
- **Open** - All year. Check in 4pm-10pm, check out 10am.
- **Beds** - 6: 2x3 (each room has one double and a single bed)
- **Price/night** - From £100 ask for details

CONTACT: Es Tresidder
Tel: 07503 775874
e.tresidder@gmail.com
www.fb.com/CoorieDoon
Coorie Doon, Old Banavie Road, Banavie, Fort William, PH33 7PZ

CORRAN
BUNKHOUSE
360r

Corran Bunkhouse, lies on the shore of Loch Linnhe, 8 miles south of Fort William and 7 miles north of Glencoe. With two fully equipped, 4* self-catering bunkhouses; one sleeping 12 (plus 9 in an annex) and the other 20, it is an ideal base for small and large groups. All bedrooms are en suite. There are fully equipped kitchen/dining areas, drying room, central heating, laundry facilities, private parking and a steam room situated in the smaller bunkhouse. Children and pets welcome.

DETAILS
- **Open** - All year.
- **Beds** - 41: 11x2, 2x3, 2x4, 1x5
- **Price/night** - £24pp, £22pp groups. £30 single occupancy. Includes bedding.

CONTACT: Alan & Halina
Tel: 01855 821000
corranbunkhouse@btconnect.com
www.corranbunkhouse.co.uk
Corran Ferry Approach Road, Onich, Fort William, PH33 6SE

BLACKWATER
HOSTEL
361

Blackwater Hostel is in Kinlochleven, surrounded by the Mamore mountains, between Glencoe and Ben Nevis. An ideal stopover for families, cyclists, walkers, climbers and those who are walking the West Highland Way. A 4* bunkhouse with private en suite rooms, free WiFi, central heating, self-catering kitchen and a dining & conference area. There are supermarkets, pubs & restaurants in the village. Glamping pods and campsite are also available with their own facilities.

DETAILS

■ **Open** - All year.
■ **Beds** - 39: 2, 3,4, 8 bed bunk rooms.
■ **Price/night** - £20 to £22 pp including bedding.

CONTACT: Patrick
Tel: 01855 831253
black.water@virgin.net
www.blackwaterhostel.co.uk
Lab Road, Kinlochleven, Argyll, PH50 4SG

GLENCOE
INDEPENDENT HOSTEL
362l

362r
KINGS HOUSE
BUNKHOUSE

Glencoe Independent Hostel lies in secluded woodland midway between Glencoe village and Clachaig Inn with access to world class cycling, walking, climbing and kayaking. The Glencoe Ski Centre and The West Highland Way are just 20 mins away. The hostel has 4 rooms with comfortable communal spaces. Also available are an alpine bunkhouse sleeping 16, 4 luxury caravans and 3 luxury log cabins.

DETAILS
■ **Open** - All year (phone in Nov and Dec). 9am - 9 pm.
■ **Beds** - 65: hostel:26, bunkhouse:16, caravans: 4x2-4, cabins: 2x2, 1x3
■ **Price/night** - From £12.50 to £50 per person.

CONTACT: Keith or Davina
Tel: 01855 811906
info@glencoehostel.co.uk
www.glencoehostel.co.uk
Glencoe Independent Hostel, Glencoe, Argyll, PH49 4HX

The Kings House Bunkhouse is right on the West Highland Way amid spectacular Scottish mountain scenery. With 32 beds across 10 rooms there is ample storage for your bags and each bunk has a locker, reading light, power socket, linen and towels. Ideal for travellers needing a stopping point or as a base to explore all that Glencoe has to offer and beyond. You'll find skiing, walking and mountain biking on the doorstep. The Way Inn café also offers all day dining and packed lunches from 7am to 11pm each day.
Jan 2018: King House is closed, hoping to reopen later in the year.

DETAILS
■ **Open** - All year. All day.
■ **Beds** - 32: 1x6, 4x4, 5x2
■ **Price/night** - From £20pp

CONTACT: Jessie Cattanach
Tel: 01855 851 259
contact@kingshousehotel.co.uk
www.kingshousehotel.co.uk
Glencoe, Argyll, PH49 4HY

BACKPACKERS
PLUS OBAN

363

Many people's favourite hostel thanks to its friendly atmosphere, the beautiful seaside town setting and its excellent facilities. Enjoy free WiFi, free breakfast, free all-day hot drinks, clean spacious rooms, secure bike storage, laundry service, communal areas, strong hot showers, comfortable beds and a well-equipped self-catering kitchen. The lively town of Oban has direct ferry access to the many beautiful Scottish Isles.

DETAILS

■ **Open** - All year. Reception 8am to 10:30am and 4pm to 10pm.
■ **Beds** - 50-60 dorm beds, family, double, twin rooms, some en suite.
■ **Price/night** - Dorms from £17pp, private rooms from £21pp.

CONTACT: Receptionist
Tel: 01631 567189
info@backpackersplus.com
www.backpackersplus.com
The Old Church, Breadalbane St,
Oban, Argyll, PA34 5PH

OBAN
BACKPACKERS

364

Perfectly situated in the heart of Oban, "the Gateway to the Isles", just 10 mins' walk from the bus, train & ferry terminals. This friendly hostel is a great place to stay and unwind. The fabulous sociable lounge has a real fire, pool table, free WiFi, comfy sofas and unlimited free hot drinks. The kitchen is fully equipped, perfect for cooking your favourite meals. Large dorm beds come complete with bedding including 2 comfy pillows. The hot powerful showers are legendary! Knowledgeable and friendly staff will help you make the most of your time in Oban.

DETAILS

- **Open** - March - Nov. 7am - 10pm.
- **Beds** - 54: 1x12, 1x10, 1x8, 4x6
- **Price/night** - From £15. Whole hostel bookings please email for quote.

CONTACT: Reception
Tel: 01631 562 107
info@obanbackpackers.com
www.obanbackpackers.com
Breadalbane Street, Oban, PA34 5NZ

CORRAN
HOUSE
365

Experience a warm welcome & value accommodation in Oban for singles, couples, families and groups. Enjoy a large self-catering kitchen, spacious TV lounge, comfortable rooms & big beds. Corran House is perfect for exploring Argyll and the inner Hebrides & is close to the bus, train and ferry. Downstairs try MarkieDans bar for tasty meals, live music and great Highland hospitality.

DETAILS

■ **Open** - All year. Reception 3-9pm. Check in only after 3pm
■ **Beds** - 52: 26 bunks, 5x4 1x6. Plus guest rooms: 26
■ **Price/night** - Bunks £18/£20 en suite. Guest rooms £27.50-£40pp (2 sharing). Singles from £45. Winter discounts.

CONTACT:
Tel: 01631 566040
enquiries@corranhouseoban.co.uk
www.corranhouseoban.co.uk
1 Victoria Crescent, Corran Esplanade,
Oban, Argyll, PA34 5PN

CRAIGNURE
BUNKHOUSE
366l

Craignure, a superior eco-sensitive bunkhouse, purpose built in 2014, is the perfect base for your Mull adventure. Set on the water's edge close to the ferry port, there's the Craignure Inn next door for traditional island hospitality. The 4 well-appointed bunkrooms have en suite showers and there's a spacious well appointed communal area with kitchen, ample dining and relaxing space.

DETAILS
- **Open** - All year, closed 11am-4pm for cleaning.
- **Beds** - 20: 2x4, 2x6
- **Price/night** - £22 per person per night. 4 berth rooms, £80 per night. 6 berth rooms, £120 per night. Whole hostel, £380 per night, by prior arrangement.

CONTACT: Chris, Nina or Eli
Tel: 01680 812043 Mob:07900 692973
info@craignure-bunkhouse.co.uk
www.craignure-bunkhouse.co.uk
Craignure Bunkhouse, Craignure, Isle Of Mull, Argyll And Bute, PA65 6AY

SHIELING
HOLIDAYS
366r

The perfect base for all Mull has to offer. Right on the sea, with views to Ben Nevis. Your accommodation is in shared Shielings, unique carpeted cottage tents which are clean, spacious and have real beds for 2, 4, or 6 people. Or hire a private Shieling or a self-catering cottage. There are super showers, a communal Shieling with woodburning stove, TV & launderette. Free WiFi. Campfire. Stroll to the ferry, pub, café, shops, and swimming pool. Catch the bus for Tobermory, Iona and Staffa.

DETAILS
- **Open** - April to October, 24 hours (reception 8am - 10pm).
- **Beds** - 18: 6 x 2, 1 x 6.
- **Price/night** - £16 pp. Under 15s £12 pp. Bedding etc £4.50 pp

CONTACT: David Gracie
Tel: 01680 812496
sales@shielingholidays.co.uk
www.shielingholidays.co.uk
Craignure, Mull, Argyll, PA65 6AY

ROSS OF MULL
BUNKHOUSE

This new bunkhouse is located less than a mile from the ferry link to Iona at Fionnphort. Ideally situated for exploring the exciting wildlife, rich history, dramatic cliffs, white shell-sand beaches and unspoilt environment of the Ross of Mull. Also a perfect base for day trips to Staffa, the Treshnish Isles and Iona. There is a well equipped kitchen, wood burner and stunning views. Larger groups could consider Achaban House next door. (see page 368)

DETAILS

- **Open** - All year. All day.
- **Beds** - 8: 2x4
- **Price/night** - Bunk: £22, 4 bunk room:£88 (4 people), £75 (3 people) £62 (2 people), £44 (1 person). Sole use £176. Towel hire £2

CONTACT: Rachel Ball
Tel: 07759 615200
info@rossofmullbunkhouse.co.uk
www.rossofmullbunkhouse.co.uk
Fionnphort, Isle of Mull PA66 6BL

ACHABAN
HOUSE

Perfect for those wanting a luxurious B&B on the Ross of Mull with the option to self-cater. Achaban House is close to Fionnphort with its ferry to Iona and day trips to Staffa, Lunga and the Treshnish Isles. Ideal for walkers, cyclists or wildlife lovers. Rooms are en suite or with private bathrooms, breakfast is included. Larger groups could consider Ross Of Mull Bunkhouse next door (Page 367)

DETAILS

- **Open** - All year. All day.
- **Beds** - 14: 1x5, 2x2 (twin), 2x2 (double), 1x1
- **Price/night** - Single room: £46. Double/twin rooms: £75. Family 5 bed room: £101-135. Sole use £440 (£400pn for 2 or more nights)

CONTACT: Matt Oliver
Tel: 01681 700205
info@achabanhouse.co.uk
www.achabanhouse.co.uk
Achaban House, Fionnphort, Isle of Mull, PA66 6BL

IONA HOSTEL

Tucked into the rocky outcrops on a working croft, Iona Eco Hostel has spectacular views of the isles and mountains beyond. The land has been worked for generations, creating the familiar Hebridean patchwork of wildflower meadow, crops and grazing land. It offers quiet sanctuary for those that seek it, within easy reach of island activities. Whether travelling on your own, with friends, or as a group, Iona Hostel promises a warm welcome. Tourist board 4 star. Green Tourism Gold.

DETAILS

■ **Open** - All year. Closed 11am-1pm for cleaning - no curfew.
■ **Beds** - 21: 1x2, 2x4, 1x5, 1x6.
■ **Price/night** - £21.00 adult / £17.50 under 10's (bedding included).

CONTACT: John MacLean
Tel: 01681 700781
info@ionahostel.co.uk
www.ionahostel.co.uk
Iona Hostel, Iona, Argyll, PA76 6SW

COLONSAY
BACKPACKERS

Come to Colonsay Backpackers
Lodge and savour the idyll of this
Inner Hebridean island. Explore the
magnificent sandy beaches, ancient
forests and beautiful lochs. Wildlife
abounds; spot dolphins, seals, otters and
many rare birds.
The pub, café & shop are 3 miles away.
Or buy fresh lobster, crab and oysters
from the fishing boats. The lodge is a
refurbished former gamekeeper's house
with bothies. Centrally heated, it has 2
twin, 3 twin bunk and 2 three-bedded
rooms.

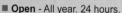
DETAILS

- **Open** - All year. 24 hours.
- **Beds** - 16: 5 x 2; 2 x 3
- **Price/night** - £28pp twin, £22pp bothy

CONTACT: The Manager
Tel: 01951 200312
cottages@colonsayholidays.co.uk
www.colonsayholidays.co.uk
Colonsay Estate Cottages, Isle of
Colonsay, Argyll, PA61 7YP

COLL
BUNKHOUSE
371

Coll Bunkhouse 5* self-catering hostel accommodation is a mile from the ferry terminal & close to local amenities. Ideal for groups or individuals, short or longer stays. A half hour from the mainland by plane, under 3 hours by ferry. This beautiful Hebridean island is ideal for walking, stargazing, wildlife, cycling, water sports or chilling amidst stunning scenery. Visit quiet and beautiful spaces and beaches and enjoy fine island hospitality. A warm welcome awaits you.

DETAILS
■ **Open** - All year. 24 hours.
■ **Beds** - 16: 2x6, 1x4
■ **Price/night** - £22pp (dorm). Private rooms from £110 (quin), £80 (quad), £65 (triple), £50 (twin). Discount of 10% to 55% for sole use for 2 nights or more.

CONTACT: Jane
Tel: 01879 230217
jane@developmentcoll.org.uk
www.collbunkhouse.com
Arinagour, Isle of Coll, Argyll, PA78 6SY

MILLHOUSE
HOSTEL
372

Tiree is an idyllic Hebridean island surrounded by white beaches and crystal clear seas. Perfect for outdoor pursuits & wildlife enthusiasts, Millhouse offers you 4* facilities and free WiFi. You can hire bikes, visit the lighthouse museum, watch the seals or enjoy watersports at Loch Bhasapol (200m away). For walkers Tiree Pilgrimage route passes close by. Tiree has a resident RSPB warden and there are handy bird and otter hides for you to use.

DETAILS

- **Open** - Mar-Oct (Winter by arrangement).Open all day. Check in 4pm. Check out 10am.
- **Beds** - Hostel 16 : 2 x 2/3, 2 x 5.
- **Price/night** - Dorm from £24pp. Twin from £28pp. Family £72-£120 per room.

CONTACT: David Naylor
Tel: 01879 220892
mail@tireemillhouse.co.uk
www.tireemillhouse.co.uk
Cornaigmore, Isle of Tiree, PA77 6XA

LISMORE
BUNKHOUSE
373

This a warm, cosy and comfy bunkhouse is the perfect base from which to explore the beautiful Inner Hebrides Isle of Lismore and its surroundings.

The bunkhouse sleeps 12 in a mix of dorms and private rooms whilst Lismore's only campsite has 5 pitches and hook ups for 2 camper vans. The Isle of Lismore is just 7 miles by car ferry from Oban and is a tranquil, unspoilt island surrounded by stunning mountain scenery. Perfect for wildlife and history lovers as well as walkers, cyclists and those wanting to get away from it all.

DETAILS

- **Open** - All year round
- **Beds** - 12:
- **Price/night** - From £18pp.

CONTACT: Clare
Tel: 07720 975433
lismorebunkhouse@gmail.com
www.fb.com/thelismorebunkhouse/
Isle of Lismore, PA34 5UG

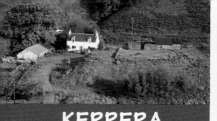

KERRERA
BUNKHOUSE
374l

GLENFINNAN
SLEEPING CAR
374r

On the island of Kerrera off the coast from Oban, overlooking the coast and stunning Gylen Castle. Self-cater using the small kitchen. No shops on the island but lunches are available in the Kerrera Tea Garden next door. Larger groups can hang out in the Byre, with wood stove and sofas. Or try bell tent glamping with bed, wood burner and stunning views of the surrounding islands.

Glenfinnan Sleeping Car provides unique accommodation in an historic railway carriage next to the station and close to Glenfinnan Viaduct (used in Harry Potter films). An ideal location for the mountains of Lochaber, Rough Bounds, Moidart and Ardgour, a good starting point for bothy expeditions and a useful stop-over en route to Skye. The Sleeping Car has a fully equipped kitchen, showers & drying room. The dining coach provides excellent meals in the daytime to give you a break from self-catering.

DETAILS
- **Open** - All year. 10am to 6pm. No curfew.
- **Beds** - Bunkhouse 7: 1x4, 1x3 double/ twin + single. Bell tent: 1x2
- **Price/night** - Bunkhouse: sole use £100, £80 thereafter. The Byre £25 (inc firewood), Bell tent: £45 (inc firewood)

CONTACT: Aideen and Martin Shields
Tel: 01631 566 367
info@kerrerabunkhouse.co.uk
www.kerrerabunkhouse.co.uk
Lower Gylen, Isle of Kerrera, By Oban, Argyll PA34 4SX

DETAILS
- **Open** - All year. 24 hours.
- **Beds** - 10
- **Price/night** - £15 pppn, £5 for hire of bedding and towels, £130 for sole use.

CONTACT: John or Hege
Tel: 01397 722295
glenfinnanstationmuseum@gmail.com
www.glenfinnanstationmuseum.co.uk
Glenfinnan Station, Glenfinnan, nr Fort William, PH37 4LT

KNOYDART
BUNKHOUSE

Knoydart is a remote peninsula on the west coast of Scotland reachable only by boat or long hike. A community enterprise, the bunkhouse runs on green principals and is just 2 mins' walk to the beach and 10 mins to Inverie with its pub, post office, shop and ferry. There are 4 bedrooms and comfy communal areas. Bed linen and duvets provided.

Ranger service and deer stalking available. Bring your own food and torch!

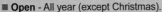

DETAILS

- **Open** - All year (except Christmas).
- **Beds** - 25: 1x10, 1x7, 1x8
- **Price/night** - £18 per adult, £10 for children under 16. Block bookings £395. Special rates for schools, youth groups and Duke of Edinburgh Award Scheme.

CONTACT: Fiona
Tel: 01687 462163
bunkhouse@knoydart.org
www.knoydart-foundation.com
Inverie, Knoydart, By Mallaig, Inverness-shire PH41 4PL

SHEENAS
BACKPACKERS
376l

ISLE OF MUCK
BUNKHOUSE
376r

The Backpackers Lodge, the oldest croft house in Mallaig, offers a homely base from which to explore the Inner Hebrides, the famous white sands of Morar and the remote peninsula of Knoydart. Mallaig is a working fishing village with all the excitement of the boats landing. You can see the seals playing in the harbour and take whale and dolphin watching trips.

The hostel provides excellent budget accommodation with central heating, a well equipped kitchen/common room and free WiFi. Hot water and heating provided by renewable energy.

This self-catering hostel can also be hired as a holiday cottage. The bunkhouse overlooks the ferry port of Port Mor, it is near to The Craft Shop & Tearoom and to the island's Community Hall. The Isle of Muck is just 2 miles long by 1 mile wide and has a population of 38 people. With a rich cultural heritage and amazing wildlife, Muck is the perfect place to unwind. BYO towel, sleeping bag and supplies. There are no shops.

DETAILS

- **Open** - All year. 9am-8pm
- **Beds** - 12: 2 x 6
- **Price/night** - £21 per person.

DETAILS

- **Open** -All year. Monthly lets available out of season.
- **Beds** - 8: 3x2(bunks) 1x2 (double)
- **Price/night** - £20pp (plus £5 per stay if bed linen is required). £80 sole use. £490 for a weeks sole use.

CONTACT: Norman or Sheena
Tel: 01687 462764
backpackers@btinternet.com
www.mallaigbackpackers.co.uk
Harbour View, Mallaig, Inverness-shire,
PH41 4PU

CONTACT:Georgia Gillies
Tel: 07833 195654
bunkhouse@isleofmuck.com
www.isleofmuck.com
Isle of Muck, Port Mor, Isle of Muck,
PH41 2RP

GLEBE BARN

Glebe Barn offers 4* homely accommodation on the extraordinary Isle of Eigg within 1 mile of the island shop & cafe/restaurant. Outstanding sea views and sleeping up to 22 in twin, triple, family & dorm rooms. Perfect for individuals, families or groups. Also two person mezzanine apartment.

DETAILS

■ **Open** - Groups all year; individuals from April to October. Open 24 hours.
■ **Beds** - 22: 1x2, 2x3, 1x6, 1x8.
■ **Price/night** - Dormitory bed: £20 (1-2 nights), £18 (3+ nights), £16 (6+ nights). Twin room £45 (1-2 nights), £10 (3+ nights), £36 (6+nights). Triple room £60 (1-2 nights), £54 (3+ nights), £48 (6+ nights). Contact for quote for groups.

CONTACT: Tamsin or Stuart
Tel: 01687 315099
mccarthy@glebebarn.co.uk
www.glebebarn.co.uk
Glebe Barn, Isle of Eigg, Inner Hebrides, PH42 4RL

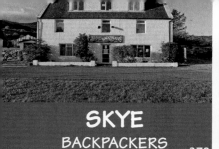

SKYE
BACKPACKERS

Whether your visit to Skye is to tackle the mighty mountains, meet the legendary faeries or simply to chill out, Skye Backpackers is the place for you. Located in the fishing village of Kyleakin surrounded by mountains and sea, the hostel has dorm, double and twin rooms. All beds come with sheets, duvets and 2 pillows. There is a fully equipped self-catering kitchen, a sunny dining area, as much free tea, coffee & hot chocolate as you can drink, free WiFi, a cosy lounge with a real fire and spectacular views.

DETAILS

■ **Open** - All year, All day. Reception 7am-12am & 5pm-10pm (times may vary).
■ **Beds** - 39
■ **Price/night** - From £14 pppn. ID required for check in.

CONTACT: Receptionist
Tel: 01599 534510
info@skyebackpackers.com
www.skyebackpackers.com
Benmhor, Kyleakin, Skye, IV41 8PH

PORTREE
INDEPENDENT HOSTEL
379l

BROADFORD
BACKPACKERS
379r

Originally the post office, Portree Hostel on the Isle of Skye sleeps 60 in small family rooms and dorms. All bedding is provided and there is a well-equipped launderette. Close to the bus terminus it is an ideal base for touring the island and is within an easy walk of a wide variety of shops. From the hostel there are pleasant coastal & woodland walks. Bike and car hire are available locally. Portree holds an annual Folk Festival in July & the Highland Games are in August.

Broadford is well connected for enjoying the Isle of Skye and Broadord Backpackers is a clean, cosy, child-friendly hostel with helpful staff for advice and information. There is a large kitchen for self-catering and a pleasant dining room overlooking the garden.
The communal area has a TV and comfortable seating with plenty of board games and tea or coffee. Put in a lovely house cat and you've got yourself a home away from home.

DETAILS

- **Open** - All year. No curfew
- **Beds** - 60
- **Price/night** - Prices start at £21pp

DETAILS

- **Open** - All year. 9am-1pm & 5pm-10pm
- **Beds** - 38:1x7, 1x6, 1x4, 2x3, 2 x family, 2 x dbl, 1 x twin
- **Price/night** - Low: Dorm £15pp, dble/twin £40. High: Dorm £20, dble/twin £60

CONTACT: Patt
Tel: 01478 613737
skyehostel@yahoo.co.uk
www.hostelskye.co.uk
The Old Post Office, The Green, Portree, Isle of Skye, IV51 9BT

CONTACT: Reception
Tel: 01471 820333
broadfordbackpackers@gmail.com
www.broadfordbackpackers.co.uk
High Road, Broadford, Isle of Skye, IV49 9AA

SKYE BASECAMP

Skye Basecamp is a luxury hostel with dorm beds, private rooms and a private self-contained apartment. Facilities are aimed at lovers of the great outdoors, with hot showers, comfy beds and a good drying room. Active staff and guests create a fantastic atmosphere and you'll find a whole lot of reasons to hang out at the Basecamp. Located on the shores of Broadford Bay. Shops and bars all within walking distance as is the beach with its resident otters.

DETAILS

■ **Open** - All year. All day. Check in 5-10pm.
■ **Beds** - 37
■ **Price/night** - Seasonal from £20pp. Discounts for groups/sole use.

CONTACT: Ellie MacLennan
Tel: 01471 820 044
bookings@skyebasecamp.co.uk
www.skyebasecamp.co.uk/
Lime Park, Broadford, Isle of Skye
IV49 9AE

RAASAY
HOUSE

381l

WATERFRONT
BUNKHOUSE

381r

Raasay House is a real 'hidden gem' for backpackers and budget travellers. Near to the Isle of Skye ferry and bus terminals, it has 4* deluxe hotel rooms and shared hostel style rooms. The shared rooms are low cost but give you access to the same facilities as the rest of the house. Bedlinen is supplied and towels can be hired. There are no self catering facilities but good value bar meals are available. Raasay House is an outdoor activity centre organising sea/loch kayaking, coasteering, climbing, sailing, abseiling and much more.

Feet from the edge of Loch Harport, Isle of Skye, with breathtaking views of the Cuillins, this purpose built, stylish & comfortable bunkhouse is an ideal base for hill walkers or sightseers. There is spectacular scenery and abundant wildlife in the surrounding hills and glens. The bunkhouse has a kitchen and common room with a balcony overlooking the loch and 5 bunkrooms, one en suite. The Old Inn, a traditional highland pub provides breakfast, lunch and dinner if required.

DETAILS

- **Open** - All year. 24 hour reception.
- **Beds** - 28: 1x2,1x3, 1x4, 1x5, 1x6, 1x8
- **Price/night** - From £15 to £22 pp in dorm (not including breakfast).

DETAILS

- **Open** - All year, all day.
- **Beds** - 24: 2x6, 2x4, 1x4 en suite.
- **Price/night** - £23pp, en suite: £26pp. Sole use £500. Booking essential

CONTACT: Reception
Tel: 01478 660300
info@raasay-house.co.uk
www.raasay-house.co.uk
Raasay House, Isle of Raasay, IV40 8PB

CONTACT: Calum
Tel: 01478 640205
enquires@theoldinnskye.co.uk
www.theoldinnskye.co.uk
The Old Inn, Carbost, Isle of Skye, IV47 8SR

SKYEWALKER
HOSTEL
382l

GEARRANNAN
382r
HOSTEL & BUNKHOUSE

Skyewalker Hostel, continually voted as the discerning traveller's favourite, offers wonderfully unique accommodation in the converted, former schoolhouse in Portnalong. Clean, comfortable and cool....well, except for the warm welcome! Highland hospitality is our speciality! An excellent base from which to explore all the wonders of the magical Isle of Skye. Rooms range from sociable dorms to twin en suites and even Jedi Huts! The force is strong with this one!

Part of the Gearrannan Blackhouse Village on the Isle of Lewis, the Gearrannan Hostel has been refurbished to sleep 13 including a 3 bed family room. Warm and cosy it has a well equipped kitchen & two modern shower rooms. The bunkhouse (groups only) sleeps 14 in bunks. The perfect base for many local attractions from surfing to country walks, archaeology to cycling. There are also 3 holiday cottages.

DETAILS

■ **Open** - 1st April - 30th Sept (or all year for group bookings). Check in between 3pm and 9pm.
■ **Beds** - 50.
■ **Price/night** - From £18.00 per person.

DETAILS

■ **Open** - All year.
■ **Beds** - Hostel: 13: 1x10 1x3. Bunkhouse: 14: 2x6 1x2. Black houses: 1x2, 2x3-5
■ **Price/night** - From £15.00 per person. Family room £47.00.

CONTACT: Brian or Lisa
Tel: 01478 640250
enquiries@skyewalkerhostel.com
www.skyewalkerhostel.com
Old School, Portnalong, Isle of Skye,
IV47 8SL

CONTACT: Mairi
Tel: 01851 643416
info@gearrannan.com
www.gearrannan.com
5a Gearrannan Carloway Isle of Lewis
HS2 9AL

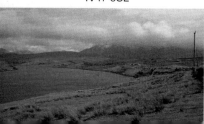

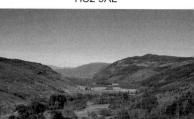

HEB
HOSTEL

The Heb Hostel is a family-run backpackers hostel in the heart of Stornoway on the enchanting Isle of Lewis. It is an ideal stop/stay for travellers visiting the Hebrides. Cyclists, walkers, surfers, families and groups are all welcome. Clean, comfortable, friendly and relaxed, Heb Hostel aims to provide you with a quality stay at budget prices. There are many facilities, including a common room with peat fire, free WiFi, local guides and information.

DETAILS

■ **Open** - All year. All day. Please phone for access code if warden not around.
■ **Beds** - 26: 1x8, 2x7,1x4 (family dorm).
■ **Price/night** - £19 pp. Family dorm: £75 for family, £84 for adults only.

CONTACT: Christine Macintosh
Tel: 01851 709889
christine@hebhostel.com
www.hebhostel.com
25 Kenneth St, Stornoway, Isle of Lewis,
HS1 2DR

GALSON FARM
HOSTEL

This fully equipped hostel on the Isle of Lewis enjoys stunning views of the Atlantic coast towards the Butt of Lewis Lighthouse. It provides the perfect haven from which to explore the crofting township of Ness and the west side of Lewis, with sandy beaches, wildlife, historic sites and culture on the doorstep. A short walk through the croft, with its network of footpaths, takes you to the shore and river, where otters are regular visitors. The hostel has one dormitory with up to eight beds, two shower/toilet rooms and a kitchen/dining room.

DETAILS
- **Open** - All year. All day.
- **Beds** - 6 / 8:
- **Price/night** - £20pp. Sole use £110 .

CONTACT: Elaine & Richard
Tel: 01851 850492 Mob: 07970219682
GalsonFarm@yahoo.com
www.galsonfarm.co.uk
Galson Farm House, South Galson, Isle of Lewis, HS2 0SH

OTTER
BUNKHOUSE

385

Otter Bunkhouse is on the shores of West Loch Roag, in Carishader on the Isle of Lewis. It offers a cosy hideaway with modern facilities for walkers, climbers & cyclists, unspoiled natural beauty, deserted beaches and wildlife. The 8 bed bunkhouse has a lounge with self-catering facilities, a bedroom with 8 bunk beds (bedding provided) and a deck with stunning views over the Loch. A double en-suite cabin will also be available in April 2018.

DETAILS

■ **Open** - Open all year, all day access available.
■ **Beds** - 8: 1 x 8
■ **Price/night** - £25 per person. Sole hire of the bunkhouse is available.

CONTACT: Michele
Tel: 07942 349755
otterbunkhouse@gmail.com
www.otterbunkhouse.com
Otter Bunkhouse, Carishader, Uig, Isle of Lewis, HS2 9ER

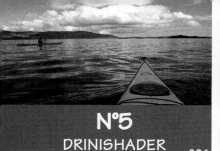

N°5
DRINISHADER

N°5 Drinishader is on the Isle of Harris, 5 miles from Tarbert and 8 miles from the famous white sandy beaches. Situated above Drinishader harbour, overlooking the beautiful East Loch Tarbert, the hostel and self-catering units provide a variety of accommodation for individuals, families and groups. Pick-up services from Tarbert can be arranged for a small cost. Your perfect base for coastal/hill walking, cycling, kayaking, boat trips, sightseeing and bird/wildlife watching. Breakfast and packed lunches can be provided.

DETAILS

- **Open** - All year. 7am-10pm.
- **Beds** - 20
- **Price/night** - From £21pp. Reductions for families, groups and longer stays.

CONTACT: Alyson
Tel: 01859 511255
info@number5.biz
www.number5.biz
5 Drinishader, Isle of Harris, HS3 3DX

BACKPACKERS
STOP

387

Situated in the village of Tarbert on the Isle of Harris, the Backpackers Stop is a comfortable hostel for travellers. Close to the ferry, bus, shops, café, bars and restaurants. The Backpackers Stop is a handy base for exploring Harris, as well as whilst walking or cycling the islands. Ideal when arriving by ferry. Self-catering kitchen, lounge and shared dorms. Linen, duvets and towels provided. USB sockets, free WiFi.Tea & coffee available all day. Basic self service breakfast provided. Keycode entry.

DETAILS

- **Open** - 1st March - 10th November. All year round for large groups/private use.
- **Beds** - 22: 4 rooms
- **Price/night** - £22 per person.

CONTACT: Lee
Tel: 01859 502742 Mob: 07708746745
bpackers_stop@hotmail.com
www.backpackers-stop.co.uk
Main Street, Tarbert, Isle of Harris,
HS3 3DJ

DUNARD
HOSTEL

388

Dunard is a warm, friendly, family-run hostel on the beautiful island of Barra in Scotland's Outer Hebrides. The hostel has a cosy living room with a lovely fire, hot showers and spacious kitchen. There are bunk, twin, family bedrooms and two garden cabins. Situated in Castlebay, the hostel has views over the castle to beaches and islands beyond. Close to the ferry terminal, a handful of shops, and bars which often fill with live music.

DETAILS

■ **Open** - All year, except Christmas and New Year. All day.
■ **Beds** - 18: 3x4 5x2
■ **Price/night** - £20pp twin cabins and dorms. £45 per twin room. £65 per family room (sleeps 4). Sole use from £350.

CONTACT: Katie or Chris
Tel: 01871 810443
info@dunardhostel.co.uk
www.dunardhostel.co.uk
Dunard, Castlebay, Isle of Barra,
Western Isles, HS9 5XD

LAXDALE
BUNKHOUSE
389l

SANACHAN
389r
BUNKHOUSE

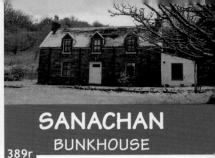

Laxdale Bunkhouse, on the Isle of Lewis, lies within Laxdale Holiday Park, a small family-run park set in peaceful leafy surroundings. Just 1.5 miles away from the town of Stornoway, it's an ideal base for exploring the island. Built in 1998, the bunkhouse has four rooms of four bunks. There is a drying room, a spacious fully equipped dining kitchen, a comfortable TV lounge and BBQ area. Toilets/showers are located in the building & are suitable for the disabled. Wigwams are also available

Sanachan Bunkhouse, in Kishorn, is the perfect base for walking, climbing, kayaking, cycling & sailing in Wester Ross. After a fun filled day, your group can return to a warm fire, comfy bunks, hot showers and simple living.

There is parking for six cars and beds for fifteen, split between two rooms (bring a sleeping bag). The bunkhouse is well equipped for self-catering, with enough tables & chairs for everyone. Laundry/drying, outside recreation and BBQ.

DETAILS

- **Open** - March to Nov. 9am - 10pm.
- **Beds** - 16:   4x4.
- **Price/night** - £18 adult, £16 child, £65 room (3 or less people) £250 sole use.

DETAILS

- **Open** - All year.
- **Beds** - 15: 1x7, 1x8
- **Price/night** - £16.50 pp. Discounted student rate of £15 pp.

CONTACT: Gordon Macleod
Tel: 01851 706966 / 01851 703234
info@laxdaleholidaypark.com
www.laxdaleholidaypark.com
Laxdale Holiday Park, 6 Laxdale Lane,
Stornoway, Isle of Lewis, HS2 0DR

CONTACT: Sean and Sophie
Tel: 01520 733 484
bookings@ourscottishadventure.com
www.ourscottishadventure.com
Sanachan Bunkhouse, Kishorn,
Strathcarron, Ross-shire, IV54 8XA

GERRYS
HOSTEL
390l

Gerry's Hostel is situated in an excellent mountaineering and wilderness area on the most scenic railway in Britain. It is on the Cape Wrath Trails, The T.G.O Challenge Route and is 0.5 miles from the Coulin Pass at Craig. It sleeps 20; 10 in a large dormitory with comfy beds, the rest in 5/6 bed family rooms. Meals and draught ale are a 15 min drive away. Your perfect base for many activities including walking, climbing, fishing, cycling, golfing and wildlife watching.

DETAILS
- **Open** - All year. Check in after 2pm.
- **Beds** - 20: 1x10, 2x5/6
- **Price/night** - From £17.50 pp main dorm. Family room from £18.50 (min 3 guests). Twins and doubles £25.

CONTACT: Simon Howkins
Tel: 01520 766232 Mob: 07894 984294
s.howkins@gmail.com
www.gerryshostel.com
Craig Achnashellach, Strathcarron, Wester Ross, IV54 8YU

KINLOCHEWE
BUNKHOUSE
390r

Walkers, climbers and mountain bikers enjoying the Torridon Mountains and wilderness areas will be warmly welcomed at the Kinlochewe Hotel and Bunkhouse. Situated on the North Coast 500 road route, within 20 miles of over 20 Munros, the bunkhouse boasts a well equipped, self-catering kitchen, an efficient drying room, hot showers and a 12 bunk dormitory. The hotel bar serves excellent home-made food and is in the 2018 Good Beer Guide.

DETAILS
- **Open** - All year. 8am - midnight.
- **Beds** - 12.
- **Price/night** - £17.50pp. Discount for group bookings with sole occupancy for 2 nights or more.

CONTACT: Dave and Karen Twist
Tel: 01445 760253
info@kinlochewehotel.co.uk
www.kinlochewehotel.co.uk
Kinlochewe by Achnasheen, Wester Ross, IV22 2PA

SAIL MHOR
CROFT

391l

Sail Mhor Croft is a small rural hostel which is perfectly situated at Dundonnell on the shores of Little Loch Broom and on NC500 route. The mountain range of An Teallach, which has the reputation of being one of the finest ridge walks in Great Britain, is right on the doorstep and the area is a haven for walkers of all experience. Whether you wish to climb the summits, walk along the loch side, visit a beautiful sandy beach or just soak up the tranquillity you will love it here.

DETAILS

- **Open** - All year, except from mid Dec until mid Feb. Flexible opening hours.
- **Beds** - 16: 2 x 4: 1 x 8
- **Price/night** - £18.00 per person self-catering only. £235.00 per night sole occupancy.

CONTACT: Dave or Lynda
Tel: 01854 633224
dave.lynda@sailmhor.co.uk
www.sailmhor.co.uk
Camusnagaul, Dundonnell, IV23 2QT

BADRALLACH
BOTHY

391r

On the tranquil shores of Little Loch Broom overlooking one of Scotland's finest mountain ranges, Badrallach Bothy and Campsite offer a fine base for walking and climbing. Fish in the rivers, hill lochs and sea or simply enjoy the flora and fauna. Hot showers, spotless accommodation, an unbelievable price, and total peace makes the Bothy and Campsite a firm favourite. There is also a holiday cottage for hire.

DETAILS

- **Open** - All year. All day.
- **Beds** - 12+ (alpine style platforms) 20 at a squeeze. Mats required.
- **Price/night** - £8pp, £2 per vehicle. £100 sole use. See @badrallachcampsite facebook page for camping/cottage fees.

CONTACT: Chris Davidson
Tel: 07435 123 190
mail@badrallach.com
www.badrallach.com
Croft No 9, Badrallach, Dundonnell,
Ross-shire, IV23 2QP

THE CEILIDH PLACE
BUNKHOUSE
392l

The Ceilidh Place, in the centre of Ullapool, is a unique small complex, consisting of a music venue/performance space, restaurant, hotel, bar, bookshop, coffee shop, gallery and bunkhouse. There are regular ceilidhs, concerts & plays. The bunkhouse (group only) does not have self-catering facilities but the coffee shop is open from 8.30am to late evening, all week including weekends. Rooms are also available in the hotel. The village of Ullapool is a small exciting port and fishing town, with ferries from the Outer Hebrides. Hill walkers and families especially love staying here.

DETAILS
- **Open** - All year.
- **Beds** - Bunkhouse: 32,
- **Price/night** - Get in touch for prices.

CONTACT: Effie
Tel: (01854) 612103
stay@theceilidhplace.com
www.theceilidhplace.com
14 West Argyle St. Ullapool, IV26 2TY

INCHNADAMPH
LODGE
392r

Inchnadamph Lodge has been tastefully converted to provide luxury hostel accommodation at a budget price. There's a large self-catering kitchen, a games room, a lounge and a dining room. Food is usually available at the Inchnadamph Hotel just across the river. Based at the foot of Ben More Assynt, and overlooking Loch Assynt, explore one of the wildest areas in the Highlands from the door.

DETAILS
- **Open** - Mid March to Mid Oct. All day
- **Beds** - 30: 8x2, 6x2, (dormitory). 14 (twin/double).
- **Price/night** - £20-22 (dormitory), £28-£32(twin) per person including continental breakfast and linen. Group discounts.

CONTACT: Chris
Tel: 01571 822218
info@inch-lodge.co.uk
www.inch-lodge.co.uk
Inchnadamph, Assynt, Nr Lochinver, Sutherland, IV27 4HL

BLACK ROCK
BUNKHOUSE
393l

BUNKHOUSE
@ INVERSHIN HOTEL
393r

Situated in beautiful Glenglass and sheltered by Ben Wyvis, this comfortable bunkhouse is an ideal base for touring the Highlands. The bunkhouse is at the eastern end of a hikers' route across Scotland and on the Lands End to John O'Groats route. The village has a general shop, Post Office, bus service and an inn (serving good bar meals and breakfasts) 250m away. There is also a camping ground. All areas of the bunkhouse are easily accessible by wheelchair and suitable for the disabled.

Situated within a small hotel in the north Highlands the bunkhouse consists of 4 rooms which share a shower room and toilet. Guests can enjoy all the hotel facilities; the cosy bar with it's roaring fire and real ale. Cyclists, walkers, bikers, fishermen, Munro baggers, families and lone travellers are all welcome and the bunkhouse is on the North Coast 500 road route. No self-catering facilities, but breakfast and a small selection of home cooked evening meals are available.

DETAILS

- **Open** - April 1st to October 31st. 24hr access. New arrivals 12noon - 9pm.
- **Beds** - 16 : 4 x 4.
- **Price/night** - £15 per person. 10% off for groups of 8+.

DETAILS

- **Open** - April-end Oct. Check in from 4pm.
- **Beds** - 10: 2x twin, 2x triple (bunkbeds)
- **Price/night** - £20pp. Breakfast: £5 or £10. Discount for groups 6 or more.

CONTACT: Lillian
Tel: 01349 830917
janemacpherson@btconnect.com
www.blackrockscotland.com
Evanton, Dingwall, Ross-shire, IV16 9UN

CONTACT: Angus or Cheryl
Tel: 01549 421 202
enquiries@invershin.com
www.invershin.com
Invershin Hotel, Lairg, Sutherland,
IV27 4ET

SLEEPERZZZ.COM

394l

Stay on a first class train in Rogart in the heart of the Highlands, halfway between Inverness and John O'Groats! Two railway carriages have been tastefully converted. One sleeps 9, and one is subdivided to sleep 4 and 2. There are two beds per room, a kitchen, dining room, sitting room, showers & toilets. All bedding is included. There is also a showman's wagon sleeping 2/3. Close by you will find a shop, post office and pub with restaurant.

DETAILS

■ **Open** - April to Oct inclusive. 24 hours.
■ **Beds** - 18: 1x9, 1x4+1x2, 1x3
■ **Price/night** - From £20pp, under 12yrs £14 pp. (£1 discount if you arrive by cycle or rail). Stay 2 nights save £1pp per night.

CONTACT: Kate
Tel: 01408 641343
kate@sleeperzzz.com
www.sleeperzzz.com
Rogart Station, Pittentrail, Sutherland, Highlands, IV28 3XA

HELMSDALE
HOSTEL

394r

Set in the scenic coastal village of Helmsdale, the hostel offers spacious en suite accommodation including a fully equipped kitchen and comfortable lounge area with log burning stove. On the main NC500 and Lands End John O'Groats route, the hostel is popular with 'end to enders' and walkers exploring the Far North Marilyn Hills. It is also a perfect stop on the way top Orkney.

Dogs welcome on request. Groups welcome, discount for sole use.

DETAILS

■ **Open** - Re-opening May 2018
■ **Beds** - 24: 6x4
■ **Price/night** - Adults from £22. Children from £14. En suite rooms from £60.

CONTACT: Irene
Tel: 07971 516287 or 07971 922356
irene.drummond@btinternet.com
www.helmsdalehostel.co.uk
Helmsdale Hostel, Stafford Street, Helmsdale, Sutherland, KW8 6JR

BBS BUNKHOUSE
EAST MEY

395l

SANDRAS
HOSTEL

395r

The mainland's most northerly hostel. In East Mey on the highly praised NC500, BB's enjoys magnificent views over to Orkney and Dunnet Head. A perfect base for walking, cycling, surfing, fishing & stargazing. BB's provides everything you need to relax and recharge. Gill's Bay ferry terminal (regular Orkney crossings) and the Castle of Mey are a few mins' drive, John O' Groats and Dunnet Head are close by. Experience a switched off, yet modern, take on hostel accommodation - affordable & luxurious.

Thurso is the northern-most town on the UK mainland. The cliffs are alive with guillemots, kittiwakes, fulmars and puffins, while the sea is home to seals and porpoises. The 4* hostel has en suite facilities in all rooms, (some have TVs). Using their own backpacking experience, the owners ensure you will enjoy a level of comfort and service second to none. Surfing, pony trekking, fishing, quad biking, coastal walks and boat trips are all available in the area.

DETAILS

- **Open** - All year. All day.
- **Beds** - 10: 1x6, 1x4
- **Price/night** - £30 including breakfast and bedding with linen.

DETAILS

- **Open** - All year
- **Beds** - 26: 3 x 4, 1 x 5, 3 x 2 (or 3)
- **Price/night** - Dorm £18pp. Double/twin £42. Family room £72 (4 people), £80 (5 people). Breakfast is included in the price.

CONTACT: Bronagh Braidwood (BB)
Tel: 01955 611499
bronagh.braidwood@yahoo.com
www.bbsbunkhouse.com
St Johns, East Mey, Caithness
KW14 8XL

CONTACT: George or James
Tel: (01847) 894575
info@sandras-backpackers.co.uk
www.sandras-backpackers.co.uk
24-26 Princes Street, Thurso, Caithness,
KW14 7BQ

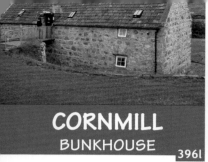

CORNMILL
BUNKHOUSE
396l

KYLE OF TONGUE
HOSTEL
396r

Cornmill Bunkhouse is situated on a traditional croft. The mill was built in the early 1800s and was active until 1920s. It is now 4* accommodation for individuals or groups. Guests are reminded of their historic setting; the smaller bunkroom has a patio door looking onto the workings of the old mill with its large wooden cog driving wheels. Activities can be organised for groups including laser tagging & shooting. Hen and stag parties welcome.

Kyle of Tongue Hostel is a stone lodge, magnificently situated on the romantic shores of the Kyle of Tongue on the north coast of Scotland. It has supreme panoramic views of Castle Varich, Ben Hope and the queen of Scottish mountains - Ben Loyal. Beautifully furnished, like a boutique hotel, but with all the friendliness of a hostel. There are comfortable private bedrooms, roomy shared dormitories and relaxing communal areas. Camping also available.

DETAILS
■ **Open** - All year, advanced notice required 1st Oct - 1st April. All day.
■ **Beds** - 14: 1x8,1x6
■ **Price/night** - £15 per person. Discounts available for group bookings.

DETAILS
■ **Open** - All year. Check in from 4pm.
■ **Beds** - 36
■ **Price/night** - Dormitory beds from £19, Private rooms from £44

CONTACT: Sandy Murray
Tel: 01641 571219   Mob: 07808 197350
sandy.murray2@btinternet.com
www.achumore.co.uk
Cornmill Bunkhouse, Achumore,
Strathhalladale, Sutherland, KW13 6YT

CONTACT: Richard Mackay
Tel: 01847 611789
kothostelandhp@btinternet.com
www.tonguehostelandholidaypark.co.uk
Kyle of Tongue Hostel & Holiday Park,
Tongue, By Lairg, Sutherland, IV27 4XH

ORCADES
HOSTEL
397

Orcades Hostel in Kirkwall, the capital of Orkney, is an excellent base for exploring the Isles. Accommodation is in doubles, twins, 4 & 6 bedded rooms. Each bedroom has en suite toilet/shower rooms. TVs and all bedding is provided. There is a stylish kitchen, a lounge with DVD & games and WiFi throughout the building. A warm and friendly welcome awaits you at this comfortable 4 star hostel.

DETAILS

■ **Open** - All year. Check in after 2pm. Check out by 10am on day of departure.
■ **Beds** - 34: doubles, twin, 4 and 6 bed
■ **Price/night** - £20 pp in a shared room, £26 pp in a double or twin room (£52 for the room), £40 for single occupancy of a double/twin room. Winter rates available.

CONTACT: Erik or Sandra
Tel: 01856 873745
orcadeshostel@hotmail.co.uk
www.orcadeshostel.com
Muddisdale Road, Kirkwall, KW15 1RS

HOY
CENTRE

Surrounded by magnificent scenery, the Hoy Centre is ideally situated for a peaceful and relaxing holiday and is also an ideal venue for outdoor education trips, weddings, workshops, clubs or family gatherings. Offering high quality, four star accommodation, the Centre has a well equipped kitchen, comfortable lounge area and a spacious dining hall. All rooms are en suite with twin beds and one set of bunk beds. Hoy is an RSPB reserve comprising 3,500ha of upland heath and cliffs with a large variety of wildlife including arctic hares.

DETAILS
- **Open** - All year.
- **Beds** - 32
- **Price/night** - Please phone for prices.

CONTACT: Stromness Customer Services
Tel: 01856 873535 ext 2901
stromnesscs@orkney.gov.uk
www.orkney.gov.uk
Hoy Centre, Hoy, Orkney, KW16 3NJ

BROWNS
HOSTEL & HOUSES 399

Providing nightly or weekly self-catering accommodation in the captivating small town of Stromness, Orkney. Within walking/cycling distance of the ancient Maeshowe, Ring of Brodgar and Skara Brae. Stromness has a museum, art centre, festival, scuba diving, free fishing and ferries from mainland Scotland. Facilities include well equipped kitchens, comfy sitting rooms and beds in single, double, twin, triple and family rooms, all with towels and bedding provided. Computers with internet and WiFi. Cycle storage & free car park up the lane.

DETAILS

- **Open** - All year. All day. No curfew.
- **Beds** - 28: 3x1,4x2,3x3,2x4
- **Price/night** - From £20.

CONTACT: Sylvia Brown
Tel: 01856 850661
info@brownsorkney.co.uk
www.brownsorkney.co.uk
45/47 Victoria Street, Stromness,
Orkney, KW16 3BS

HAMNAVOE
HOSTEL
400l

RACKWICK
HOSTEL
400r

Accommodation on the waterfront at Stromness, Orkney, close to the ferry. Single, family and twin rooms with glorious views. Light, airy kitchen and a large dining table with views of the harbour. Lounge with comfortable seating, TV, DVD's and books. Laundry room, WiFi, free long stay car park. Visit the nearby islands of Graemsay and Hoy, check out the World Heritage Sites. Relax in the tranquillity of island life.

Three Star Rackwick Hostel in Hoy has 2 bedrooms containing 4 beds each (2 bunk beds per room). In the scenic Rackwick Valley in the north of Hoy, the hostel overlooks Rackwick Bay considered one of the most beautiful places in Orkney. There's a small kitchen with a good range of utensils, and a separate dining area. Singles, families and groups are welcome for private room or whole hostel bookings. Car parking and bike storage behind hostel. Walkers and Cyclist Welcome

DETAILS

■ **Open** - All year. All day. No curfew. Check in after 2pm (reconfirm if not arriving before 7pm), check out by 10am.
■ **Beds** - 13: 1x4, 1x1, 4x2.
■ **Price/night** - From £21pp. Private rooms £23pp

DETAILS

■ **Open** - April - September
■ **Beds** - 8: 2x4
■ **Price/night** - For prices please phone 01856 873535 ext 2901 or check online.

CONTACT: Mr George Argo
Tel: 01856 851202
info@hamnavoehostel.co.uk
www.hamnavoehostel.co.uk
10a North End Road, Stromness,
Orkney, KW16 3AG

CONTACT: Orkney Islands Council
Tel: 01856 873535 ext 2901
stromnesscs@orkney.gov.uk
www.orkney.gov.uk
Rackwick Hostel, Rackwick, Hoy,
Orkney, KW16 3NJ

BIRSAY
OUTDOOR CENTRE
401l

ROUSAY
HOSTEL
401r

Birsay Hostel in the northwest corner of the Orkney mainland offers comfortable accommodation for up to 28 in 5 bedrooms. An ideal venue for outdoor education trips, weddings, clubs or family gatherings. It has a well equipped kitchen, dining area, drying room, disabled access and all bed linen is provided. There is a campsite in the extensive grounds. Close to spectacular coast, RSPB reserves and the remains of early Christian, Neolithic and Norse settlements. UNESCO heritage sites.

The island of Rousay is a walker's and birdwatcher's paradise with many footpaths and a nearby bird reserve. Often called "the Egypt of the North" Rousay contains some of the best preserved archaeological sites in the north of Scotland, set in spectacular scenery rich in wildlife, plants and flowers. The small, friendly community creates a unique welcome for the visitor to this beautiful island. Rousay Hostel is situated on a working organic farm within easy walking distance of shops, restaurant, pub, bike hire and the pier.

DETAILS

- **Open** - April - Sept. Open all year for group bookings.
- **Beds** - 26:2x4,1x2,1x6,1x10+camping.
- **Price/night** - Prices on enquiry. Private rooms and sole use of hostel available.

DETAILS

- **Open** - All year. All day
- **Beds** - 11
- **Price/night** - £15.00 (£17 with linen), £7 camping.

CONTACT: Orkney Islands Council
Tel: 01856 873535 ext. 2430
stromnesscs@orkney.gov.uk
www.orkney.gov.uk
Birsay, Orkney, KW17 2LY

CONTACT: Carol or Eric
Tel: 01856 821252 Mob: 07545 374029
trumland@btopenworld.com
Trumland Organic Farm, Rousay,
Orkney, KW17 2PU

AYRES ROCK
HOSTEL
402l

STRONSAY
FISHMART
402r

Sanday is the perfect place to take time out, with long stretches of unspoiled sandy beaches, an abundance of birds, seals and other wildlife, glittering seas, clear air and spectacular skies. Those lucky enough to live here enjoy a rare quality of life in a small, friendly and safe community. Enjoy the views over the Holms of Ire & Westray from the new conservatory in this 4* hostel.

DETAILS
- **Open** - All year. 8am to 10pm.
- **Beds** - 8 : 2x2 (twin), 1x4 (en suite).
- **Price/night** - From £19.50pp. Twin room single occupant £23.50. Groups from £60. Camping pods from £18.50pp Twin pod £35. Cooked breakfast £7.50 Evening meals from £12.50

CONTACT: Julie or Paul
Tel: 01857 600410
allanpaul67@googlemail.com
www.ayres-rock-hostel-orkney.com
Ayre, Coo Road, Sanday, Orkney
KW17 2AY

This family run hostel is ideally situated in the small fishing village of Whitehall, on the island of Stronsay, Orkney. Built on the sea front, just 100yds from the ferry. Some rooms overlook the harbour where you can see seals and other wildlife from the comfort of your room. Stronsay Fishmart Hostel has four bedrooms and a self-catering kitchen with dining area. The Fishmart also includes a café which serves lunches throughout the week and a heritage centre showing the history of Stronsay.

DETAILS
- **Open** - All year. All day
- **Beds** - 10: 3x2; 1x4
- **Price/night** - £20 per adult £15 per 16yr and under.

CONTACT: Richard or Evelyn
Tel: 01857 616401
fishmartstronsay@gmail.com
www.stronsayfishmart.uk
Whitehall Village, Stronsay, Orkney,
KW17 2AR

CHALMERSQUOY
ACCOMMODATION

Chalmersquoy offers four-star hostel accommodation and camping on Westray in Orkney, the Queen of the Isles. The barn hostel has an excellent kitchen and lounge. There is a double room, a family room and three twin bunk rooms, all with sea views.

Explore the cliffs, beaches and seabirds on the island or visit the Heritage Centre and local crafts. Bar and food available at Pierowall Hotel. Famous fish and chip shop open Wednesdays and Saturdays.

DETAILS

- **Open** - All year. If we're in, we're open.
- **Beds** - 12: 3x2 (bunk), 1x2 (dbl), 1x4
- **Price/night** - £22pp or £190 per night for exclusive use.

CONTACT: Michael & Teenie Harcus
Tel: 01857 677214
enquiries@chalmersquoywestray.co.uk
www.chalmersquoywestray.co.uk
Chalmersquoy, Westray, Orkney,
KW17 2BZ

OBSERVATORY
HOSTEL
404l

404r

GARDIESFAULD
HOSTEL

On a 34 acre croft managed by the North Ronaldsay Bird Observatory on the most northern isle of Orkney. Adjacent to a shell sand beach visited by seals and unique seaweed-eating sheep. Spectacular bird migrations and outstanding views. Ideal accommodation for those interested in wildlife but welcomes all. The hostel sleeps 10 in three dormitories with a self-catering kitchen. Lounge bar and meals available in the Observatory Guest House.

Gardiesfauld Hostel is on Unst, the most northerly of the Shetland Isles with spectacular cliffs sculpted by the Atlantic Ocean on the west and secluded, sandy beaches on the east with rocky outcrops where seals and otters appear. On the picturesque shore at Uyeasound, this refurbished hostel has good facilities and a relaxed atmosphere. There is a kitchen, dining room, lounge, conservatory and rooms with en suite facilities as well as a garden when you can pitch a tent and a 5 berth caravan.

DETAILS

- **Open** - All year. All day. No curfews.
- **Beds** - 10: 2x4,1x2 + Guesthouse.
- **Price/night** - Hostel £18-£19, half board from £39.50. Guest house private rooms £56 - £73.50 half board.

DETAILS

- **Open** - April to October. Open in winter for pre-bookings, All day.
- **Beds** - 35: 1x11, 2x6, 2x5, 1x2
- **Price/night** - Adults £16, U16's £9. Camping £8, U16s £4, Hook ups £18

CONTACT: Duty Warden
Tel: 01857 633200
nrbo@nrbo.prestel.co.uk
www.nrbo.co.uk
NRBO, North Ronaldsay, Orkney
Islands, KW17 2BE

CONTACT: Warden
Tel: 01957 755279
enquiries@gardiesfauld.shetland.co.uk
www.gardiesfauld.shetland.co.uk
Uyeasound, Unst, Shetland, ZE2 9DW

SHETLAND
CAMPING BÖDS

A network of low cost accommodation in various historic buildings across Shetland, each one set in fantastic scenery. The smallest böd sleeps four and the largest sixteen. Electricity, hot water and showers are available in some böds, with solid fuel stoves in all. Each böd has a story to tell. One even produced the jumpers used in Hillary's expedition to Everest. Tour the beautiful Shetland isles staying in böds en route.

DETAILS

■ **Open** - 1st March – 31st October. Böds are unmanned. Contact custodian up to 9pm on day of entry.
■ **Beds** - 4 to 16 (depending on böd).
■ **Price/night** - £10 to £12. Group discounts are also available.

CONTACT: Reception
Tel: 01595 694688
info@shetlandamenity.org
www.camping-bods.co.uk
For info: Shetland Amenity Trust,
Garthspool, Lerwick, Shetland, ZE1 0NY

60 TOP QUALITY
INDEPENDENT HOSTELS
THROUGHOUT GERMANY

CASTLE NEUSCHWANSTEIN, FÜSSEN

BOOK WITH BEST
PRICE GUARANTEE HERE:

WWW.GERMAN-HOSTELS.DE

Photo: maennlichen.ch

Exclusive insurance cover tailored for Independent Hostels UK (IHUK) members

IHUK have negotiated an exclusive insurance deal with award winning* insurance brokers Jelf, for the benefit of IHUK members.

Call Jelf for a quote and choose the covers you require whilst receiving excellent advice and peace of mind.

✆   01905 892 366

✉   IHUK@jelfgroup.com

BENEFITS FOR ACCOMMODATION OWNERS

We support your own existing marketing to provide direct bookings from the right kind of people.

We actively promote your accommodation on Twitter, Facebook, Google+ & Pinterest.

We promote your accommodation on our website, in this book, in leaflets supplied to Tourist Information Centres and on the Long Distance Walkers' website.

Our group booking service promotes your accommodation directly to all types of group leaders.

We promote your accommodation at leading outdoor shows in the UK. We provide you with IHUK branded signs, mugs, leaflets and books.

Our message boards host conversations between accommodation owners. We keep you in touch with industry news and we provide exclusive deals on insurance. Always with a friendly efficient service.

Official (IH) Member
Independent Hostels UK
The largest network of hostels, bunkhouses & group accommodation in England, Scotland and Wales

WHAT IS
INDEPENDENT HOSTELS UK ?

IHUK IS THE LARGEST NETWORK OF HOSTELS & BUNKHOUSES IN THE UK.

The network's website is viewed by 300,000 individuals each year. We distribute 10,000 guidebooks and 60,000 leaflets via bookshops, hostels, Tourist Information Centres and at events.

To join IHUK visit
independenthostels.co.uk/
advertise-your-hostel
or phone 01629 580427

INDEX

INDEX

INDEX

INDEX

INDEX